NEVER DATE A DEAD ANIMAL

The Red Flags of Losers, Abusers,
Cheaters and Con-Artists

Nancy Nichols

EPIPHANY IMPRINT

EPIPHANY IMPRINT
Email: info@epiphanyimprint.com
www.godpleasefixme.com

Disclaimer: This book is designed to provide accurate information with
regard to the subject matter covered. It is sold with the understanding
that the publisher and author are not engaged in rendering legal, psychological, or other professional advice. If expert assistance is required,
the services of a competent professional person should be sought.

*Names, locations and identifying characters of people in the book
have been changed to protect the extremely guilty.*

ISBN: 978-0-9795791-1-0

Library of Congress Control Number: 2013930209
Printed in the United States of America

This book is available for quantity discounts for bulk purchases.
For information, please email info@epiphanyimprint.com.

Editor, Denise Nall
Interior Design, Susan Leonard

To my vibrant, creative daughter, Krissy;
you make me laugh like no other.
I am in awe of your determination
and inner strength.

To my son, Roger,
who supported and encouraged
through my difficult writing journey.
Your wisdom is my blessing.

To my brothers, Harry and Todd,
the bright stars in my eyes.

Contents

PART FOUR
HALL OF SHAME

Acknowledgements

To my fascinating "Shoe Sistas" who supported
my writing journey:

Denise Nall, my longtime friend and editor, thank you for the
extensive hours you gave me working through a complicated book.

Ann McMains Prince and Tracy McGowan,
my best friends forever.

Aly Sands, my first Nashville girlfriend,
you opened your home and your heart to me.

Terri Smith, a dedicated reader of my first book
who became my trusted friend.

Sherry Stevens, my savvy go-to-girl, you rock!

Amy Smith, thank you for your unconditional
friendship and support.

Lorraine Barnett, Helene Vivian and Janet Adams,
thank you for your Memphis bedrooms.

Renee Abel, my special friend, thank you
for your keen reading eyes.

Melissa Reeves, my long-standing friend
and Houston getaway.

Sue Leonard, it's special when generous, talented
people connect long-distance.

To red high heels, a woman's expression of confidence, personal
power and our ability to have fun.

Introduction

ever Date a Dead Animal reveals the complex and covert warning signs of men who present themselves as charming, stable, desirable partners—but in fact, are the anti-social personalities of this world. This book presents the true stories of women who ignored the red flags of men with dysfunctional, unreliable, deceptive, self-absorbed, abusive behavior, fell in love with and committed to these men—and in retrospect, what they would do differently.

Sometimes the red flags of a man's bad behavior are blatant, observable and undeniable. Other times the warning signs are vague, seemingly insignificant and concealed by a veil of seduction and deceit. It is our job as women to learn the behavioral indicators of anti-social personalities and to stop, look, listen and question a man's character, intentions, compatibility, stability and relationship worthiness.

Never Date a Dead Animal will open your eyes to a man's shallow, self-serving and deceitful relationship tactics. It will illustrate *why* women gravitate towards men who are unworthy of their love, affection and loyalty. It will inspire you to stop dating the jerks, deceivers and bad boys. It will gain you the confidence to stand up to a man who wants to manipulate and control you. It will give you the courage to leave a boyfriend or husband who demeans and abuses you.

This book is for you if:

- You have a history of attracting, dating and committing to the wrong man.

- You fall in love quickly and easily.

- You secretly question a man's motives, behavior and honesty— but you keep dating him anyway.

- You ask a girlfriend for advice about a man and then you go against her counsel.
- You have a track record of failed relationships or divorce.
- You feel needy or incomplete without a man.
- You allow men to run over you, mistreat, and even abuse you.
- You are trying to leave a hurtful relationship, but you can't seem to muster up the courage.
- You recently broke off a relationship with a man who fits the description of a "dead animal" man.

Never Date a Dead Animal is a personal growth book. It will increase your understanding of man's hurtful behavior and a problematic relationship. It will give you insight into your faulty belief system which causes you to attract, fall in love with, commit to and remain with men who maltreat you.

If you are a single woman *Never Date a Dead Animal* will help you reserve emotional involvement with a man until you are certain he is the right man. If you are a married woman or you are in a committed relationship it will help you deal with the reality of a destructive, abusive relationship.

Falling in love with an abusive man is a debilitating event in a woman's life. Disengaging from a charming man who is deceptive, manipulating and controlling seems almost impossible for many women; in fact, some women never sever the emotional grip these men hold on their hearts.

Never Date a Dead Animal will empower you to:

- Read the early warning signs of a man's potentially harmful behavior—and avoid involvement with him.
- Trust your instincts about a man. Trust your ability to comprehend the dynamics of a dysfunctional relationship.
- Resist the charm, seduction and empty promises of an insincere man.

- Recognize the courting tactics and protect yourself from the manipulative, controlling man.

- Stand up to a man's self-serving, demanding, demeaning behavior without fear of his anger or rejection.

- Ask for the things you want and need in a relationship without worry of saying the wrong thing, making a man angry or losing him.

- Find the courage to get out of a relationship with a man who neglects, disparages or verbally or physically abuses you.

- Break the emotional cycle of a hurtful addictive relationship—and begin the healing process.

To realize positive change in one's life, one must change the defective thoughts and beliefs which cause us the bulk of our unhappiness.

The problem is Shoe Sistas ...

Most people do not believe there is anything wrong with the way they think. They blame their friends for a misunderstanding. They blame their boss and co-workers for their difficulties at work. They blame their parents for their adult problems. They blame their spouse for their relationship problems. They blame their boyfriend or girlfriend for their relationship failures. When in truth, we are each responsible for our own realities.

Our thoughts attract the people in our lives. Our thoughts affect the quality of our relationships. Our thoughts ultimately shape our realities. If you are unhappy with your life and your relationships, and you want to change it—you must change *your* thoughts. And that dear reader will alter your destiny. I know ... because it happened to me and it can happen to you.

The purpose of *Never Date a Dead Animal* is to neither batter nor stereotype men as a defective, offensive gender. I write books for women because I am a woman, and therefore, I identify with women's low self-esteem issues, lack of relationship understanding and heartbreak. However—I plainly state that women are often "dead animals" with *their* deceptive, self-serving, manipulative, co-dependent agendas. They are often unfaithful, controlling and abusive to men.

I empathize with men's relationship difficulties, confusion and heartbreak. If I had a magic wand I would grant everyone, men and women alike, happiness, personal security, and especially true and lasting love. But, alas, I've not been able to find this lavish accessory in any of the department stores.

In the meantime, *Never Date a Dead Animal* tackles the traits of anti-social personalities, the manipulating tactics of these personalities and the dynamics of abusive relationships. It is my hope that my book will enlighten women, and men, who struggle with dating and relationship difficulties.

Shoe Sistas, put on your Louboutins ... your Hummer H2 limo is pulling off. Guys, you can ride alongside on your motorcycles.

Girlfriend Within

You are the wind beneath my wings.

With super-strength and super-speed My Girlfriend Within suddenly appears when I need her most. She's worldly wise, startling intuitive and strikingly self-assured. She does and says the things I dare not do or say. My Girlfriend Within is a styling, strutting fashionista; she loves designer labels, handbags, jewelry and shoes. She feels especially sassy in her red patent-leather high heels. My Girlfriend Within is my super-sized, uber-magnificent alter-ego.

I can depend on my Girlfriend Within. She helps me conquer my fears, empowers my confidence, illuminates my femininity, and embraces my life with gusto. She protects me from my naivety, gullibility, poor judgment and impulsive lovesick emotions. When I am smitten by a smooth-talking, sugar-dripping, boasting man, she furrows her brow, shakes her French manicured finger and cautions me to resist emotional entanglement with him. When I struggle with a man's duplicitous, blaming double-talk, she scoffs at his dim-witted attempt to confuse and control me. When I date a man for the wrong reasons, she holds me accountable for my self-serving, needy, co-dependent agenda. If a man maltreats me, she reminds me that I am a beautiful, gifted, competent woman who is worthy of the respect, loyalty and the love of a wonderful man.

My Girlfriend Within inspires me to think large, be discerning, relish life and contribute to the betterment of others.

Thank God for my zany, brainy, fearless Girlfriend Within. You are the wind beneath my wings.

I devote my book to your *Girlfriend Within*.

Part One

A Woman's Curse

"You can't mature as a woman without at least one miserable man in your life."

—Nancy Nichols

My *1* Story

My life has been a succession of dating mishaps, relationship failures, divorce and the wretched heartbreak that accompanies these events. My self-improvement books are a culmination of the knowledge and insight I acquired from my hurtful experiences. *Never Date a Dead Animal* is the crowning wisdom I gained, or I should say—I earned, from dating and falling in love with a highly dysfunctional man.

Dating was once a confusing and disappointing activity for me. I doubted my worth as a woman. I mistrusted my judgments about men. I repeatedly dated and fell in love with the wrong man.

My relationships were once heartbreaking encounters. I repeatedly committed to emotionally unavailable or dysfunctional men. I questioned my understanding of a difficult relationship situation. My romances ended in heartbreak. My marriages terminated in divorce.

Men were once a perplexing gender for me. I was afraid I would say or do the wrong thing and reap a man's displeasure. I was scared to ask for the things I wanted and needed in a relationship because I might anger him. I was afraid to confront a man for his hurtful or questionable behavior because he might reject or leave me.

My life's quest has been to understand men, dating and relationships, all of which lead me to write self-improvement books for single women, who like me, struggle with the difficulties of finding a desirable partner. Who, like me, find themselves in a relationship which robs them of their joy, sanity and personal security. After years of counseling, self-discovery and even writing a dating and relationship book, I thought I was mentally armed to attract and fall in love with the right man. And then life blindsided me with a consummate life-altering, life-shattering lesson for dating, falling in love with and committing to a man who was destined to ill-treat me.

The most hurtful, dysfunctional, destructive relationship I have ever experienced was with the man I called my "soul-mate."

David (of course it's not his real name) was a charming, talented, successful man and although he was not the most handsome man in the world, his playful boyish spirit and affectionate nature instantly captured my heart.

When David and I met we fell quickly and deeply in love. We believed fate had somehow magically thrown us together. The first six months of our relationship was a euphoric state of romantic exploration, and then, as if overnight, a complicated, even disturbing side of David began to emerge. His once carefree social cocktails became nightly drinking episodes that seemed to trigger his cynical and irrational behavior. He became secretive, hyper-critical and unpredictable. Eight months into our relationship I recognized him to be the most controlling and verbally abusive man that had ever crossed my path. As I watched his cruel personality unfold I was numb with disbelief. Then the sickening realization set in: I had come face to face with a bona fide narcissistic, pathological lying, anti-social personality, who in twelve short months robbed me of my joy, security and mental stability.

"How did this happen?" I asked myself. "How did I, the expert and author of a successful dating and relationship book screw up so horrifically by falling in love with an arrogant, schizophrenic, noxious con-artist who lacked all sense of compassion, moral values and social conscience?"

*If you have no frame of reference, you might
not know what you're dealing with.*

I have met a legion of men who tell the everyday garden-variety of lies: "I'm divorced," he says, when he's really married. "I'm a successful real estate investor," he boasts, while rubbing two dimes together. Or a man boldly pursues me and the moment I fall for him I find out he is poking other women. But *never* had I dated a man who so skillfully mastered the art of dupery. Like the women who dated David before me, I bought into his polished phony façade—*hook*, *line* and *sinker*.

In my own defense I will tell you I did ask David the right questions in the early stages of dating to determine if he was relationship worthy. I asked him, "Are you married?" "How long have you been divorced?" "Why did you get a divorce?" "What are you looking for in a relationship?" "Are you looking for a committed relationship?" But he, with intent and purpose, lied to me telling me what he thought I wanted to hear to steal my love, affection and commitment.

It took three dates for me to fall in love with David. It took a year for his abusive nature to maim my spirit. It took two additional years to break the crippling love addiction I had for him and undo his covert brainwashing. In total, I sacrificed three years of my life for but one simple detail—I ignored the warning signs of a highly dysfunctional man.

He was the gift that came in an ugly package.

My life was never the same after David. It was this devastating relationship which opened my eyes to *why* I allowed the Davids of this world into my life. *Why* I discounted the obvious signs of a man's bad behavior. *Why* I gave my heart to a man I suspected to be highly dysfunctional. *Why* I stayed with a man who demeaned and verbally abused me. And *why*, after we broke up I clung to the memory of a love that never existed.

Warning! Dead Animal Ahead!

Is there a clinical term for "scumbag"?

What is a "dead animal," you ask?

A dead animal is a man (or woman) who is mentally, emotionally, physically or financially unavailable to participate in a loving, healthy, stable relationship. He's an alcoholic, sportsaholic, workaholic, gambler, womanizer, verbal or physical abuser, liar, cheater; drug, sex or porn addict, con-artist, criminal, commitment phobic or emotionally unavailable. Or he may have emotions—but he's married and they belong to his wife.

A dead animal is a man who takes great interest in his hobbies, friends, job, comforts and concerns—but he takes little to no interest in the things that are important to the woman in his life. He'll happily drink beer, golf, hunt or play cards with his buddies 24-7, but when it comes to a moment of meaningful conversation with his girlfriend or wife, he turns a deaf ear. He's considerate, patient and understanding in the workplace, but when dealing with her problems, he alienates her with his unsympathetic, hyper-critical, blaming comments. He loves to spend money on his electronics, tools and cars, but the last bouquet of flowers or piece of lingerie she received was after the first time she slept with him.

A dead animal doesn't call when he says he will. He disappears for hours and even days without a plausible explanation. When you press him for a reason he becomes angry or he casts blame on you. A dead animal is unreliable, unpredictable and untrustworthy. He spends his paychecks on casinos, hookers, booze and drugs. He boasts of success, possessions and fabricated financial worth. He borrows money that he never intends to pay back.

A cheating dead animal man secretly exchanges emails with other women. He plays "lover boy" on online dating services and he surfs internet porn sites late at night while you are in bed asleep, oblivious to his online affairs and addiction.

A dead animal will adore you one minute, and in the next minute, manipulate, criticize and condemn you without reason or provocation. He'll flirt with women to make you jealous and boost his ego. He'll lie to you, cheat on you, and verbally demean you. And no! *Hell no!*—did that jerk just slug you? And when you complain, threaten or plead with him to straighten up his act, he will give you lip service and accuse *you* for all the relationship problems.

If you're a single woman, a married dead animal man will lie to you about his marital status so he can have sex with you. If you're married to a dead animal, he'll cheat on you with his mistress and then he'll cheat on his mistress with your female marriage counselor, all the while concealing his assets should you finally get the guts to divorce him.

Anyway you look at it, a dead animal is a precarious relationship risk.

A dead animal is not always that easy to detect; sometimes the red flags of his hurtful nature are a vague pink.

A dead animal man appears to be a normal functioning creature. In the beginning he seems to be trustworthy, considerate, generous and stable. He is, of course, charming, debonair, seductive and exceedingly fun to be with. You may even be thinking, *"This could be the man of my dreams."* But as you peel away the layers of his attitudes, character and personality, and you take a closer look at his behavior, values and belief system, you'll see the tell-tale signs of a highly dysfunctional man. A man who will break your heart if you give him half the chance.

Understand—you can't change the spots on a leopard, the stripes on a zebra or the distorted value system and destructive behavior of a dead animal man. You can scream at him and threaten him. You can beg, plead and try to reason with him. But he's dead, dead, dead and you'll wear yourself out trying to make him participate in a meaningful relationship because he thinks YOU are the one who is broken.

Stay in a relationship with a dead animal man long enough and he will drain the joy, life and spirit right out of you. Or he will unexpectedly leave you for another woman and destroy your emotional and financial stability, and your ability to love and trust.

Women Love a Charming Dirtbag

He's confident, cocky and in-control—and she laps it up!

The man a woman chooses to date, fall in love with and marry is one of the most important decisions she will make in her lifetime. A woman's partner will impact the quality of her existence, influence her destiny and even affect the future of her children—be it good, bad or indifferent. Living with the wrong man in a dysfunctional or abusive relationship will destroy a woman's self-esteem, happiness and stability.

Why in planet's name do we, as women, ignore and minimize the obvious warning signs of a man's hurtful and dysfunctional behavior? Why is it so hard for us to walk away from a man who has shown himself to be inconsiderate, pretentious, non-communicating, deceptive and untrustworthy? More importantly, why do we continue to date a man once his toxic behavior is realized?

God help women who buy into a man's dazzling personality, romantic dinners, convincing verbiage, flowers, gifts and designer jeans; fall madly in love with him and submit to his sexual conquest—only to discover later that he is incapable of a meaningful relationship.

Remember, David, my soul-mate?

I met David through social contacts. He was a charming, successful, intelligent doctor (I call him Dr. Dirtbag). He was the most enchanting, attentive, entertaining man I had ever known and with his social references and impressive resume I considered him to be a safe relationship prospect.

Wrong, wrong, wrong—a jillion, zillion, gabillion times wrong!

Dr. Dirtbag was all about presentation, his custom clothes, his Mercedes, his garish jewelry—why his diamond studded Rolex watch alone was worth a petite house.

On our first date Dr. Dirtbag took me to a fancy restaurant. He seated me at our table, took my cloth napkin and with much ado flung it open and dramatically draped it across my lap. For two hours he smiled at me, served my plate with grilled sweetbread, buttered my roll and poured me wine, all the while aggrandizing his medical career, financial success, extensive travels, his homes, Maserati, small airplane, and his knowledge of wine, cooking and art. Dr. Dirtbag was a fascinating braggart, who was intent on winning my affection and commitment.

The reality was Dr. Dirtbag had a severe anti-social personality disorder. He lied when the truth was a plausible explanation. He verbally battered is wife into long-term depression. He hated his children and they hated him. And his Rolex watch, well, it was a Shanghai counterfeit. And yet, (fooling myself into believing that he was the best thing that had ever happened to me) I loved him hopelessly for three years before I could uncoil the life-sucking tentacles he had wrapped around my heart.

It would have been less painful to take a hammer and beat the crap out of my hand.

What causes women to fall prey to the bad boys? Are we that desperate for a relationship? Are we total suckers for a man's charisma, flattering words and his implied promise of a future together? Are we so blind that we can't see through a man's peacock feathers and false bravado? Or do we slide into a convenient coma so we can hold onto the players, scumbags and bad eggs.

Jerry, an ex-Air Force Major and commercial pilot captain, pursued Myra like she was the last woman on Earth.

Their first date for lunch was on a freezing, snowy day. Jerry arrived at Myra's townhouse with an impressive bouquet of yellow roses. As he helped Myra into his SUV he draped a plaid wool blanket over her lap and legs to keep her warm. It was one of the most endearing gentlemanly gestures Myra had ever experienced.

From the beginning Jerry wanted to occupy Myra's every minute. He cooked for her several nights a week, he visited her at work and took her to lunch, he took her to dinner, parties and movies, and he surprised her with an invitation for ten luxurious days at his Caribbean condo.

Everything Jerry said and did demonstrated that he was genuinely serious about Myra. He helped her with small household repairs. He bragged about her to his family and friends. He professed strong feelings for her and he talked about their future together. After only three weeks of dating he asked Myra for an exclusive relationship.

Myra was certain Jerry was the real deal. He was tall, successful, intelligent and worldly. He was attentive, affectionate, fun-loving and verbally articulate. He seemed perfect for her—or had she lost her mind? Two weeks after consenting to Jerry's "exclusive" dating request she saw him to be a self-serving, emotionally immature mama's darling whose flyboy status inflated him with a false sense of superiority and entitlement.

The moment Jerry knew he had captured Myra's heart his behavior changed; he became withdrawn and unreliable. Once he answered her phone calls immediately with a cheery, "Hi, Babe." Now she went straight into his voice mail and she would wait an hour for his return call. If she texted him it was an even longer wait. Previously he talked of their future travel plans; now he complained of their spending while still planning costly vacations with his friends—that didn't include her!

The kick-in-the-stomach was that he continued to socialize with his previous girlfriends. He had lunch with his wealthy ex-lover (the one he said that the sex wasn't that good). And he went to a dinner party which he couldn't invite Myra because, yet, another ex-girlfriend was attending. "I would feel uncomfortable," he told Myra. Myra expressed her hurt feelings at his inconsiderate, insensitive conduct. His amazing response was, "I think we need to rethink the exclusive dating thing ... things are moving too fast."

What the bullcrap?!?! What was this idiot thinking?!?!?! Jerry selfishly believed that he could have an exclusive dating contract with Myra with a disclaimer of ex-girlfriend privileges.

The reality was when he got his way with Myra—he became apathetic, inconsiderate and blaming. The jerk-off pilot could fly a MD11 upside-down but he didn't have a clue of how to work at an honest relationship.

We want to believe that our charming, attentive suitor is truthful, genuine and totally into us.

When a man tells me, "You're the most beautiful woman in the room," I want to believe, that in his eyes, I am. When he says he adores me and he wants a committed relationship with me, I want to trust that not only is he sincere, I want to believe that my dream man has found me and my search for true love is over. But when our co-dependency issues, emotional longings and physical urges cloud good sense and reasoning—regret and heartbreak will always find us.

In retrospect Myra said:

I take my share of responsibility for this plane wreck. I was impressed with Jerry Jerk-Off's lofty pilot career and I hastily bought into his skillful presentation of a caring, generous, forthright man who was capable of a give-and-take relationship. I succumbed to my emotional desires because I wanted to be in love. I wanted him to be real. I wanted him to be my dream man. Jerry went back to seeing his old flames and I was left with a ailing heart.

My Blue Angel Girlfriend Within flies her F/A-18 Hornet over Jerry Jerk-Off's house, does a triple somersault and skywrites ...

Loser!

When a woman gives her mind, body and soul to the wrong man she is no longer available to meet the right man. Years later her relationship crumbles and she is past her prime, companionless and longing for the love of a man.

It's Not My Fault–Or Is It?

Her heart struggled to distinguish between the good and bad in a man.

W omen eternally hope to meet, fall in love and even marry the love of their lives. We can't help it—it's in our genes. We long to share life's pleasurable moments with our special man; someone we enjoy conversation with, someone to hold hands and snuggle with, someone to share the holidays and travel with, someone to build memories and grow old with. But as time passes and the right man doesn't show up we become disheartened, we compromise our standards and we hastily, recklessly become involved with the wrong man—a man who is less than what we want and deserve.

It's a woman's curse to want and need a man so much that we will date, fall in love with and commit to a man we suspect in our hearts is not right for us.

Life's original design was for man to love, honor, protect and support (emotionally and financially) his equal, yet physically weaker female mate. Prehistoric man secured a suitable cave dwelling for his woman, brought home a nice bison steak for her to grill, and kept the fires stoked for warmth and protection. Likewise, modern man courts his gal, weds his bride, buys her a lovely two-story Tudor house and doles out the grocery money.

Women were created to love, honor, comfort and emotionally uphold their man. Cavewoman sewed her troglodyte's pelts together for clothing, she praised him for his masculine hunting abilities, and she basked in her man's safeguard. Similarly, modern woman admires her hubby's intellect, she encourages him after a hard day's work, and she draws comfort from his relationship commitment, while enjoying her own successful career.

Women are relationship-driven creatures. We yearn for the companionship, touch and affection of a man and the security of a relationship. Even the most independent, successful and esteemed women, try as they may to deny it, long for the love of a man and the intimacy of a relationship.

> *Jessie, an attractive 47-year-old single and New York magazine editor: I know I'm a beautiful, intelligent, competent woman. I have creative talents, an exciting career, interesting hobbies, a large social life and I have friends and family who love me. Why do I feel incomplete without a man?*

> *Wanda, a 39-year-old divorced professional: I try to be open-minded and trusting about men, but just when I think I have found the right guy he does something unreliable or deceptive. It's so depressing, it makes me want to throw in the towel on men.*

> *Sharon, a 45-year-old widow: I can't help it, I long for a man to be in my life. If I've had a bad day loneliness feels like a block of stone sitting on my heart. Or when I have a personal problem or a household repair that needs fixing, I so wish I had a man to lean on. It's then I can't seem to shake the emptiness.*

> *Carmen, a 52-year-old twice-divorced nurse: I don't feel I have to have a man all the time. It just feels that way when*

*my life slows down, when I'm alone on the weekends or when
a special occasion or a holiday rolls around. During the week
I eat most of my meals alone in front of the TV. When I go to
sleep I feel completely isolated. Sometimes I wonder if I disappeared forever, except for my family and a few friends, who
would miss me?*

It is no surprise that women become disheartened and cynical
towards men and give up on having a quality relationship.

Women Choose Mates Who Court Them

It's not our fault, as women, that we fall head over heels for a man
who ardently pursues us.

Relationship author Patricia Evans says that in the early stages
of dating, "Women usually experience an attentive and affectionate
person because while he's courting her, his approach to her is
conciliatory." In other words, during courtship a man's intention is
to gain a woman's goodwill and win her favor.

Men are experts at concealing their dysfunctional behavior
in the early stages of dating. They know they must put their most
charming foot forward to gain a woman's interest and sexual
commitment. They will trim their mustache and nose hairs, they'll
give their beat-up loafers a slipshod shine, they will wash their cars,
and they'll hide their girlie magazines before taking you to their
home. They will call you daily, text frequently, open doors for you
and send you flowers and cards. They will defer to your choice
of restaurants and movies, give your teenagers baseball tickets,
take you to an early church service on Sunday, and buy front row
tickets to the Broadway show you just *happened* to mention. In
the beginning men will exhibit their most creative, irresistible
courtship techniques because they know it's their job to woo and
wow you.

*Amy: My boyfriend was constantly looking for ways to please
me. One day he placed a red rose and a greeting card under*

my car's windshield wiper for me to find after work. If I said I liked a song, the next day it was playing in his car's CD player. I was constantly shuffling through business cards looking for a phone number; he surprised me with a business card organizer. Two weeks into dating him he took my hand, stared at my rings and watch and he said, "Do you prefer silver or gold jewelry?" I, of course, thought he was thinking about buying me jewelry, which also meant a committed relationship.

It's not our fault as women that a man touches our heart with his seemly genuine romantic gestures.

When a man senses a woman is needy, lonely or co-dependent he intuitively knows what to say and do to steal her heart and promote a sexual connection. An insecure, naive woman is an easy mark for an insincere man. He listens to her conversations of longing, hurts and fears, self-doubt and uncertainty, and then he shrewdly feeds her lines that influence her to give up her goodies.

I met David at a low point in my life. My job was very demanding. Traveling was extensive and grueling. Dining out-of-town alone most evenings was lonely. It was a Friday night and I had returned home from a trip to find myself eating out again— alone. I remember whining to myself, "I'm tired of traveling. I'm tired of being alone. I'm tired of feeling unloved. I want a man in my life." And then, abracadabra, like fricken fairy-tale magic, David (aka Dr. Dirtbag) unexpectedly came into my life.

David and I bonded instantly. We thought alike. We enjoyed the same things. We laughed and we played like teenagers. He professed to want a loving, committed relationship. In a very short time he told me he would love and care for me always. I thought my search for true love was over; I would never be alone again until I was shriveled up and ready for my grave. Months later David's dark and murky side began to surface and my euphoric world began to crumble.

I believe that it was my negative prayer that willed David into my life. When I met him I was afraid of being alone, unloved, and of one day being penniless. A tiny voice in my head said, "What if you get sick and you can't work? Who will take care of you? What if you get old, wrinkled and decrepit and no man will want you? What if you never find another man (a doctor for Chrissakes) who will love you as David does?" So I closed my eyes to his obvious hurtful behavior and I continued to date him.

In the beginning it was David's enchanting, persuasive behavior which caused me to fall for him. In the end it was Dr. Dirtbag's deceitful, abusive nature that almost destroyed me. Like my girlfriend so wisely put it, "Be careful what you wish for because you might get it."

It's not our fault that our core is trusting, naive and insecure. It's not our fault that we were taught to depend on a man for our financial and physical safety, and consequently, we believe that the center of our happiness revolves around having a relationship. It's not our fault that we repeatedly fall in love, or we are currently in love with a man whose daily life's pleasure is to maltreat and abuse you—*OR IS IT?*

My Lonely Confused Girlfriend Within goes to the medicine cabinet to look for a pill to cure her penchant for playboys, slimeballs and dead animal men.

Part Two

So You Think You Can Spot One?

"Knowledge is power and knowing the warning signs of men with harmful, self-serving, abusive personalities can you save you heartbreak, financial ruin, and possibly your life."

—Nancy Nichols

The Controlling, Abusive Personality

Recognizing the warning signs of a manipulative, controlling, abusive man is the first step to avoiding him.

I am not a degreed psychologist or counselor, nor am I a tarot card reader, and I would not attempt to explain the intricacies of the varied personality mental disorders. I do, however, profess to have first-hand knowledge into the red flags of men who are antisocial, abusive, narcissistic and sociopathic. I have unsuspectingly dated these men. I was in a serious relationship with this type of man. I have absorbed the many amazing and unpleasant stories of my female friends who have loved and been duped by these men.

Where to Start?

The relationship road is paved with dead animal men. Men who are alcoholics, drug users, gambling and porn addicts. Men who are non-communicating and non-committal. Men who pursue you, but are secretly involved with someone else. Men who will commit to you, but are married. Men who declare to be wealthy, but in truth are insolvent. Men who are chronically unemployed. Men who pretend to be caring, devoted, sensitive partners, but in reality are verbally and physically abusive. Men who pathologically lie about anything and everything. Men who are boasting, self-serving narcissists or ruthless sociopaths. Men who literally charm the pants off you and then instantly disappear.

Did I leave any dead animal man out?

For the purpose of brevity I use the clinical term anti-social personality, or ASP, to loosely refer to men with deceitful, self-absorbed, abusive personalities.

Dating an Abusive Personality

In the beginning the red flags of a skilled conniving sociopath are ambiguous, intangible and indefinable.

> *There was something about my new guy David that I just couldn't quite put my finger on. On the surface he was charming, attentive and intelligent. He was a talented and successful doctor. But there were times his behavior was perplexing and his explanations vague and conflicting—not so much that I would want to question him and possibly insult him. After all, I was smitten with this exciting, accomplished man who in just a few short weeks had charmed his way into my life, professed his love for me and gained my trust. Why, he had even hinted at matrimony. The last thing I wanted to do was to run him off with my insecurity and imagined accusations.*

When a woman is smitten by a man's charm, she is more apt to assess him with her wants, needs and desires—rather than sound judgment. If she is overly impressed by a man's appearance, accomplishments and bank account—all the harder it is for her to see through his manufactured façade. Once she is intimately entangled with him, the more apt she is to dismiss the evidence of his deceptive behavior, accept his lame alibis, excuse his hurtful words and stay in a relationship that promises to inflict heartbreak—or worse.

> **"Abusive men are never abusive in the beginning. If they were, women would dump the abusive men immediately in search of a good man."**
>
> —Stephany Alexander, *Top 10 Signs of an Abusive Man*

Something's not right in your new relationship; you sense it but you can't define it. He seems to say and do all the right things, but your heart has moments of uneasiness and your gut keeps questioning his sincerity.

A month went by, and I was perplexed by David's capricious behavior. But I had never dated nor been involved with a man with an extreme personality disorder. I was, therefore, oblivious to the warning signs—and so I continued to date him.

Understand—I had encountered dysfunctional men in the past who were quasi-controlling, unreliable and phony— and I quickly dumped them. But David's behavior was oddly paradoxical. In many ways he was the most adoring, devoted, affectionate man who had ever crossed my path. I thought I had met the love of my life. And yet there were facets about him which confounded me. For example, he was extremely jealous of any man looking at me or talking to me—he rationalized his jealousy, saying he was very protective of his loved ones. He had a contentious relationship with his daughter—but she was innately condescending so I judged her to be the problem. He was an excessive braggart—he's a man! And when he drank he was overtly flirtatious with other women—I repeat, he's a gawddarn man! Two months into dating him I was at his house when he zinged me about my past relationships. His derogatory comment stung and insulted me. In anger I grabbed my purse and I flew out the door to drive myself home.

David ran after me and he begged me to stay. "I didn't mean it; I'm sorry," he pleaded. His apology was weak but his passion for me was compelling, so I forgave him and I stayed. A month later he ambushed me with another snide remark. An intelligent woman would have dumped this jerkiod after the third date. I just thought we were having relationship difficulties and I justified his hurtful behavior.

A woman who is accustomed to dysfunction and discord in her relationships may not recognize the subtleties of man's verbal abuse.

Signs of an Abusive Personality

Men with an abusive personality disorder, or APD, are often charming and can be good actors. They use flattery, excessive attention, flowers and gifts (large and small), elaborate dinners, creative outings and trips to draw you into the relationship. Recognizing the signs of an abusive personality is your best protection to avoiding him.

Extreme jealousy or possessiveness: Jealousy is a sign of insecurity and lack of trust, but the abuser will say that it is a sign of love. He overacts to a man looking at you or talking to you. He calls and texts you constantly interrupting your work or private time. He wants to spend every evening with you. His constant contact is flattering—in reality, he's keeping tabs on you, establishing that you are his domain.

Pushes for quick involvement: He comes on strong at the beginning of the relationship. He claims "love at first sight" and "I've never met anyone like you before." He brags about you in front of his family and friends. He makes you feel special and needed. He uses charm, gifts and talk of the future to "wow" you. He tells you he's stopped dating anyone else and he wants you to do the same.

Blames others for his problems and mistakes: An abuser does not take responsibility for his mistakes or harmful behavior. It's always someone else's fault if something goes wrong. He blames his boss, his children or you for his problems. He talks badly about his ex-wife(s) or ex-girlfriend(s). He blames his previous partners for his break-ups and divorce—but he never mentions his part in his failed relationships.

Bragging: Self-obsessed behavior is frequently seen in an abusive man. He talks in length about himself, bragging about his accomplishments, connections, money and possessions.

Deceit and lying: He's evasive, his facts don't match up or you catch him telling lies. There may be some areas of his life he doesn't want you to find out about because he thinks he may lose you.

Dominance: He boldly pursues you and he takes charge of the relationship. He chooses what nights you go out, what you do and where you will go. You're attracted to his confidence, determination and masculinity, but these aggressive qualities can be a red flag of an abusive personality.

Controlling behavior: He is easily irritated or upset if you do not follow his lead. If you make a request of him he becomes aggravated and he throws up a road block. If you go against his plans or question his abilities he becomes disagreeable, confrontational and angry.

Hypersensitivity: He is easily insulted, he takes everything as a personal attack and he blows things out of proportion. He claims that his feelings are hurt when really he is mad. He'll rant about the injustice of things that are just a part of life.

Seems too good to be true: An abusive man draws you into a premature relationship with flattery, gifts, adoration and empty promises. Feelings of instant and extreme utopia—as in, "I met my soul-mate" are your signal to slow down and assess the man and the relationship he is offering.

History of abuse: He was abused as a child; abused men are at risk of becoming abusers. He intuitively seeks out women who are submissive and can be controlled. He admits to hitting women in the past, but he says they made him do it, or the situation brought it on.

History of drug or alcohol abuse: He drinks excessively or he uses drugs socially, or he has an arrest history of DUI or drug possession.

Poor relationships with women: He has a poor or no relationship with his mother, ex-partners or daughter. He speaks negatively and disparaging about women in general, an indication that he doesn't like women and he blames them for all his problems.

Cruelty to animals and to children: He may kill or punish animals brutally or be insensitive to their pain. He may expect children to do things that are far beyond their years.

The abusive man's actions don't match his words.
He says he loves you but he blames and abuses you.
He constantly breaks his promises because
he doesn't respect you.

In a Relationship with an Abusive Personality

The honeymoon is over. Once your suitor was caring, attentive and generous—now your guy is blaming, withdrawn, self-serving and angry. Abusers draw you into the relationship with their charm and generosity. They create your dependency on them with a distorted sense of security. When the relationship turns abusive they use lies and misrepresentation to keep you confused and off-balance. They use adoring words, empty promises and "make-up" gifts to keep the relationship going. They use guilt, fear, shame and intimidation to keep you under their thumb.

> You need to understand, "Abuse is used for one purpose and one purpose only: to gain and maintain total control over you."
>
> —Helpguide.org

Frank's pathological lying and abuse had taken its toll on Fran. After his last brutal verbal battering Fran told Frank she was leaving him. This time he knew she meant it and he needed to do something extravagant to patch things up. He surprised Fran with a trip to Spain to take the heat off of him and pull her deeper into their tumultuous relationship. Four weeks later they were in Barcelona celebrating a luxurious 10-day vacation. Fran had never been abroad and she was duly impressed by Frank's efforts to make her happy. Their vacation came to an end and a week later they were having highballs on their backyard terrace when Frank began to dig into Fran with his degrading remarks.

Abusers get what they want in life by manipulating, exploiting, dominating and bullying others.

"You dress like a skank," he announced abruptly, a satirical comment in that Frank always insisted that she reveal extreme cleavage when they went to a party or the country club. But when Fran wore a low-cut blouse in the privacy of their home he saw it as an opportunity to ridicule her. "Men talk about the way you dress. You should see how they look at you—it's embarrassing!" he exclaimed accusingly.

Frank berated Fran for over an hour about her appearance. When she finally stood up to him he became angry and proclaimed, "You don't appreciate anything I do for you! I spent a fortune taking you to Spain, I just can't please you!"

Fran felt guilty for yelling at Frank—and Frank got his money's worth by taking out his hostility out on Fran.

Signs of an Abusive Relationship

As the abusive relationship progresses, the courtship ends, the abuser is less apt to show his adoration, or it ceases altogether—and his behavior becomes more and more erratic, controlling, demeaning, aggressive and explosive.

Extreme jealousy and possessiveness: In his mind, you are his property. He wants to know where you've been and with whom. He accuses you of flirting or having an affair. He's jealous of the time you spend with your friends, family or children. He visits you unexpectedly at home or at work. He prevents you from going to work because "you might meet someone."

Isolation: He tries to cut you off from your family and friends—he accuses them of "causing trouble." He may deprive you of a phone or car or try to prevent you from having outside interests, holding a job or going to school. He may want you to quit your job to have a baby. He may sabotage your job by making you miss work. You may have to ask permission to do anything, go anywhere or see anyone.

Denies responsibility: He minimizes, denies or blames you for his mood swings, outbursts and hurtful behavior. He claims, "It's your fault; you made me mad." It's always someone else's fault when something goes wrong.

Unrealistic expectations: He is easily upset or angered and is unreasonable with his demands and expectations. He expects you to be the perfect woman and meet his every need.

> *In the movie "Sleeping with the Enemy" Julia Roberts plays Laura. Laura was married to NPD (narcissistic personality disorder); her husband was brutally obsessed with her flawlessness as a wife, housekeeper and lover and he would fly into a violent super-rage if a hand-towel was hanging slightly crooked or the cans in the food pantry were not symmetrically aligned. After his explosive wrath he expected immediate reconciliation with Laura, with his smothering, contrived apology, leaving Laura in a constant state of trepidation.*

Manipulating: The abuser twists your words in an argument, avoids your direct questioning and offers varying excuses for his hurtful behavior. He abuses you and then he solicits your forgiveness and sympathy with feigned remorse. He makes you responsible for his actions, saying, "You made me angry." "You're hurting me by not doing what I tell you." And, "I can't help being abusive."

Dominance: He needs to feel in charge of the relationship. He will make decisions for you and the family, tell you what to do and expect you to obey without question. Your abuser may treat you like a servant, child, or even as his possession.

Controlling behavior: He is overly demanding of your time and he must be the center of your attention. He tells you how to dress, who to talk to and where to go. He is constantly "checking up" on you. He calls you to see where and what you are doing. He times you when you leave the house and he checks the mileage on your car. He interrogates you, especially if you're late. He may eavesdrop on your phone conversations, censor your mail, and check your cell phone call history, emails and computer activity.

Financial control: He controls the checking accounts and financial records. He keeps you from working, or if you work he takes your paychecks and he is in charge of your money and credit cards. He restricts you to an allowance and he demands an account of all spending. He withholds basic necessities of food, clothing, medications and shelter.

Sherry, a stay-at-home mom, was married to Ronnie, a successful land developer. In the public eye Ronnie was a devout Christian husband and father. In private he maintained rigid control of Sherry's spending, allotting her a paltry monthly allowance for groceries, their three children's school and sports activities, and living expenses—while he spent big money at sports bars, on guy trips, and his sports equipment and electronic devices. If Sherry complained he further controlled and demeaned her by reciting scriptures, reminding her of her wifely duty to obey and submit to him. Ronnie used Christianity to whip and shame his wife, and money to dominate and power over her.

Procrastination: Procrastinating is a covert form of control and manipulation. He controls your time by making you wait. He will say he is ready to talk, but will continue doing something else. He tells you he is ready to go somewhere with you or he's ready to go to bed, but then he makes you wait. The procrastinating abuser drags his feet or blocks something that he knows is important to you. Examples are: stalling on promised work, or refusing to give a direct answer to a direct question: "Are you going to do this or that?" His responses may be, "We'll have to wait and see," or "I suppose," or "Maybe," or, "I don't know how," and "I didn't know I was supposed to." If you get upset with him for giving you the run-around he condemns you for your lack of patience and trust in him.

Dr. Dirtbag gave me three excuses for not getting the car washed that day. There was a long line. He didn't have change. The automated machine was broken. I didn't buy into his stonewalling and I insisted that he wash the car. I later paid hell for standing up to his deceptive, manipulating behavior.

My Girlfriend Within scratches her head, wondering, *Why were cars waiting in line for a car wash that wasn't working?*

Superiority: Abusers are insecure and their dominance over you makes them feel better about themselves. He calls you names and he talks down to you. He blames you for everything. He is always right; he has to win and be in charge. His goal is to tear you down to build himself up.

Controlling your time and space: The abuser disrespects his partner's boundaries, privacy and need for separate activities or identity. He controls her social space by limiting her contact with friends. For example, he may say she's not home when she is, or he refuses to allow her to invite others over. He invades her privacy; he may deprive her of sleep or wake her up to interrupt her sleep.

Punishing: He withholds sex, emotional intimacy or communication. He ignores you or he plays the "silent game" when he doesn't get his way or you upset him.

Mood swings: His mood switches from sweetly loving to angry and explosive often within a matter of minutes. After the abuse he acts as if nothing happened—or he is caring and apologetic. The abuser's drastic and sudden mood swings cause the victim to think he has a mental health problem.

"Playful" use of force during sex: The abuser may pressure his partner into having sex. He may throw or hold his partner down during sex, or demand sex when his partner is tired or ill. He may ask his partner to do sexual actions she doesn't want to do.

Verbal abuse: He ridicules, insults, humiliates, intimidates, manipulates, and even threatens his partner. The abuser's underlying goal is to control and dominate his victim to mollify his feelings of low self-worth and a sense of powerlessness in his life.

Breaking or striking objects: The abuser breaks treasured possessions to punish the victim, or he strikes and destroys objects near her to terrorize her into submission.

Threats: The abuser uses violence or other repercussions to control his partner's behavior; to keep her from leaving him or coerce her into dropping assault charges. He threatens to harm her, her children, other family members or pets. He may threaten to commit suicide, file false charges against you, report you to child services or threaten to take the children away from you. He uses his physical size to intimidate, e.g., he stands in the doorway blocking your exit during an argument. He makes statement like, "I'll break your neck," or "If you ever leave me, I'll kill you." He dismisses his threats by saying, "Everybody talks that way," or "I didn't really mean it."

Force during an argument: The abuser may hold the victim down, push, shove or hold her against the wall, or restrain her from leaving the room. Also considered force is punching walls and destroying your favorite possessions (e.g., furniture, dishes or clothing);

Physical violence: The abuser exhibits violent behavior to you, your children, household pets or others; e.g., slapping, shaking, hitting, punching, kicking, choking, pushing, biting, burning, etc., as well as, use of weapons or keeping weapons around to frighten you.

Adapted from WomanSavers.com, Relationship.LifeTips.com, HelpGuide.com, Lindsey Ann Burke Memorial Fund, "Project for Victims of Family Violence" Fayetteville, AZ, and Domestic Violence Resource Center of South County.

No! Oh, Hell No! Verbal Abuse

Control and dominance seem to give the abuser a sense
of power, security, and identity as a male.

—Lundy Bancroft, *Why Does He Do That?*

Not all abusive relationships involve physical violence.

"Just because you're not battered and bruised does not
mean you're not being abused."

—Helpguide.com

Verbal Abuse Can Be Overt or Covert

The anger and contempt of overt verbal abuse are obvious;
the abuser uses shouting, yelling, temper tantrums, name
calling, profanity and threats of loss or pain to intimidate
and control his victim.

If a man hits you, you know instantly—*that's abuse!* If a man
calls you a stupid, ugly, fat pig—you know without question—*he's
demeaning you.* But if a man tells you that he can never please you,
you have a rotten attitude, you can't do anything right, you're too
brainless to get a job, or you're a bad mother, a lousy lover and no
man will ever want you—some women will minimize the fact that
those statements, and comments like them, are—*verbal abuse!*

Covert Abuse is Subtle

Covert abuse can be difficult for the victim to identify because the
perpetrator communicates in ways that are sly, vague, underhanded

and confusing. If the abuser delivers his message without anger or yelling, or he smiles sweetly while mocking his partner, or he passes his demeaning comments off as "constructive" criticisms, the victim is doubly perplexed. The abuser's tone of voice may seem normal, but if you listen closely, a trace of criticism or contempt can be heard. For example, the abuser ridicules his partner in public with sarcasms disguised as "jokes." "You're so easily entertained," he quips in front of friends (insinuating that she is dim-witted and easily amused), or "Don't bother trying to explain it to her; it's over her head." He laughs contemptuously while delivering her a left-handed compliment, e.g., "I like your dress; it does wonders for your figure," and "You're really smart for a woman."

My Texas Girlfriend Within checks out her red rattlesnake cowgirl boots; *Sweet!* She picks up her 12-gauge shotgun, cocks it in one quick motion and says, *"Hey Dickwad, Say that again like you mean it."*

A covert abuser uses guileful actions to demoralize his victim. He consistently forgets the things that are important to his partner which devalues her as a person. He trivializes her interests and accomplishments. He procrastinates to frustrate her and keep her under his thumb. If she complains about his deceptive, misleading, oppressive actions he compounds her abuse by telling her, "You're too sensitive," or "That's not what I said," or "Where did you get a stupid idea like that!"

Covert abuse is **hidden aggression**. Its aim is to **control** and **dominate** you without you knowing. It wounds deep and its psychological damage is long-lasting, and sometimes even permanent.

If you've never been exposed to the insidious nuances of a covert verbal abuser, you may not realize what is happening to you. Therefore, you may be unable to clearly explain his cruel conduct to a friend or counselor.

When Dr. Dirtbag jabbed me with his subtle cutting remarks, I struggled to explain to him how his comments hurt my feelings. He pretended to not understand what he was doing, he screeched, "If you can't tell me what I am doing wrong, how can I change?" I called my girlfriend Annie, who lived several states away, crying about his hurtful behavior. Annie listened pensively and then she said, "Nancy, I think you're over-reacting. Look at everything he's done for you. You know he loves you deeply. You need to toughen up and give this guy some slack. If you don't, you're going to run him off." I couldn't seem to make Annie understand the extent of his wounding actions because I didn't fully understand it myself. Part of the problem was, it wasn't "what" he said that was so ruthless; it was his condescending tone of voice and scornful expressions that cut like a knife.

It was easy for me to believe that I was the one in the wrong given my past relationship failures. I wanted to believe that Dr. Dirtbag truly loved me. And I didn't want to run him off with my uptight behavior and delusionary allegations. So I accepted Annie's explanation. I sucked up my hurt feelings. I forgave him and I tried harder not to react to his erratic verbal assaults.

Verbal abuse is unpredictable. No matter how discerning, guarded or alert a woman is, she is never prepared for her partner's sarcasm, spiteful put-downs or angry jabs. It is his unexpected attacks which keep her confused, stunned and off-balance.

Dee: I felt like I was walking on eggshells around Randy, try-ing to watch what I said or did to not set him off. One minute he was asking me what I wanted for dinner, and the next he was raging at me for not emptying the dishwasher. His mood swings were exhausting and kept my stomach in knots.

Verbal abuse is deliberate and not accidental. It is unimaginable to any woman that the man who professes to love her with such passion and devotion would knowingly want to berate, demean and dominate her.

In public the abuser will act like the perfect caring, good-natured husband or boyfriend. But in private he will turn on and lash out at his partner. Abusers know what they are doing and they choose when and where to abuse. Proof that abuse is a cognitive act is the moment a friend shows up unexpectedly at the door, or his boss calls, or the police arrive on the scene, an abuser is able to immediately compose himself. He may even try to convince the police you were the trouble maker.

As was Clark's normal drinking behavior, he instigated an unjust and hurtful argument with his girlfriend Cindy. One night their argument escalated and Clark threw Cindy up against the wall and grabbed her by the throat. Cindy broke loose, ran into the bedroom and called 911. Fifteen minutes later two uniformed patrolmen showed up at their door. The officers separated Cindy and Clark, taking them into different rooms to interview them. With tears streaming down her face Cindy told her officer how Clark had instigated the fight and violently attacked her. When she finished telling her story, Cindy and her policeman joined Clark and his policeman in the living room. Clark had his hand on his policeman's shoulder, laughing and telling good-old-boy stories. Clark had bamboozled his policeman with his tales of community work and political connections. Suddenly both officers downplayed the seriousness of the situation, saying, "You guys need to try to get along," and upon leaving said routinely, "Call us if you have any more problems." Clark had suckered the cops—it was a jolt to Cindy's self-esteem and a threat to her safety.

Verbal abuse is hostile. All verbal abuse is dominating, controlling and hostile. The longer you remain with an abuser, the more destructive he evolves and the more tolerant you become of his abuse.

There is an anecdote which describes a frog being slowly boiled alive. As the story goes, if you throw a frog into a pot of boiling water, he will immediately feel the heat and jump out. But if you put a frog in lukewarm water and slowly turn up the heat, he will not perceive the danger and he will be cooked to death.

And so it is in abusive relationships.

A wise woman recognizes the warning signs of a man's controlling and abusive personality and quickly stops dating him. The naïve or needy, co-dependent woman minimizes and denies a man's hurtful behavior. She covers up his abuse to her friends and family. She suppresses her fears and anxieties. She gradually adapts and adjusts to his harmful behavior and she remains in the abusive relationship.

Believe It or Not, Abuse is a Planned Event

Experts say abusers know what they are doing, but may not necessarily know why they do it. They choose when, where and whom to abuse. They don't insult, threaten and assault everyone in their life; usually it is the ones closest to them, the ones they claim to love.

Dining out with Dr. Dirtbag was his opportunity to berate, punish and publicly humiliate me. It was a brilliant scheme. He would ask me out to dinner on the pretense of a lovely evening. We would arrive at a restaurant, be seated at a table and then he would blindside me with his jabbing and berating insults. He unknowingly revealed his maiming dinnertime behavior to me when we were first dating. He told me the story of how he and his wife were dining at an exclusive 5-star New Orleans restaurant. She became angry and abruptly left the restaurant leaving him and her untouched plate of seventy-five dollar confit de canard (duck). Amazed I asked him, "Why did she do that?"

"She got mad at the chef [a culinary celebrity]," he claimed. "The chef didn't allow salt and pepper shakers on the table because he claimed his dishes were perfectly seasoned. The uppity waiter refused to bring her salt, she got mad and stormed out of the restaurant and went back to the hotel," said Dr. Dirtbag. "Her loss, it was more food for me," he laughed haughtily.

What a bitch, I thought, How could she behave so crass in such a classy restaurant? But mostly, how could she abandon such a scrumptious meal?

Having experienced countless uneaten restaurant meals with Dr. Dirtbag, and abruptly leaving him at a restaurant and driving myself or taking a cab home, I realized what really happened that night. His wife didn't flee the restaurant because of the waiter's comment. Dr. Dirtbag, in his customary "attack and paralyze" style set his wife up for an enjoyable dinner date, and before she could raise a fork to her mouth he stabbed her with an angry, cutting remark sending her wounded and crying from the restaurant. So unbelievable that he would do this, it took a year for me to realize Dr. Dirtbag's invitations to dinner were a planned event to demoralize me.

My Delilah Girlfriend Within eyeballs Dr. Dirtbag with contempt and she cranks up her gas hedge trimmer, *Time for a haircut, Dirtbag!*

Lettie's husband waited until she was in the car with him driving down the street to start his verbal assault. Said Lettie:

When I finally understood what he was doing, I insisted that we take my car when we drove somewhere together. When he started criticizing me, I slammed on the brakes and told him to "get the crap out of my car." It only took a couple of times before he learned to keep his trap shut.

The verbal abuser undermines his partner's self-perception. The abuser will try to convince you that you are the one who is the problem. He voices his berating and intimidation under the guise of "guidance" or "advice." He presents his criticisms in such a compelling way that the victim believes he knows what he is talking about and she tries to alter her behavior accordingly.

> If the partner is told with gradually increasing frequency that she is illogical, too sensitive, competitive, always trying to start an argument, etc., she may become conditioned to accept more and more abuse while experiencing more and more self-doubt. This conditioning is like brainwashing.
>
> —Patricia Evans, *The Verbally Abusive Relationship*

When the abuser denies the abuse, he also denies your reality.

Verbal abuse escalates with time, increasing in intensity, frequency and variety. Verbal abuse may begin with put-downs disguised as "jokes," but as time passes snide comments turn into blaming accusations, and the accusations evolve into verbal battering that can escalate into physical abuse.

> *In all the time I knew Dr. Dirtbag, he had never laid an abusive hand on me. He rough-housed me one night when demonstrating a martial arts self-protection technique. When I protested of his physically aggressive treatment, he growled, "You can't learn how to protect yourself without getting hurt." It sounded logical, so I shrugged it off.*
>
> *Near the end of our relationship there were occasions when he was so angry and irrational I wondered if he were capable of hitting me. The last night we were together, I got my answer.*
>
> *As was with Dr. Dirtbag's normal verbal assault tactic, he invited me out to dinner, accused me of flirting with a man and he started a verbal altercation with me. We abruptly left the restaurant, packing our dinners into doggie bags. At home*

he continued to rant and rave. He followed me upstairs to my bedroom and into the large walk-in closet where I was changing clothes. He kept berating me and he blocked my exit. I tried to push past him and he grabbed my wrists and penned them to my chest. I thrust my arms downward breaking his vice grip (a self-defense move Dr. Kung-Fu-Dirtbag taught me) and then I slapped him hard across his face to make him back off. "Good move," he sneered, and then he put me in a brutal headlock.

It was the first time I had ever feared Dr. Dirtbag's violence. I screamed and I struggled against his vicious neck hold. He released me once he felt he had made his point (that was—to power over me). That was our final fight.

I later drilled him on the phone about his vicious assault. He laughed scornfully and said, "What the hell are you talking about? You hit me first! I was just trying to keep you from hurting yourself and protect me."

Verbal abuse most often occurs in secret. "This means there may not be anyone who has seen what has happened to you," states the Rape and Abuse Crisis Center of Fargo-Moorhead.

When abuse happens behind closed doors there is no one to validate the victim's suspicions that she is being abused.

In public the abuser is the model husband or boyfriend. He acts perfectly normal showing his successful, outgoing, well-liked persona to friends, neighbors, church members, associates and unsuspecting family members. In private he uses guilt, shame and threats to demean, berate, intimidate and control his partner. He voices his blame, accusations and criticisms in such a convincing way that you doubt your perception of his abuse, as well as, your perceived experience of that abuse. Those who don't know him well may not believe your stories of deception, rage and verbal abuse. With no one to witness his hurtful behavior there is no one to authenticate your emotional injuries. You may even begin to believe you have misinterpreted everything and that there is something wrong with you, as you were told.

Verbal abuse inflicts extreme emotional suffering on its victim that can lead to low self-esteem, depression, hopelessness, and even thoughts of suicide. The longer you stay with an abuser the more time he has to tear down your confidence, self-esteem and self-opinion. The longer you stay with an abuser the more he can isolate you from your family and friends; control your time, activities and finances, and make you dependent on him for your welfare and happiness. The longer you stay in an abusive relationship the more you wonder if the abuse is your fault and you doubt your ability to take care of yourself. The longer you stay with an abuser the more you question your self-worth and you doubt if any man will ever want you again.

Lauren and Mitch dated only six months before she moved in with him into his spacious ranch home. She knew Mitch was rough around the edges, but his generosity and his passion for her were intoxicating. Lauren found his ex-wife's book "Codependent No More," a self-help recovery book, in a closet. Thumbing through the heavily underscored and yellow highlighted pages Lauren was acutely aware of a pained and troubled reader. Her eyes were drawn to a self-awareness checklist that posed the question, "Do you have suicidal thoughts?" Mitch's ex-wife had marked "yes."

Mitch told Lauren that his wife of twenty-six years was a psychological misfit. He said he accompanied her to counseling to try to save their marriage but she became more depressed and their marriage finally ended in divorce. Lauren believed Mitch. She dismissed his ex-wife's suicide admission, thinking her to be, indeed, a distraught, unstable woman.

Months passed and Lauren began to experience a different side of Mitch—he was controlling, demeaning and verbally abusive. A year passed and Lauren was completely demoralized from Mitch's relentless verbal attacks. Her thoughts drifted back to his ex-wife's book. She realized that his ex-wife was not the innately crazed, wretched woman he had portrayed her to be. She was a woman trapped for twenty-six years, raising two children in a cruel and abusive marriage. She had lost her dignity. She had lost her ability to think rationally and function normally—and according to her book—she had lost her will to live. After living with Mitch for slightly over a year, Lauren's happiness and security was also replaced with desperation and hopelessness.

- Verbal abuse is hostile.
- Verbal abuse is unpredictable.
- Verbal abuse is deliberate and not accidental.
- Verbal abuse escalates with time.
- Verbal abuse precedes physical abuse.
- Verbal abuse causes severe emotional suffering.

Shoe Sistas ... verbal abuse is UN-acceptable!

Psychological Warfare

Do not argue with an idiot. He will drag you down to his level and beat you with experience.

—Anonymous

An abuser's goal is to affect and control the emotions, objective reasoning and the behavior of his victim. Covert abuse is disguised by actions that appear normal, but it is clearly insidious and underhanded. The covert abuser methodically chips away at his partner's confidence, perception and self-worth with his subtle hints, unnecessary lying, blaming, accusing and denial. He fosters an atmosphere of fear, intimidation, instability and unpredictability, steadily pushing his victim to the edge—and if she erupts in anger, he condemns her and justifies his hurtful actions.

Darlene's husband, a covert abuser, used insignificant daily happenings to control and demean his wife.

John would argue about anything, Darlene said. He once made a huge issue over my jacket hanging over the back of a chair in the dining room.

"Why is your jacket hanging on the chair in the dining room?" John said angrily.

"Oh ... I'm sorry ... I just got home ... I put it there temporarily."

"But WHY (he's now yelling) did you do that?"

"Really, I'm sorry ... It's no big deal ... I'll hang it in the closet."

"It's no big deal," he said, mockingly, menacingly.

"John, please stop yelling—and stop mocking me."

His face looked like a red-hot chili pepper. He shouted, "I'll do whatever the hell I please! And I'm NOT raising my voice!"

"John, I don't know what to say ... I'm sorry ... I won't leave my jacket out again."

"Quit saying you're sorry! I'm sorry doesn't cut it!" he screamed.

"Okay," I said and I started to walk away.

"Great!" he shouted. "Great job fixing the issue! Just walk away!"

My Irate Girlfriend Within looks up from her Cosmo magazine, glares at her Chauvinist Pig Husband and says, *That's it! I've heard enough! Where's my wallet? I'm going shopping for shoes!*

Psychological Forms of Verbal Abuse

Withholding

Withholding includes refusing to listen, refusing to communicate, and emotionally withdrawing. The withholder may give you the "silent treatment" to punish you. He may refuse to give you information about where he is going, when he is coming back, about financial resources and bill payments. He withholds approval, appreciation, affection, information, thoughts and feelings to diminish and control his partner. He may refuse to answer questions or make eye contact and ignore you.

The verbal abuser who withholds may respond to you by saying:

There's nothing to talk about.

What do you want me to say?

You wouldn't be interested.

It doesn't matter what I say; you'll just do the opposite.

Connie: My fiancé Robert was a knowledgeable, excellent investor. He was always bragging about his increasing wealth.

His money seemed to double and triple effortlessly while mine barely earned a return. I asked him repeatedly to help me invest more wisely. He would say, "Yeah, sure," and then he would turn his attention to something else. He knew it was important to me and he willfully withheld his knowledge to trivialize and control me.

April: When my boyfriend Ricky answered his cell phone, he always walked into another room or outside to talk. When he returned he said nothing as to who he was talking to or what he was talking about. I finally started asking him, "Who was that?" He'd say, "Oh, it was nobody, it was just a client." I asked him, "What did they want?" He would reply, "Nothing. They just called to say hello." It was as if he wanted me to think I was missing out on something important.

Blocking and Diverting

Blocking and diverting prevents or controls a discussion when the abuser changes the topic or he refuses to discuss an issue. Diversion happens when the abuser inappropriately interrupts the conversation. He twists his partner's words, he watches TV or he walks out of the room while she is talking, or he criticizes her in some way so that she ends up defending herself and loses sight of the original conversation. For example, A woman tries to discuss a problem within their relationship and he responds with, "Oh, I guess you never do anything wrong, do you!" Or, "I don't see where this is going! I'm not discussing this with you!" Or, "Where did you get a stupid idea like that!"

Angie: When Michael doesn't like what I am saying he just stops talking and walks out of the room and ignores me the rest of the night.

Other blocking and diverting statements are:

> *You're talking out of turn!*
>
> *You heard me. I'm not going to repeat myself!*
>
> *Who asked you?*
>
> *You're just trying to get the last word!*
>
> *You don't know what you're talking about!*
>
> *Will you get off my back? Just drop it!*
>
> *Quit your bitching!*

With diversion the verbal abuser obstructs the partner's legitimate question. Examples are:

> *What are you worried about? I pay the bills!*
>
> *It's useless to try and explain anything to you; you won't understand.*
>
> *If you think it's so easy then you do it!*
>
> *You're always trying to start an argument!*
>
> *That's not the way it is; you're twisting my words.*

> *Dr. Dirtbag would bait me by making me think he was going to share some important information with me. He would say something like, "I got some good news from the bank today," or "I talked to a friend about a great job opportunity," or "I got a lead on a vacation property." When he knew he had my interest he would pretend to be distracted and turn his attention to something else, or he would say, rather absentmindedly, "Oh, it's not important, I'll tell you later."*

My Psychologist Girlfriend Within arches her eyebrow, folds her arms across her chest, scowls at me, *And you love this asshole—WHY?*

Countering

The verbal abuser sees his partner as an adversary.

A normal conversation is an opportunity to share one's thoughts, feelings and opinions. The counterer, however, sees it as a chance to undermine, demean and control his partner by contradicting, opposing and correcting her thoughts, perceptions, or her experience of life itself. No matter what she says he will use elaborate contradicting arguments to wear her down. If you say, "It's a beautiful day," he'll say, "What's great about it, the weather's crappy." If you say you like sushi, he'll say, "Are you kidding, it will give you parasites." Countering prevents all possibility of discussion and denies the victim's reality about everything.

> *In the beginning I shared my freshly written manuscripts with David. But he began to hyper-criticize and argue against my thoughts.*
> *"You can't say that," he said. "That's wrong!"*
> *I tried to explain my essay so he would better understand my point of view, but it gave him more ammunition to chastise my beliefs. I learned to hide my manuscripts and keep my mouth shut.*

Discounting

Discounting denies the reality and experience of the partner. It is extremely destructive because it discredits and distorts the partner's perception of the abuse.

If the partner says, "I felt hurt when you said . . ." and the abuser says, "You're making a mountain out of a molehill. You're imagining things. You're too serious. You can't take a joke, etc . . ." he is sending the message that your feelings don't count and your experience is wrong. The victim then wonders if her partner is right, that she is hypersensitive or imagining things, and she begins to mistrust her perception of his abuse and her emotional experience.

If the victim does not recognize discounting for what it is she may spend years trying to figure out what is wrong with her and her inability to understand and communicate. Examples of discounting are:

> *You blow everything out of proportion; it's all in your head.*
>
> *You have a negative attitude about everything.*
>
> *You're always trying to start a fight.*
>
> *You can't be happy about anything.*
>
> *You don't understand anything.*

Verbal Abuse Disguised as Jokes

Verbal abuse can begin as small digs disguised as jokes. The abuser teases, ridicules and humiliates his partner with sarcastic remarks about her appearance, personality, abilities and values. As time goes by these put-downs destroy the victim's self-esteem and she begins to have doubts about her capabilities. If the victim says, "I don't think that's funny," or she asks him to stop "poking fun at her" he may become irritated or angry. He again says, "You're too sensitive," or "You can't take a joke." These statements in themselves are abusive, causing the victim to believe she did overreact and wonder what's wrong with her sense of humor.

Some abusers purposely scare us and then laugh, as though it were funny when it was actually designed to frighten us.

Comments made in front of others that mock or belittle a partner are abusive. For example:

> *Margaret is so funny. She burns everything she cooks.*
>
> *It's easy to poke fun at you because you're so cute!*
>
> *She's afraid of her shadow.*
>
> *She can't remember anything; she has sticky notes everywhere.*
>
> *She can't find her way to the grocery store without a GPS.*
>
> *Having a bad hair day?*
>
> *You act just like your mother.*
>
> *Doris is a wild woman in the bedroom; I can't keep up with her!*

You would forget your name if it weren't on your driver's license.
You're not going to wear that are you?

> "Disparaging comments disguised as jokes often re-
> fer to the feminine nature of a woman, to her intel-
> lectual abilities or to her competency."
>
> —Patricia Evans, *The Verbally Abusive Relationship*

Bessie: My date was helping me prepare a beef stir-fry recipe in
my kitchen. When I put the top on a pot of boiling rice the water
boiled over onto the burner making a gigantic gooey mess. He
mockingly said, "Wow, Betty, you sure are entertaining." I
laughed, but inside I knew he was ridiculing me.

Jokes which exaggerate your faults in front of others are verbal abuse.

Melody, a four-time divorcee, runs into her ex-husband (a verbal
abuser) at mutual social settings. Said Melody:

Arthur loves to tear me down in public. We'll be at a
party standing in a group of people. He'll manage to segue
a conversation, asking me, "Well, tell me, Melody, are you
working on your next marriage? Let me count, how many
times is that for you?

Accusing and Blaming

Accusing and blaming shifts the responsibility and the emphasis
from the abuser onto the victim.

Ramona's out-of-town quasi-boyfriend told her he was
coming to see her for the weekend, saying he would arrive on
Friday—and then she never heard from him. Ramona called

him on Monday and she asked what happened to him. He said, "Where have you been? I thought you were going to call me?" making it her fault that he didn't come to see her.

An abuser blames his partner for his mood swings or violent outbursts. The woman may think that his berating is a product of his "bad temperament" or she assumes that his abusiveness comes from something that has gone wrong inside of him, or that he drank too much. She believes his stories of a bad day, a bad childhood, his ex-wife mistreated him, and his other misfortunes and failures.

"What else is she to conclude," says Lundy Bancroft, "given how wonderful he was at first?—so she pours herself into figuring out what happened."

Dr. Dirtbag blamed everyone for his outbursts and sullen behavior. He blamed his ex-wife for their dysfunctional marriage. He said, "I think my wife was cheating on me in our first year of marriage; it's where my insecurity comes from." He blamed his daughter for their estranged relationship, saying, "I'm nothing but a bank account to her." He blamed me for his punishing behavior, saying "I have abandonment issues. When you get mad at me I can't think straight." Nothing was ever his fault.

Carla blamed Andrew's mother for his cruel, abusive personality, states Carla:

When Andrew was a youngster his father was a traveling salesman, earning a mediocre salary. He said his mother blamed him for her unhappiness. She constantly berated him, saying, "It's your fault your father is gone all the time," and "You'll never amount to anything." His mother was the rudest, nastiest person I'd ever met, and so I believed Andrew's hurtful childhood stories. I believed his motivation to become a wealthy businessman was to prove his self-worth and his mother wrong. His entire existence was to attain money and power, but in doing so he suppressed his concern for others. I thought my love could help him get rid of the demons from his past—instead, he became more determined to demean and control me.

Examples of blaming:

> *If you didn't spend so much money, I wouldn't have to work all the time.*
>
> *If you didn't act so stupid, I wouldn't get upset.*
>
> *If you weren't so emotional we could talk.*
>
> *I did it because you ...*
>
> *It's your fault.*
>
> *You didn't remind me.*
>
> *Nothing I do is ever enough.*

Gaslighting

The other person denies your perceptions of events and conversations.

Gaslighting is a form of psychological abuse in which false information is presented to the victim, making her doubt her own memory and discernment. Gaslighting can cause the victim to feel confused and second-guess herself, have trouble making simple decisions, feel as though she can't do anything right, and even cause her to apologize for things that are not her fault.

> *Dr. Dirtbag's favorite game was the triple threat: deny, shift and blame. He was always flirting with younger women. When I confronted him he would tell me I was overreacting. I would then believe myself to be controlling and insecure and I found myself apologizing to him for giving him a hard time.*
>
> *We were at a casino nightclub one evening. It was standing room only and he invited two attractive young women to*

share our table. He asked the two girls to dance with him. Song after song they danced as a threesome while I sat at the table alone, watching him grinning, twirling and lusting after the scantily dressed trixie twins. We left the club and a horrible argument ensued. I screamed at him, "Your behavior was completely inappropriate and I'm not going to tolerate it." He glared at me as if I were a Linda-Blair-head-spinning-lunatic and he bellowed, "WHAT THE FUCK IS WRONG WITH YOU?!?! I was just being polite. Why do you always have to ruin our evening?!?!" The next morning, when I awoke, my heart wrenched with regret. I thought I had overreacted and wrongly accused him. I begged him for his forgiveness. He punished me for an hour with his sullen silence and then he finally took me in his arms and proclaimed, "Of course I forgive you. Don't I always forgive you? You're the love of my life!"

Dr. Dirtbag never did take responsibility for his conspicuous flirtatious behavior and I worked harder to stifle my overactive jealous imagination.

Psychologist Susan Meindle says the gaslighting abuser attempts to make the victim doubt her own perceptions and judgments and accept those of the abuser. This may be done intentionally, or unconsciously, but when the victim loses confidence in her judgment they become easily swayed and they accept their perpetrator's point of view, plan or decision.

I once had a psychologist girlfriend who enjoyed poking fun at me in front of our friends. I challenged her on her hurtful behavior and insisted that she cease her ridicule of me. She told me she thought I was bi-polar and I needed medication and psychiatric counseling. She even went so far as to tell me she spoke to a psychiatrist colleague about me.

"Here's her phone number," she said, and she handed me a piece of paper with the psychiatrist's scribbled phone number. "She said she would see you as a favor to me."

Her abuse was passive-aggressive, sinister and threatening. She used her professional knowledge to try to control and demean me, while avoiding responsibility for her harmful, toxic actions. My so-called-psycho-doctor-friend accused me of what she was guilty of being—a mentally unbalanced verbal abuser.

If anyone consistently accuses you of being too sensitive, paranoid, controlling, unreasonable, too stressed, forgetful, or mentally unstable—you may be the victim of gaslighting.

Crazy-Making

The abuser will use a combination of distortion, blaming, forgetting, stonewalling and denial to confuse, frustrate and drive his victim to the edge of insanity. His language is vague and tentative. He will twist your words, putting you on the defense. He wants you to second guess yourself and doubt your reality. Here are some examples of crazy-making:

He has a way of making me doubt myself. He tells me, "That's not what I said." "You're misinterpreted what I said." And, "Have you lost your memory?

I can never get a clear-cut answer from him. His favorite lines are, "I'll let you know." "I'll think about it." And, I'll take care of it"—and, of course, he never does.

My boyfriend ripped me apart one night. The next morning when I appeared in the kitchen visibly depressed and unhappy, he half-asked me, incriminating, "What's the matter with you?"

My husband gets mad over nothing. When I ask him what's wrong he denies he's upset, when clearly he is. And when I don't guess what wrong with him, he gets more upset and gives me the silent treatment.

Don't try to reason with a crazy maker. If you do, he will work harder to confound and upset you. And when you become unglued, explode and bombast him, he will make you look like the guilty, offending party.

Judging and Criticizing

Verbal abuse is often disguised as "constructive" criticism.

> The verbal abuser may judge his partner and then express his judgment in a critical way. If she objects, he may tell her that he is just pointing something out to be helpful, but in reality he is expressing his lack of acceptance of her.
>
> —Patricia Evans, *The Verbally Abusive Relationship*

I was sensitive about my weight, and although I was only five pounds over my ideal size, Dr. Dirtbag would make demeaning comments to me about my body. One evening while we were eating dinner he said, "I thought you were trying to lose weight?" It felt like a hard jab to my heart. When I told him his remark was unkind he looked at me in disgust and exclaimed, "Geez! I was just trying to help you with your dieting. I'll keep my mouth shut from now on."

Statements like, *"Are you sure you need another serving?"* and *"You know that cake goes straight to your hips,"* and *"That dress makes you look fat!"* are verbally abusive.

"Most 'you' statements are judgmental, critical and abusive," states Patricia Evans.

You're never satisfied.

You're a lousy winner.

You're lazy.

You can't do anything right.

You can't let well enough alone.

How dumb (you are).

Paraphrased from The Verbally Abusive Relationship

Trivializing

Trivializing says directly, or indirectly, that what you have done or said is not important. An abuser will downplay your efforts, interests, hobbies, achievements and concerns. He may ignore or minimize what is important to you, or he may focus on what is *not* done. When this is done in a frank and sincere manner, it can be difficult to detect. The victim then becomes confused, thinks her partner simply doesn't understand, and tries harder to explain the importance of her thoughts or interests, only to be met with more criticism, trivializing and discounting.

The trivializing-abuser may "set you up" by first praising you and then following it with his hyper-criticisms. "Your report is good but it makes no sense. No one will understand what you are trying to say." Or, "I like your red dress, but don't you think it's a bit vulgar for the event."

The trivializing-abuser may undermine the importance of your time or work.

Thomas knew how much Arlene enjoyed her women's ministry work, and although it only required a couple of hours of weekly preparation and one night a week away from home, he constantly complained about her participation. "All you ever do is church stuff. If you put that much effort into being a wife I might enjoy being a husband."

Undermining

The undermining abuser not only withholds emotional support, but he erodes his partner's confidence by breaking promises, failing to follow through on agreements, and renouncing his fair share of responsibilities, e.g., he refuses to help with the children or housework. He crushes his partner's self-assurance with a single comment, "That ridiculous," he says and laughs contemptuously. "How did you come up with a crazy idea like that?" He degrades her thoughts, actions and suggestions; e.g., she suggests a restaurant to dine or vacation destination, and the abuser says, "The food is awful at that place!" "Why would you want to go to Florida; it's nothing but a tourist trap!" He talks in ways to confuse or baffle his partner. He undercuts her self-worth by making light of his bad behavior. He tells her the abuse didn't happen or that she caused it. He tells her she is unable to function without him.

The undermining-abuser interrupts you when you are doing something that is important to you.

It took concentration and privacy for me to finish my writing projects. Dr. Dirtbag knew this. When I was working in my home office he would constantly barge into the room to ask me inconsequential questions, like, "How's it going?" "You need anything?" "You got anything you want me to read?" I would tell him, "I'm busy. I'm writing. I'll quit in an hour. Can you please not disturb me until then?" He would concede and withdraw. Fifteen minutes later he was back at my door, asking me something asinine, like, "Do these slacks make me look fat?" It was a game to him. He wanted to see how many times he could disrupt my thoughts before I finally exploded.

He sabotages your ideas by pointing out the way you might fail. Examples of undermining comments that squelch your enthusiasm are:

You wouldn't understand.

Who asked you?

You don't know what you're talking about.

You'll never succeed.

What makes you think you're so smart?

Who are you trying to impress?

Threatening and Intimidation

Intimidation (also called cowing) is a tactic designed to scare you into submission; such as, threatening to leave you, threatening to get a divorce, or threatening to take a mistress. He will make menacing looks or gestures, smash things in front of you, threaten to hit you or hurt your pet, insinuate physical harm to your loved ones or possessions, or put weapons on display. The message is: if you don't obey there will be violent consequences.

> *Roberta's boyfriend always carried a loaded pistol with him thinking he was a badass. At home his pistol was always nearby. When he watched TV in the living room he sat in his overstuffed chair with a loaded Glock semi-automatic next to him. In his back yard, lying by the pool, he laid his gun on a table next to his lounge chair, in case "someone climbed over the fence," he said. He slept with it next to him in bed should someone manage to get past his many deadbolts and alarms. He told Roberta, "Don't worry, I will always protect you." His psychotic behavior frightened Roberta and made her co-dependent on him for her safety.*

Some examples of intimidation:

> *If you don't leave me alone, I'll leave.*
>
> *If you break up with me, I'll call your boss and get you fired.*
>
> *Iron my shirt now or I'll make the dog sleep outside in the snow tonight.*
>
> *Hang up the phone or I'll hurt you.*

Intimidation is delivered in pressure tactics: e.g., rushing you to make a decision through "guilt-tripping," sulking until he gets his way, withholding money and manipulating the children.

Emotional Blackmail

Emotional blackmail is any behavior that attempts to threaten and control you. The abuser plays on your fear, guilt, compassion, values, or other "hot buttons" to get what he wants. This could include threats to end the relationship, totally reject or abandon you, giving you the "cold shoulder," withholding money or financial support. He may say, "If you don't come back to me I will quit paying your car note." It can also be manipulation to appeal to your sense of responsibility or obligation to achieve his personal goal; e.g., "If you really loved me, you would do this."

Name Calling

Name calling is an overt obvious form of verbal abuse, designed to hurt or degrade someone. Terms of endearment such as "sweetheart" can be used in an abusive way when spoken with obvious sarcasm. Calling someone "stupid" because she isn't as intelligent, or calling her a "klutz" because she is not as coordinated is abusive.

Archie Bunker repeatedly insulted his wife Edith's intelligence by calling her a "dingbat."

Marilyn's boyfriend demeaned her by calling her "Muggy Quacks" because he said she walked like a duck. Because he said it in a semi-loving manner, she accepted it as a caring pet name—when secretly it stung her feelings.

Forgetting

Forgetting involves both denial and covert manipulation. The declaration by the abuser that what occurred didn't occur is abusive.

—Patricia Evans, *The Verbally Abusive Relationship*

Everyone forgets things from time to time, but when the abuser regularly forgets appointments, agreements, promises and incidents, he is saying, "I'm in control of your time and reality."

Robert accidently on purpose forgot to do the things he knew were important to Inez.

Inez moved in with her fiancé Robert, a successful investor. She wanted to return to school to finish her teaching degree. With

Robert's approval she quit work, enrolled in college and Robert took over her living expenses. Said Inez:

When my credit card bills arrived I would present them to Robert for payment. He would put them on the kitchen counter until the final due date, giving me the distinct feeling that he "might" or "might not" pay my bills. He told me he would add me to his health insurance and get me a cell phone on his business plan. Every month I would ask him, "Did you add me to your health insurance?" He would say, "Oh, I'm sorry. I was really busy today. I'll take care of it tomorrow." I would ask, "Did you take care of my cell phone?" He repeatedly said, "I'm waiting for my representative to call me." Month after month I asked him about my credit card bills, insurance and phone and he screamed at me, "I told you I would take care of it dammit! Will you get off my back. When I say I will do something, I do it! Give me a break, will ya!" I worried myself sick about my bills and insurance. It was how me controlled and punished me.

Tanya's boyfriend had selective amnesia. He constantly forgot the things that were important to her. He forgot to pick up her dry cleaning, to make a household repair, to call the travel agent, or to purchase theatre tickets. He would agree to take care of her requests; time would lapse and she would ask him, "Did you do so and so?" He would get a stupid look on his face and say, "Oh, jeez. I'm sorry. I forgot. Oops! My bad!"

Abusers who selectively forget previous incidents of verbal abuse deliver a double whammy to their victims. First with the verbal abuse, and second by denying the victim's reality of the abuse.

The day after an argument with Dr. Dirtbag I sought him out for an explanation and an apology for his hurtful behavior. I said to him, "It really hurt my feelings when you talked to me the way you did last night." He looked at me as if I had lost

He conveniently forgets the verbal bashing he gave you last night!

my mind, frowned and screamed, "**WHAT THE HELL ARE YOU TALKING ABOUT? I never said that. You always blow everything out of proportion.**" I knew that he said it, but he was so convincing he caused me to doubt my cognition and memory.

Ordering

"Ordering denies the equality and autonomy of the partner," states Patricia Evans. "When an abuser gives orders instead of respectfully asking for what he wants" he is treating his partner like a slave or subordinate; someone who exists to fulfill his wishes. The abuser is saying, "I have a right to dominate and have power over you."

Examples of ordering:

You're not wearing that.

Bring me something to drink.

Clean this mess up.

Get this off of here.

Be quiet; I'm watching TV.

Turn that off.

Denial

Denial renounces the reality of the partner. A verbal abuser will outright deny his hurtful and unacceptable behavior and he will refute that any hurt or upset has occurred. Denial is exceedingly damaging to the victim because it denounces her experiences and causes her to doubt her perceptions.

Examples of denial:

You think I'm hurtful to you? Look at the way you treat me!

He says, "I'm not upset," (when clearly he is).

I never said that, you can't get anything straight.

You're lying; you're making that all up to make me look bad.

It's no big deal; you're getting upset over nothing.

Abusive Anger

Abusive anger is hostile and threatening. The abuser uses irritable outbursts, sarcasm, sneering, cursing, arguing, temper tantrums, yelling, raging, explosiveness, hitting things or aggressive body language to intimidate, control and dominate his victim. The abuser may physically block you, or follow you from room to room. Angry outbursts may lead to physical violence.

> **If your partner is abusive, it is not your fault, nor is it your responsibility. Your efforts to bring reconciliations, mutual understanding and intimacy will most likely be rejected because your partner will view them as adversarial and undermining of their desire to control.**
>
> —Rape and Abuse Crisis Center of Fargo-Moorhead

I tried to ignore Dr. Dirtbag's verbal abuse. I'm strong, I thought. He doesn't really mean it. I'll show him how much I love him and together we'll work through this. When he saw me trying to resist his hostility and maintain my composure he increased the force of his abuse.

> "This is one of the reasons that verbal abuse increases over time. As the partner adapts—trys [sic] to ignore the behavior, possibly hoping it will stop or hoping she won't inadvertently provoke him or that she'll figure out what she's 'doing wrong' or why she's 'feeling wrong,' the abuser increases the intensity and/or the frequency of the abuse."
>
> —Patricia Evans, *The Verbally Abusive Relationship*

Humiliation

Humiliation uses insults, name-calling, shaming and public put-downs to erode the victim's self-esteem and make her feel powerless. The abuser will say bad things about you, behind your back and in front of you, to family and friends saying you are the unstable and abusive one. After all, if the abused partner believes she is worthless and no one else will want her, she is less likely to leave him.

> *Zonda, a 50-year-old divorcee: Ron used my relationship failures to shame me. "I bet you've slept with a lot more men than I have with women," he sniped at me. And, "What everyone says about you is true." He never told me who "everyone" was and what they were saying. He didn't have to; he knew my self-deprecating imagination would fill in the blanks.*

Psychological Forms of Verbal Abuse: Category headings from The Verbally Abusive Relationship, by Patricia Evans. Content paraphrased in part from The Verbally Abusive Relationship, Helpguide.com and Dr. Irene's Verbal Abuse www.drirene.com/control.htm.

Controlling with Body Language or Gestures

The verbal abuser uses body language to control his partner, with the words and gestures often going together. Examples of controlling body language and gestures:

- Refusing to talk or make eye contact
- Sulking, strutting and posturing, stomping out of the room
- Boredom-crossed arms, eyes closed, head down
- Inappropriate sounds, deep sighs, words like, *"Soooo!"*
- Showing disgust, rolled eyes, frowning
- Refusing to give her something
- Hitting or kicking something
- Driving recklessly
- Withdrawing or withholding affection

Paraphrased from Dr. Irene's Verbal Abuse (Site)! and the The Verbally Abusive Relationship by Patricia Evans.

Controlling Behavior Intended to Diminish the Partner:

- Patronizing, laughing at your opinion, mimicking or smirking
- Using a tone of contempt, absolute certainty and authority (defining your reality)
- Interrupting, ignoring, not listening, refusing to respond
- Distorting what you say, provoking guilt, playing victim
- Criticism that is harsh, undeserved or frequent
- Changing the subject to his grievances
- Yelling, out-shouting or swearing
- Starting a sentence with, "Forget it."

My Wounded Girlfriend Within finishes reading *Never Date a Dead Animal*, stretches out on her shrink's sofa, and glances at her Lorus wrist watch ... *Doc, we only got a few minutes ... Saks is having a Friends and Family Sale!*

Don't You Dare Hit Me!

*A batterer will beat any partner if she is
with him long enough for the violence to begin.*

Short, but not so sweet chapter—*physical abuse!*

Women and men of all races are vulnerable to violence by an intimate partner. The National Institute of Justice and the Center for Disease Control estimates that 1.5 million women and 835,000 men are the victims of domestic violence each year.

> **People whose partners abuse them physically and sexually are at a higher risk of being seriously injured or killed.**
>
> **—Helpguide.com**

Stay clear of a man who has a record of domestic violence. Beware of a man who admits to hitting his wife or girlfriend. He may claim his previous partner provoked him to do it, or he has changed and he is no longer that person. Situational circumstances do not cause a person to be abusive—either they are, or they are not.

Think twice about dating a jealous and controlling man. Don't take his word for it—call a previous girlfriend or ex-wife about a suspected batterer (hopefully she will talk to you). I once dated a man who admitted to hitting his former wife. He began to demean me and I contacted his ex-wife, hoping to confirm my suspicions about his abusive behavior. No surprise, she was afraid to talk to me.

True stories from the Internet:

Maggie: My boyfriend verbally and physically abused me for three years. He yanked my hair, jerking my head so hard that it cracked my neck and I can't move my head. I know I'm worthless to him and I never do anything right. What really drives me to depression is how he calls me worthless, dumb, retard, stupid, the fat part of meat, etc. I asked him to stop calling me names and his response was, "Well, don't be one and I will stop."

Alice: I was in the hospital twice with violence-related injuries inflicted by my husband. I was in the psych ward twice for attempting suicide. I miscarried in the middle of one of his beatings. I gained 80 pounds through misery eating and I developed a drinking problem. I wasn't allowed to leave the house. He cut me off from my family and friends. I was required to make an appearance at church, and as soon as the service was finished, he packed me up and took me home.

My Self-Defense Girlfriend Within warns her female students, *If you visit a guy's home and he ignores a ringing phone, you see broken glass, holes in the wall, downed doors, guns on display or blood on the carpet—assume there's trouble around the corner.*

Never is there a worthwhile reason for a woman to stay with a man who is verbally and physically abusive. Not for the sake of commitment, family ties, children, finance or position.

Millions of Shoe Sistas have an empowering, awakening moment. They kick out their good-for-nothin' boyfriends and divorce their abusive husbands. They block his annoying, abusive, threatening emails and phone calls. They change the passwords to their emails, bank accounts and other online accounts. They delete the sappy breakup songs from their iPod. They pull out their Louis Vuitton luggage, pack their most obscene designer shoes, their big-girl bikinis and they book a fabulous Mediterranean cruise.

Cycle of Abuse

During every stage in the cycle, the abuser is fully in control of themselves and is working to control and further weaken the victim.

—DomesticViolentServices.com

*U*nderstanding the abuser's distorted mindset that fuels the "cycle of violence can help the victim recognize they are not to blame for the domestic violence they have suffered and that the abuser is the one responsible," states DomesticViolenceServices.com.

Six distinct stages make up the cycle of violence: the set-up, the abuse, the abuser's feeling of "guilt" and their fear of reprisal, their rationalization, the abuser's shift to non-abusive or very good behavior, and the fantasies and plans for the next episode of abuse. A sequence of events, although in variety, that happens over and over again with certainty.

—DomesticViolenceServices.com

I was crazy in love with Dr. Dirtbag and I was horribly ad-dicted to the roller coaster love-abuse-breakup-reconcile cycle of our relationship. I knew I was being slowly destroyed and I tried a hundred times to leave him permanently. But he kept sucking me back in with his pleas to forgive him, his sorry ex-

cuses, and his expressions of adoration. I believed him when he promised to stop drinking and verbally abusing me. I was optimistic when he consented to go to a counselor and he got meds for his mood swings. Then I realized—the only way I would survive this maiming relationship was to leave him— forever.

> Life with an abuser can be a dizzying wave of exciting good times and painful periods of verbal, physical, or sexual assault. The longer the relationship lasts, the shorter and farther apart the positive periods tend to become. If you have been involved with an abusive partner for many years, the good periods may have stopped happening altogether, so that he is an unvarying source of misery.
>
> —Lundy Bancroft, *Why Does He Do That?*

The abusive cycle confounds and keeps the victim off-balance. The abuser's behavior vacillates, one minute he is loving and attentive, and the next he is angry and punishing. The victim often feels as though she is walking on eggshells as her abuser becomes more temperamental and critical, or he withdraws and is irritable and moody. The victim senses a growing tension and she may placate her abuser, asking him, "Are you okay? Is something bothering you?" She tries to be extra careful to not trigger an abusive episode.

The Six Cycles of Abuse

1. **Setup:** Your abuser creates situations in which you have no choice but to act in a way that will, in his mind, justify his abuse. For example, the abuser wants to lose weight but he berates you when you serve him grilled fish and salad. Consequently, you add scalloped potatoes and rolls to the menu, and he screams, *"Are you crazy? You know I'm trying to lose weight. You know I have high cholesterol and I can't eat carbs! Are you trying to kill me?"*

2. **Abuse:** When the time and the planned circumstance are right, the abuser begins his violence. He lashes out at his partner with accusations, hurtful put-downs or frightening aggression. He may become violent, knocking over chairs, kicking in doors and hurling objects. A trivial event is often used to trigger the main event.

3. **Guilt:** After the violence, the abuser may have feelings of guilt, not over what he has done, but he worries about facing consequences for his abusive behavior. He thinks, *"I shouldn't have done that, because I might get caught."* If there are visible bruises, he will minimize his abuse telling her it was an "accident." He apologizes and he promises to never do it again so he can reconcile with his partner and minimize the effect of his abuse.

4. **Rationalization:** The abuser can't stand feeling guilty for long, so he quickly moves on to the rationalization stage. He blames the victim and he makes excuses for his violent behavior. Common excuses usually revolve around the abuser being intoxicated or he was abused as a child. But alcohol use, self-esteem issues, emotional problems, mental illness or a previous relationship with a woman who mistreated him does not cause a man's abusiveness.

5. **Normal:** The abuser does everything he can to regain control and keep the victim in the relationship. He may act as if nothing has happened. He offers no apologies or explanations for his hurtful behavior and he waits for his partner to recover from his abuse on her own volition. The abuser may turn on the charm: he is thoughtful, charming, adoring and generous. He may take her out to dinner, take her shopping and placate her with flowers and gifts. He may try to convince her that he will change. The victim is persuaded to stay or return to the abuser because she is hopeful—*that this time*—he really will change.

6. **Fantasy and Planning:** Unbelievably batterers fantasize about their past and future abuses. The fantasies feed the abuser's anger and help him to move on to the active planning stage. The abuser thinks about what you've done wrong and how he'll make you pay. He devises a plan to turn his fantasy of abuse into reality. He uses excuses to rationalize his abuse. For instance, if the abuse is rationalized due to the victim's behavior with other individuals, the abuser will decide to take his partner to a social outing. If the abuser resents his partner's spending, he will accompany her on a shopping trip. Some abusers fantasize that their partner is having an affair because she can't prove otherwise. The abuser activates the fantasy. The event brings on the abuse. The abuser experiences power over his victim ... the abuse cycle continues.

Adapted and paraphrased from Mid-Valley Crisis Center; HelpGuide.org; The Verbally Abusive Relationship by Patricia Evans; Dr Irene's Verbal Abuse Site, and Domestic Violence and Services.

Towards the end of my relationship with Dr. Dirtbag I began to recognize a logical, but schizophrenic rhythm to his abusive behavior. David would wake up every weekday morning cheerful and even-tempered and he would go to work in his scrubs, focused and sane. Midday he would come home for lunch relaxed and agreeable. After work he would arrive at home, stand at my office door appearing lucid and good-natured. He would ask me about my day, ask to read my latest manuscript, and he would go outside to drink a glass of ice tea, smoke a cigarette and unwind. An hour later, from the dark side of Mars, his agitated, irrational evil twin brother, Dr. Dirtbag, would appear. I knew the drill. I could see the irritation and displeasure in his eyes. I knew he was getting ready to instigate a disagreement that would quickly escalate into a berating episode.

It was the end of a work day, David, in his sane skin, announced, "I'm going to the grocery store. You wanna go?"

"Sure," I said willingly (it was one of the few things I still enjoyed doing with him).

Immediately he retorted, "No, I'm not going—you are. I've got to start dinner."

My Bi-Polar Girlfriend Within screams, *What?!?!? What the hell is he talking about?*

"Never mind," I told him, "I'm busy" ... and I went back to working on my computer.

David huffed and stomped off and then I heard the front door slam (he left to go to the grocery store—alone). Five minutes later he called me on my mobile phone. I knew a fracas was brewing and I didn't answer my phone. Five minutes later he was hovering at my office door, looking flustered, annoyed and ready to strike—and he did.

Dr. Dirtbag had set me up for an ambush. He plotted his assault on his drive home from work and there was nothing I could have said or done to diffuse the anger that fueled his demented soul!

Abusers Are Payback Oriented

The abusive personality is payback oriented. He keeps a mental log—a sheet of imagined checks and balances of the time you angered him, the times you stood up to him, and the occasions you exposed him for his deceit, all of which build his resentment towards you and give him the ammunition he needs to set you up for an abusive event.

At the core of the abusive man is a sense of false entitlement. When something doesn't go his way, or he is questioned about his motives or privileges, or if you defy him and expose him for his bad behavior, he will retaliate to regain his superiority. The abuser assaults you, purging himself of his built-up anger and resentment (like letting steam out of a pressure cooker), and he justifies his behavior, claiming your actions or behavior provoked his outburst. Relieved of his hostility, he is rejuvenated and he may work to restore the harmony of your relationship by offering weak excuses, flimsy apologies, token gifts or an invitation to dine out. But your head is spinning because you are confused as to why he attacked you, and you are mortified by his unfair and cruel behavior.

> *Dr. Dirtbag had a real talent for pushing me to the edge until I exploded and retaliated, and consequently, I became the bad guy. One night he made me so angry I threw my engagement ring at him, and then I wound up apologizing to him. He eventually accepted my apology. "I can't stay mad at you; I'd cut my arm off for you," he said.*
>
> *He acted like he had put his hard feelings to rest; when in reality, he had mentally filed the incident away so he could justify his next verbal assault. Sure enough, several days later, when I least expected it, and he was ready for his next hostile-fix, he invited me out to dinner, he dug into his bag of past grieves, and he bomb-blasted me the minute my entrée was served.*

Don't fool yourself thinking that your abusive man has forgiven you for standing up to him. Abusers are unfeeling and vengeful and he will mentally compute your offenses and when the time is prime—and you are unaware—he will pay you back with harsh dividends.

Ending Verbal Abuse

The first step to ending verbal abuse is recognizing that you are in a verbally abusive relationship. If you have never been in a covert abusive relationship, you may not have a frame of reference; and therefore, you may not understand the dynamics of this type of relationship. You may not know that the abuse language is "coded," the gestures are underhanded and the overall assault is scheming. You may not understand that the abuser's cruel and unpredictable behavior is designed to confuse, undermine and beat you down, while his intermittent deeds of affection and kindness are intended to suck you deeper into the cycle of abuse.

Shoe Sistas, listen up! All verbal abuse is anger driven! In case you didn't catch that, I repeat—*ALL VERBAL ABUSE IS ANGER DRIVEN!*

The goal of covert abuse is to manipulate, dominate and control the victim without her knowing, states Patricia Evans. The victim's best defense against an abusive relationship "is to find out everything you can about verbally abusive relationships and their dynamic ... Usually one person is blaming, accusing, even name calling, and the other is defending and explaining."

As time went by, my relationship with Dr. Dirtbag became increasingly worse. His lies became more exaggerated, his behavior more irrational, his verbal abuse more intense and his remorse non-existent. He masked his hurtful behavior with well-timed gifts and feigned apologies. But my head was reeling, my heart was aching and my gut was churning from the constant turbulence. I felt like I was crazy, but in my heart of hearts, I knew I wasn't. I began to look for answers. I went to the bookstore to look for self-help books. At first I didn't know what to look for—then I stumbled on a book describing verbally abusive relationships. I found books on narcissistic, sociopathic, anti-social and borderline personalities. I read about the characteristics and behaviors of people with these mental disorders and the dynamics of the verbally abusive relationship. I began to understand that was the relationship I had with Dr. Dirtbag.

Recognizing verbal abuse for what it is, an attempt to gain power and control over another is the first step to begin personal healing and regain your life.

Antisocial Personality Disorder

When dating a sociopath the only warning sign you may have is a mild sense of doubt and skepticism—it's a warning sign you should heed.

ooner or later you will have a run-in with a man (or woman) with an antisocial personality disorder; aka sociopath or psychopath. There are just too many of them, possibly being between "3 million to 12 million sociopaths in the United States," states lovefraud.com, an online dating and relationship website.

Antisocial personality disorder is characterized by persistent disregard for, and violation of the rights of others without guilt feelings, as well as impulsive, irresponsible and aggressive behavior. Among the most common characteristics of those with antisocial personality disorder are superficial charm, shallow emotions, lack of a conscience, pathological lying, extraversion, egocentricity and delusions of greatness, excessive hedonism, high impulsivity, lack of responsibility, a desire to experience sensations of control and power, and manipulation of others without remorse or empathy for the victim.

Sociopath or Psychopath

Experts do not agree on how to differentiate the sociopath and psychopath; but both have been recently accredited as subsets of the Antisocial Personality Disorder. Some say it depends on who is defining the mental illness. Psychiatrists often class sociopaths and psychopaths together, while criminologists differentiate between them based on their outward behavior. Generally, sociopaths are said to behave in a disorganized, erratic manner; they lack impulse control and they can't seem to keep a job or sustain relationships. While psychopaths tend to be extremely organized, have the tendency to be better educated than sociopaths and can keep successful careers and relationship intact for years. Sociopaths are equated with dysfunction. Psychopaths are typically equated with serial murders (*nice!*). Sociopaths are random in victims and actions; psychopaths are very calculated in both. Both are often extremely charismatic and likeable and generally behave outwardly normal, but are secretive, manipulative and ruthless.

In the interest of brevity I will use the term "sociopath" to discuss antisocial personalities.

The Romantic Sociopath

In the book *Snakes in Suits* authors Dr. Robert Hare and Dr. Paul Babiak talk about the potent charm of the sociopathic personality:

> One of the most effective skills psychopaths [sociopaths] use to get the trust of people is their ability to charm them. Some psychopaths lay the charm on too thick, coming across as glib, superficial, and unconvincing. However, the truly talented ones have raised their ability to charm people to that of an art, priding themselves on their ability to present a fictional self to others that is convincing, taken at face value, and difficult to penetrate.
>
> —*Snakes in Suits*

Sociopaths can be very romantic, extremely charming, exceedingly generous and seductive. They shower their targets with excessive attention, flattery and gifts—yet they are covertly hostile and domineering. Lying, deceiving and manipulation are second nature to a sociopath and they are extremely convincing. When caught in a lie they are seldom embarrassed; they simply rework the facts to camouflage the first lie. The result is a series of contradictory statements that confuse, frustrate, demoralize, and even anger the listener.

The hallmark of a sociopath is intense charm and lack of conscience.

Sociopaths have a false sense of entitlement; their severe self-interest makes them narcissistic, self-indulgent and arrogant. They feel they are superior to others and they scorn social conventions. They disregard the rights, feelings and safety of others. They see people as targets and opportunities for personal gain of wealth, power and/or sex. They are unable to empathize with the pain of their victims and they have contempt for their distressed feelings. Sociopaths do not accept blame, but rationalize and blame others, even for the acts they obviously committed.

Sociopaths don't experience emotions of normal people. Their

Sociopaths have no conscience; their only goal is self-gratification.

emotions are shallow and feigned. Where most people form genuine loyal attachments to the people they love, sociopaths are incapable of feeling "true love" and therefore their relationships are without depth or meaning. Many are hedonistic and egocentric and can easily have numerous affairs without guilt or remorse. He lies to you about his infidelity while also lying to his lovers.

Sociopaths are often angry and their self-interest makes them arrogant.

Sociopaths learn to imitate the feelings and behavior of others so they can appear normal and fit it. When they do show what seems to be warmth, joy, love and compassion it is more pretended than experienced and serves an ulterior motive. When he becomes bored with berating, punishing and terrorizing you—or he has spent all your money—or he has his next "bedmate" lined up—he can quickly abandon a loved one, revealing his true self: a cruel, raging, heartless monster who feels no remorse for the pain and suffering he has caused. The sociopath deservedly earns the name—the "empty soul."

As time goes by a sociopath's appearance of perfection begins to crack. But by that time you will have already been emotionally and perhaps financially burned.

Sociopaths live on the edge and verbal outbursts and punishing behavior are normal. Promiscuous sexual conduct, infidelity, drugs, alcoholism and gambling are common. The sociopath's rage and abuse, alternating with small expressions of love and approval, produce an addictive cycle for the abuser and the abused, and create confusion, despair and hopelessness in the victim. Sociopaths believe that they are all-powerful, all-knowing and they are entitled to their every wish with no sense of personal boundaries and no concern for their impact on others. They tend to move around a lot, make elaborate promises for the future and will change their image as needed to avoid exposure and prosecution. They frequently have a history of behavioral and academic difficulties and criminal offenses, yet they "get by" by conning others. The sociopath spends his life lying, cheating, extorting, raging, abusing and manipulating others without guilt, remorse or shame.

Adapted from www.mcafee.ccc

Successful Sociopaths Under the Radar

Some sociopaths use their professional role as a mask to hide their real personalities.

—**Dr. Martha Stout,** *The Sociopath Next Door*

Not all sociopaths end up in jail or on the streets; some become (or pretend to be) clergy, police officers, bank presidents, military personnel, writers, artists, entertainers, teachers, doctors, lawyers and Indian chiefs. These sociopathic citizens appear to function normally and are generally thriving and respected within their communities.

We assume people in these positions are trustworthy—*think again!* The sociopath's needs, wants and goals are of utmost importance to them and they use their vocations, intelligence, societal standing and social skills to manipulate, intimidate, con and swindle others with their romance scams, phony stock schemes, fraudulent business deals and embezzlement. They can escape detection and prosecution for their illegal activities because of their business connections, family ties and their ability to "pay off" the violation.

Other sociopaths do things that, although not illegal, are unethical, immoral and harmful to others, e.g., cheating on a spouse, financial or emotional neglect of family members, and irresponsible use of company resources or funds. These offenses are tricky to document, and consequently, difficult to expose

Successful, professional sociopaths often excel at white collar crime.

or prosecute. If the successful sociopathic businessman is narcissistic as well (which they normally are) they will use their stature to berate, terrorize and control their loved ones, family members and employees. Outwardly these sociopaths appear to be the epitome of an esteemed citizen, successful entrepreneur, supportive boyfriend, loving husband and father—no one would believe that he secretly steals from his friends, co-workers and clients; tells premeditated lies and betrays the people who trust him, and batters his wife or girlfriend and children behind closed doors.

> **If they happen to be intelligent, "well-bred," and physically attractive psychopaths [sociopaths], can have a devastating impact on the people they meet.**
>
> —*Snakes in Suits*

Characteristics of people with narcissistic, sociopathic antisocial personality disorders may include:

- Outgoing, gregarious and exciting. Tells unlikely yet convincing stories. Uses intense charm, verbal skills, flattery, gifts and boasting to influence and manipulate others.

- Pathological lying, deceitful and sneaky, cool under pressure, use of aliases; cons others for pleasure or personal profit.

- Completely self-centered, inflated sense of entitlement, and illusions of grandeur. Tendency to violate the boundaries of others, disregard for the safety of others, disregard for right and wrong. Marked lack of guilt, remorse and shame for the heartbreak and hardship they cause to others.

- Intimidation of others; aggressive, often violent behavior, fits of rage, prone to getting involved in fights. Vindictive when thwarted or exposed.

- Contempt for social norms and legal constraints. Criminal or DUI history, recurring difficulties with the law or committing fraud without being charged. Inability to learn from experience or punishment.

- Can be reckless, impulsive, and financially irresponsible, indulges in pretentious, extravagant shopping.

- Inability to tolerate boredom; need for stimulation and excitement, promiscuous sexual behavior, infidelity, prone to addictions and substance abuse.

- History of failed relationships and/or divorce, lack of friends, and estranged from family members. Blames everyone and everything for his problems and hurtful actions; will often portray their victim as the culprit. Can end relationships quickly when necessary or when it suits them.

- Poor behavioral controls; expressions of irritability, annoyance, impatience, aggression and anger. Secretive and paranoid; defensive when asked about his whereabouts, work, money, or how he spends his time.

- Consistent irresponsible work behavior or failure to honor financial obligations, parasitic lifestyle—or, if he is a successful businessperson he uses his stature to manipulate, intimidate, dominate and control others.

- Possess an innate ability to find the weaknesses in other; will use this knowledge to manipulate, intimidate and control people.

Adapted from Wilipedia.com, Healthtree.com, McAfee website, World Health Organization, Lovefraud.com, and Encyclopedia of Mental Disorders minddisorders.com.

The Victim

Life is reduced to a contest and other human beings seem to be nothing more than game pieces, to be moved about, used as shields or ejected.

—Martha Stout, *The Sociopath Next Door*

On the surface a sociopath appears to be a normal, decent, reasonable and caring individual. He is exceedingly charming. He flatters you, pursues you and gives you excessive attention. He wines and dines you, calls you constantly, sends you greeting cards and love notes, writes you poetry, and surprises you with flowers, jewelry, gifts and trips. He is thoughtful. He repairs your broken necklace clasp. He picks your children up from school and he brings groceries and wine to your home. He declares his love and devotion to you early in the relationship and he's quick to propose an engagement and marriage. He convinces you that he has been misunderstood and mistreated all his life and that you are the only one who understands him. You feel needed and validated by this man. He makes you feel special. He talks of a romantic and secure future together and he intrigues you with his grandiose plans.

Everything about a relationship is a game for a sociopath. They use seduction to woo their victims, pity to play them, and once the victim is engulfed in the sociopath's treacherous relationship they use blame, projecting and gaslighting to convince them they are the defective one. Said one sociopath on an online blog, "It's like playing a game ... you feel the thrill of the chase, the power of the challenge and once you feel you have conquered her, or you get bored, you end the relationship, cut your losses and move on to a different game."

A sociopath is always searching for someone who will buy into his trumped-up façade and they will generally target women who are nurturing, trusting, kind and caring.

Some sociopaths enjoy the challenge of conquering strong, successful, intelligent, confident women—it makes them feel manly to break down a woman who puts up a good fight. Dr. Dirtbag told everyone he loved me because I was the only woman who ever stood up to him. Other sociopath's prey on women who are lonely, vulnerable, naïve and needy; who have been recently hurt or victimized—the unhappily married woman, a newly divorced woman or grieving widow are easy targets for the skilled sociopath.

The sociopath is an astute observer of human behavior. He determines your beliefs, issues and passions and he adjusts his behavior accordingly. He proclaims to like what you like, dislike what you dislike, and believe what you believe—thus becoming your ideal mate. *Snakes in Suits* states that the sociopath communicates four important messages (through words and deeds):

1. I like who you are.
2. I am just like you.
3. Your secrets are safe with me.
4. I am the perfect friend or lover or partner for you.

Kenny, a 5-star sociopath, portrayed himself as a man of substance with his morally contrived questions. On his first date with Jackie he asked her, "Do you smoke? Are you a good mom?

Are you a Christian?" His questions insinuated that he was a non-smoker, a good dad and a moral person.

That is why psychopaths often feel like soul-mates in a relationship—they project your own persona back to you in their "assumed" personality.

—*Snakes in Suits*

Women tell way too much, way too soon to a man they've only just met. They disclose their wants and needs, their hurts and fears, their passions and ambitions—and with this information the con-artist can present himself as the perfect man to fulfill their dreams.

The sociopath has the uncanny ability to determine a person's weak points and who will be vulnerable to his sexual overtures. He takes note of the insecurities or weaknesses you wish to minimize or hide from view. Later, when he knows he has your love and commitment, he will use your weak spots and vulnerabilities to exploit, dominate, demean and control you.

Roberta and John were both social drinkers. When John drank he became extremely surly and abusive; Roberta became silly and vocal. Alcohol made Roberta super sensitive to John's hurtful behavior, causing her to react with her own bad behavior. One evening, while imbibing, John was especially nasty. Roberta retaliated with a tantrum of resentful anger. The following day Roberta apologized to John, confiding in him that drinking made her hyper-sensitive. John seemed supportive and he promised to adjust his behavior. That weekend they went out to dinner, John ordered a bottle of wine and as Roberta finished her first glass he blasted her, "You're doing it again. You're acting drunk and belligerent." He used her intimate confession to degrade and punish her.

Psychopaths [sociopaths] play on the fact that most of us are trusting and forgiving people.

—Michael Seto, Ph.D.

The initial charm you feel with the sociopath does not last long. After you sleep with him, or you sell your home and move in with him, or you marry him and quit your job or you have a baby with him, and he has dug his claws deep into your soul, his schizoid, sinister personality emerges. You scratch your head, wipe the tears from your eyes and ask yourself, *"Where the heck did my dream man go?"*

Sociopaths can have an overwhelming need to be admired and often portray themselves as kind, compassionate and caring people. Only their victims know the truth.

Dr. Dirtbag was a public "good guy" but underneath his counterfeit facade beat the frozen heart of a man who bilked, bullied and damaged the people who truly loved him. He was insensitive to the pain and suffering he caused me—and yet, he acted like an adoring grandpa in front of a strange baby; his eyes got all misty when he verbalized his hatred of animal abuse, and he faked pitiful crocodile tears to accompany his insincere apology after he had berated me to a pulp. The irony was, he called men who abused women—"dirtbags!"

Sociopaths always think they are right; you can't reason with them and if they are caught in a lie, they will attempt to disguise that falsehood with even more elaborate lies.

It was amazing, when I cornered Dr. Dirtbag with an obvious lie, he would counter it with a more exaggerated tale to mask his deception. When that didn't work he would give me this blank stare void of guilt or shame for his dishonesty, followed with a look of disgust that I would dare confront him, and then he would just walk away without saying a word. Even with the raw evidence of his deceit shoved in his

He wants you to believe: you are the crazy one.

gutless face, he refused to own up to his unscrupulous, hurtful behavior. He could easily do this because, as an ASP—he had no conscience.

The truly scary part about giving your heart to a sociopath is their ability to cut you out of their lives in the bat of an eye.

Narcissistic Personality Disorder

The narcissistic personality shares many of the anti-social personality traits; what is distinctive to them is their exaggerated sense of importance.

Narcissists believe themselves to be unique and superior to others and are consumed with ego, self-promotion and the need for admiration. They believe they are smarter, stronger and meant to control those around them. Many times their "god syndrome" drives them to achieve successful careers such as doctors, lawyers, politicians, etcetera—where they hold charge over others. Their false sense of entitlement causes them to believe they deserve special treatment and privileges. They feel they are blameless and beyond reproach, even when caught red-handed in a lie or dishonest act.

Highly intelligent narcissists are often extremely conniving and can distort reality with their elaborate lies, which oddly fit most of the facts—but their super egos can cause them to overlook the obvious and they trip on their own lies. If questioned or criticized they become defensive, indignant or enraged.

He had wealth, power and an evil mindset—a narcissistic triumvirate.

In the beginning the narcissist fakes integrity. They appear to be loving, helpful and potentially the idyllic husband or boyfriend, when in truth they are unfeeling and can be brutal and insensitive to the feelings of others. In their relationships the narcissist provides little emotional satisfaction for their partner but they demand absolute loyalty and responsiveness. The partner must subordinate to the narcissist in all ways; if she does not live up to his expectations he may resort to rage and projection and he withdraws his love and support.

The sadist narcissist seems to enjoy the emotional pain he inflicts on loved ones. The raging narcissist can be disproportionately irrational, intimidating and threatening. The narcissist ultimately blames their partners for the problems in a relationship and they can discard companions, spouses and family members without warning, thought, guilt or remorse.

Gail dated an extremely abusive, schizophrenic narcissistic man, who if diagnosed, would most certainly register off the chart as a sociopathic personality. Warren was consumed with his self-image. Once a handsome TV weather anchorman, he was fired from his job in his thirties, and for the next 30 years he piddled in the video recording business. At age sixty he imagined himself a Brad Pitt. His face kept a grungy 2-day stubble. His designer clothes were tattered thrift store discards. He teased and combed back his long thin hair into a 50s bouffant held in place with helmet-head hair spray. His face was wrinkled and seedy and he wore blotchy-orange self-tanner year-round on his face. He special ordered his shoes with two-inch lifters, adding height to his barely 5'7" frame. He believed himself to possess super intelligence and be uber-superior to everyone else. Every Wednesday night he would sit at the bar at the local watering hole wearing a dingy, faded T-shirt, shabby saddle-tan bomber jacket, elevated cowboy boots and extra-dark Rayban sunglasses, imaging that all the women wanted him, and all the men were jealous of him.

Gail was sucked in by Warren's superficial charm and delusions of grandeur. She slept with him, he immediately put up his wallet and became verbally abusive. His public behavior was blatant and outrageous; his temper was sudden, unpredictable and vicious. He flirted flagrantly with women in front of Gail. One evening at happy hour, they were sitting at the bar, and he brazenly flirted with a married woman.

The woman's husband came over, angrily grabbed his wife by the arm and pulled her away. Warren turned and snapped at Gail, "What the fuck is wrong with that asshole." When Gail spoke to someone he would rage at her, "Who the fuck was that? Why are you talking to him?"

One day Gail accidentally dropped Warren's cell phone in a parking lot. Warren went berserk, stomping and screaming at her, "What the fuck is the matter with you, you stupid bitch! Can't you do anything right?" Bystanders were appalled and dumbstruck. Gail learned to keep her mouth shut to avoid Warren's berating. She walked on pins and razors in his presence. Then one night he did the unthinkable. After an evening of drinking, worn-out Weatherman couldn't get an erection. He became enraged at Gail, he jumped on top of her and he screamed, "What's wrong with you, you fucking bitch. It's your fault," and he brutally slapped her across her face.

Borderline Personality

Worth mentioning is the borderline personality disorder (BPD), not to be confused with "bipolar." Their emotional instability and impulsive actions cause them to have chaotic relationships.

States the Mayo Clinic, the borderline personality frequently has a distorted, insecure and flawed sense of self and they often experience turmoil in their work, school and relationships. They idealize someone one moment and then abruptly and dramatically shift to fury and hate over perceived slights or even minor misunderstandings. Their anger, impulsivity and frequent mood swings may push others away, even though they desire loving relationships. They may be fully aware that their behavior is destructive, but feel unable to change it. Borderline personality disorder symptoms may include:

- Impulsive and hazardous behavior, such as risky driving, unsafe sex, gambling sprees or illegal drug use

- Strong emotions that ebb and flow frequently
- Intense but short episodes of anxiety or depression
- Inappropriate anger, sometimes escalating into physical confrontations
- Difficulty controlling emotions or impulses
- Fear of being alone
- Suicidal behavior

Reports the Mayo Clinic, borderline personality disorder treatment may include psychotherapy, medications or hospitalization. If you have borderline personality disorder, don't get discouraged. Many people with borderline personality disorder get better with treatment and can live happy, peaceful lives.

Great ... My Girlfriend Within thought ... Let's put Dr. Dirtbag in a straight-jacket and get him on meds!

Bonding with the Enemy

When it was good, it was the best relationship I ever had.
When it was bad—it was psychotic.

We shake our heads and ask, "How can a woman stay with an abusive man?" "What relationship could possibly be worth the horrific conflict, mental battering, bruises and busted lips from the hands of an angry boyfriend or husband?"

Some of the compelling reasons why women stay in a relationship with an abusive partner are:

- The abuse may occur over a short period of time, and she is able to shrug it off.

- He may tell her, "I'm sorry, it will never happen again," and she believes him.

- She may have been abused as a child, or witnessed her mother abused, and she accepts it as normal behavior, consciously or unconsciously.

- She may be financially dependent on him; or she may have a fear of living alone.

- She may fear her partner and may believe she has no power to change the situation.

- She may fear his suicide; he says he'll kill himself if she leaves.

- She may have religious and cultural beliefs or a misguided sense of loyalty that keeps her tied to her relationship—or she stays for "the sake of the children."

- She is in denial about the abuse. He is often loving *and lovable* which helps her excuse and minimize his episodes of cruelty or violence.

- She still "loves" him and she is emotionally dependent on him.

Yes, these reasons are valid and to some extent understandable—but there has to be a greater force that ties a woman's soul to a man who unmercifully berates and batters her.

Traumatic Bonding

The longer you have been living with his cycles of intermittent abuse and kind, loving treatment, the more attached you are likely to feel to him, through a process known as traumatic bonding.

—Lundy Bancroft, *Why Does He Do That?*

Traumatic bonding may be described as the development of strong emotional ties between two people in which one person maltreats the other with psychological or physical abuse, alternating with sporadic acts of kindness, affection, intimacy and generosity—whereby—creating a victim.

The "honeymoon" phase, that is, acts of kindness and intimacy, is critical to forming traumatic attachments. After an abusive event, the abuser demonstrates compassion towards his victim. The victim feels relief from his abuse, and she is grateful for his affection. She is relieved that he remains committed to their relationship, prompting her to pardon his offense and renew her relationship vows. Consequently, her love and loyalty deepen for her abuser and "traumatic bonding" takes hold.

Sex with an abuser can be compelling and habit-forming. The woman becomes addicted to erotic and intense sex, creating an irrational, destructive attachment to her abuser.

Jackie was sexually addicted to her abusive boyfriend. Said Jackie:

Sex with Kenny was seductive, passionate and exciting. I did things with him I thought were taboo. He introduced me to sex toys. He taught me new sexual positions and he gave me bodily sensations I had never experienced. When we were in public places, when no one was looking, he would slip his hand into my panties, touch me and arouse me. In private he gave me unbelievable orgasms. But his abusive nature was maiming. I felt myself gradually being destroyed. I hated him and wanted him out of my life but I was hooked on having sex with him—like a junkie needing a fix.

Sex can operate like a drug; it numbs the woman's emotional pain and keeps her coming back for more of his abuse. The cycle of abuse resumes. The abuser gains additional power over his victim—while the victim loses her sense of self, her ability to fend for herself and she loses hope of her situation changing.

My Fifty Shades Girlfriend Within appears, *It's hard to go back to plain old vanilla when you've had spank-me, cuff-me, oh lawd, don't you dare butt plug me.*

Intermittent Abuse

The longer a woman stays with an abusive man the more abuse she will experience. It is the constant battering of the victim's spirit which causes her to crave his acts of kindness; and consequently, depend on him for her happiness and welfare.

The victim's life becomes a constant act of emotional survival. If she defies him or tries to leave him he may threaten her into submission, or manipulate her with his insincere and short-lived promises to change. Suddenly he is thoughtful, attentive and caring. He reminds her of the man she fell in love with, her heart melts and she forgives him. She adapts to his abusive behavior and she is pulled deeper into a relationship that progressively destroys her self-worth, her trust, her ambition, her enthusiasm and her sexuality.

When physical abuse is administered at random and intermittent intervals, and interspersed with tolerant and friendly contact, the phenomenon of traumatic bonding seems most powerful.

The three phases involved in the cycle of violence (tension building, battering and "honeymoon") provide a prime example of intermittent reinforcement. The unpredictable duration and severity of each phase serve to keep the victim off balance and in hopes of change. The "honeymoon" phase is an integral part of traumatic bonding. It is this phase that allows the victim to experience calm and loving feelings from the abuser and therefore strengthens her emotional attachment.

—Domestic Violence Intervention Services

Traumatic Bonding Scenario

You meet and fall in love with the most wonderful man you've ever known. He adores you. He understands you and he showers you with attention, affection and gifts. You allow him into your life because you trust him. He develops close relationships with your family, friends, co-workers, and even your children. He gets in your head. He gets in your heart. And he gets in your bed. You are overwhelmed by the love you feel for him. Time passes and he begins to criticize, control and demean you. You are conflicted by his abuse. *"How could he do this to me,"* you ask, and you think, *"I gave him my heart, body and soul."* You know you deserve better and so you break up with him.

Your sweetheart apologizes profusely for his abusive behavior and the battering phase ends. He appears contrite. He is quasi-agreeable, considerate and attentive. He may agree to quit drinking or go to counseling. You are grateful for his change of heart and you are optimistic that his remorse is genuine—so you forgive him. You let him back into your life and you enter the "calm loving respite phase" or the "honeymoon phase."

The honeymoon phase is the most psychologically victimizing phase because the batterer fools the victim into believing he has changed and his abuse has ended. Having forgiven him you are doubly-emotionally invested in the relationship. Inevitably your sweetheart begins to again batter you. The destructive cycle of abuse commences, and you are drawn deeper into the traumatic bonding experience.

Seduction, deception and betrayal are core components of the abusive relationship. The more times you are abused—the more times you experience your abuser's rejection, cruelty and treachery. His acts of malice and betrayal wound you deeply. Your emotional suffering is profound. The loss of his emotional and sexual intimacy, his financial support, and your fear of life keep you coming back for more of his abuse. You are traumatized. The only cure for the pain that grips your heart, *as your psyche sees it*, is to regain his love, acceptance and approval.

The cycle of abuse is deadly—each time you reconcile with your abuser ...

- You are telling your abuser you condone his abusive behavior, giving him the green light to increase the frequency and intensity of his abuse.

- You adapt and learn to cope with the abuser's disapproval, rejection, deception, cruelty, betrayal and anger.

- You incur more and more self-doubt, confusion, disbelief, depression, guilt, shame, isolation, anxiety, fear and hopelessness.

- You become addicted to experiencing the "honeymoon phase," craving his love, acceptance and approval.

- Your sense of helplessness and dependency on your abuser increases.

Lack of Information

We repeatedly hear the question asked of battered women, *"Why do you stay?"*

"Because I love him," battered women reply.

If you don't have accurate information, you might not understand what is happening to you.

When a battered woman says she stays with her abusive husband or boyfriend because *"she loves him,"* she is describing the Stockholm syndrome—a psychological condition in which the hostage (the victim) emotionally bonds to their captor (the abuser).

Battered women are conflicted by the intense feelings they have for their abusers. Unaware of the dynamics of the abuse-trauma-bonding process, they describe their acute emotions as best they can—*calling it love.*

True Stories from Domestic Abuse Blogs

Catt: My boyfriend and I have lived together for four years and he abuses me daily. One moment he is fawning all over me and the next he's calling me every name in the book. At times he is perfect and loving—and then he gets mad at me over the smallest things; he kicks and hits me and gives me the silent treatment for weeks. I try to appease him but he hangs me out to dry. I keep searching for that one thing or piece of knowledge that will make it click for me—that will make me want to leave him.

Catt is acutely aware that there is something horribly wrong within her relationship. She feels intense emotional pain from her boyfriend's abuse causing her to long for his acceptance and intimacy. She misinterprets these powerful feelings as the loss of his love. In truth; she is experiencing mental anguish caused from traumatic bonding.

Rosebud: I left my abusive boyfriend. I thought I loved him, but now I see what I was feeling was the "bond." I hated leaving him, but I can't go back to him because I know he will punish me for leaving and start beating me again. It took me four months to realize I was being manipulated.

Ursula: I found myself in a terrible relationship that was dangerous to my physical and emotional well-being. I left him constantly but I would crawl back to him because I missed him. I missed him so much I craved him—like I was trying to give up cigarettes. When I told people how he treated me they would look at me in aghast. I kept trying to understand why I, as an intelligent and financially independent woman, would accept his treatment—it was "trauma bonds." Then one day he went too far and something changed deep inside me. I moved 400 miles to get away from him. I didn't give him up right away but my mindset had finally changed. A month later I finally let go of him completely.

"By recognizing abuse for what it is," explains Patricia Evans, "the partner dispels the illusion of security in the relationship" and can then act to protect herself, protect her own spirit and regain the security of her "natural state of personal power."

In other words, she can muster up the courage to leave the scumbag and regain her life.

In all, I spent six months basking in the adoration, excitement and generosity of Dr. Dirtbag. I spent a year trying to figure him out while enduring the cycle of his abuse—and another two years healing from Post Traumatic Stress Disorder ... a costly price to pay for ignoring the red flags a lying, controlling, abusive, malfunctioning man.

Pop Singer Rihanna just announced that she's back together with her abusive ex-boyfriend Chris Brown. Yes. The same Chris Brown who pled guilty to a felony and was subject to a restraining order for attacking her on the eve of the Grammys back in 2009. She says he's changed.

My Social Services Girlfriend Within looks at the police photos of Rihanna's bruised face and bloody lip. *Nuh uh! Don't go there girl. That crazy black pimp will stomp yo' ass again!*

Shell Shocked

The trauma bond can persist after the victim leaves the relationship; sometimes taking months, or even years, for the victim to completely break the bond.

Physical symptoms of trauma can include insomnia or nightmares, being startled easily, racing heartbeat and anxiety attacks, aches and pains, fatigue, excessive weight loss, difficulty in concentrating, edginess, agitation and muscle tension—and, *oh, God, oh, pleazee no*—the shingles. Victims of traumatic bonding will often

> *I felt unbearably empty inside; as if someone had hollowed me out with a melon scoop.*

shut down emotionally, describing themselves as having felt "robotic." Intellectually they know what happened to them but they feel frozen or numb inside and are unable to take action.

The emotional and physical side effects of trauma will gradually fade as you process the trauma. But even when you've moved on with your life and you're feeling better, you may experience painful memories or emotions triggered by a sound, an image or a situation which reminds you of your abuser or the traumatic experience.

Remember Almira Gulch, a.k.a. the pointy-wart-nosed Wicked Witch of the West in the Wizard of Oz? She rode her bicycle, amidst the threat of a tornado, to Dorothy's house to seize Dorothy's little dog Toto. The witch furiously peddled her bicycle to the instrumental theme song, "ta-tada-tada-da-da ta-tada-tada-da-da."

For years, after Dr. Dirtbag and I broke up, whenever I heard a certain cell phone ring tone my heart constricted, jolting me back to the times Dr. Dirtbag terrorized me with his abusive phone calls. Or when I saw an old model dark blue Mercedes, like his, driving down the road, I impulsively envisioned him with his piercing rodent eyes, hunched down in his car seat with his hands on the steering wheel while my mind spontaneously played the Wicked Witch's song, "ta-tada-ta-da-da-da ta-tada-tada-da-da" as he raced down the road to his next evil deed.

It's been six months since My Traumatized Girlfriend Within last saw her Shithole Boyfriend. She's battled to purge him from her mind—every week she thinks of him less and less. She has moments when she feels like her old self: confident, cheerful and optimistic. She pours herself a Skinnygirl® Cosmo, lights a lavender candle, and she plops down into her comfy recliner—*ahhh*—life is almost back to normal. She picks up a Glamour magazine ... unexpectedly a cologne insert floats from its pages. The scent of Dolce and Gabbanna reaches her nostrils and her mind jolts back to the time the Shithole abused her.

Grieving is normal following a traumatic relationship. We cope with the loss of the relationship and we eventually regain our sense of well-being.

The good news is, *Shoe Sistas* ... now that you know the warning signs of a pathological lying, abusive, narcissistic, sociopathic, anti-social personality—you can make the decision to not follow that wacky wabbit into his wretched hellhole.

Dead Animal in Therapy

A woman keeps trying to fix her dead animal.
The problem is—he's permanently broken.

What causes the antisocial personality disorder?

Antisocial personalities (ASP) come from all walks of life and from a variety of economic backgrounds. They can easily be a family member, a co-worker, a business partner, a friend, or a spouse or partner. Personality disorders are reported to be a result of genetic factors, childhood upbringing, societal factors and a dysfunctional environment. They frequently have histories of childhood neglect or abuse, and parents who abused alcohol or other substances.

Signs of antisocial personality disorder first become evident in young children and adolescents who display aggressive behavior which causes or threatens physical harm to other people or animals; while their non-aggressive behavior exhibits deceitfulness and causes property loss or damage, theft, and serious violations of rules that can lead to "illicit drug use, dropping out of school, violent behavior, severe family conflict, and frequent delinquent acts." It is crucial that a child who is genetically predisposed for antisocial personality disorder be placed in a stable environment which reinforces positive behaviors and communication skills—otherwise, this child is at great risk of developing antisocial personality disorders later in life. By the time a child hits their late teens, states Psychologist Michael Seto, "the disorder is almost certainly permanent." Moreover, research shows that people with antisocial personality disorders have an increased risk for "passing down" the antisocial personality disorder to their children—an added reason to "break the cycle" while a child is still pliant.

> *Gail's boyfriend, Warren Weatherman, sociopathic behavior was glaringly evident at a young age. As an only child, his narcissistic mother battered his father while putting him on a pedestal, fostering his adult delusions of grandeur and a false sense of entitlement. At age thirteen Warren killed his neighbor's cat. His neighbor complained repeatedly about Warren's dog barking, causing his parents to get rid of his dog. Warren took revenge on the neighbor by driving a nail through the neighbor's cat's throat nailing it to a tree. Gail minimized Warren's behavior, thinking it was a sick adolescent prank, but internally she was disquieted by his morbid behavior. "He always carried a concealed revolver and an 8-inch serrated knife," said Gail. "He would pull the knife out in front of me and run his finger along the blade and in a bone-chilling guttural voice say, 'Can you imagine what this would do to a black man's gut?' I'm certain he had morbid fantasies of killing someone. When we broke up I was terrified that he would show up at my back door with his gun and say, 'You owe me and I'm here to collect.'"*

Part of what kept me emotionally tied to Dr. Dirtbag was his claim to an abusive childhood. I thought my love and understanding could heal the pain of his hurtful past. But he seemed content as a permanently disturbed, ill-tempered adult who demeaned and bullied others.

I have read repeatedly that the cure rate for antisocial personalities is virtually zero—that their frontal lobe, the area of the brain which governs judgment and planning appears to be different in them. Their moral and value systems are corrupt and they lack the emotions and the conscience of a normal person.

Psychotherapy is a recommended treatment for the adult antisocial personality. (Psychotherapy helps the patient to uncover unhealthy, negative beliefs and behavior and replace them with healthy, positive ones, and learn coping strategies and problem-solving skills.)

In their eyes, everyone else is stupid, naïve and inferior

The problem is these personalities are severely self-serving and typically narcissistic. They view themselves as superior to others, beyond reproach, incapable of making mistakes and they think they should bear no responsibility for their hurtful behavior. They see no reason to change and will agree to therapy only when they are pushed into it by a desperate relative, demanding partner or court order.

The heartache is we keep hoping our dead animal will be healed.

I believe that emotional healing is possible for anyone. An alcoholic can quit drinking, a gambler can quit gambling, a cheater can stop cheating, a porn addict can quit "porning," an abuser can cease the mental and physical battering of his partner—*but it will happen only if someone passionately wants to change.* It's not going to happen because you pray to Buddha or you count your rosary beads; nor will it happen if you cry, scream, beg and threaten your sick, dysfunctional partner. It will certainly **not happen** if he submits to therapy to appease you or the court.

Change happens when a person gets to that low place in their life—*a nadir of despair*—where they can no longer stand the misery that engulfs them. Change happens when one admits to their wrongdoings and flawed behavior. Change happens when a person seeks forgiveness and emotional and spiritual healing, and they go to work on the negative aspects of their character and personality. Then, and only then, will a restoration of the mind, heart and spirit take place.

Antisocial personalities may project confidence and superiority—but behind their mask of ultra-confidence are low self-worth issues which make them sensitive to criticism or defeat. They tear down others to numb their feelings of insecurity and self-loathing. They don't want to change because to do so, they would have to relinquish their chronic need for domination and self-importance; and thereby, forfeit their ill-gained feelings of power and superiority.

Qualifying the Therapist

Finding a qualified therapist is tantamount in counseling an antisocial personality.

Therapy for the abusive, narcissistic, sociopathic, antisocial personalities is complex and multi-faceted. I will not attempt to discuss the endless sly ways these personalities undermine, resist and maneuver the psychological process. Nor am I qualified to recommend psychological and medical treatments for these mental disorders. I do, however, know this: abusive, antisocial personalities can be slick impersonators in sheep's clothing and will manipulate and deceive the unsuspecting or inexperienced therapist to fulfill their own self-serving agendas.

My Dr. Laura Girlfriend Within turns off the Dr. Phil show, pries a popcorn kernel from her tooth, sits down to her computer and googles, *How to outwit a lying, conniving, narcissistic anti-social dirtbag.*

If you are the victim in an abusive relationship, and you are seeking individual or couples counseling, it is extremely important that the therapist be verified as someone who is knowledgeable about the traits and conning techniques of abusive, sociopathic, antisocial personalities. Otherwise, you may find yourself twice victimized.

Dr. Dirtbag and I went to three counselors in eight short months. Our first psychologist, Dr. Amory, a woman in her mid-thirties, was transparently impressed with Dr. Dirtbag's triple degree in medicine, psychology and law, and his lofty community status. I got the distinct feeling she felt an alliance with Dr. Dirtbag because their professions made them— supposedly—superior to the general population.

For two months I tried desperately to explain the complexity of Dr. Dirtbag's verbal abuse to Dr. Amory. For two months he claimed he didn't understand what he was doing wrong. Dr. Amory offered little help. She listened to me whine and complain about Dr. Dirtbag's mistreatment of me—while Dr. Dirtbag and the Psyche shared doctor-lawyer stories.

Dr. Dirtbag was extremely composed and agreeable in our counseling sessions—making him the ideal, credible patient. He listened attentively and he answered Dr. Amory's questions politely. He said very little about my misgivings and he didn't admit to any wrongdoing. He nodded like he understood what I was saying. He said calmly, "That's news to me," and "I understand; I'll try to do better." He seemed to bask in the cerebral process ... while I remained depressed and frustrated with the psychosomatic system.

Two months into our counseling Dr. Amory broke ground in our complicated case. We were sitting in a three-way session. I had just reported Dr. Dirtbag's latest and greatest assault on me. Surprisingly, Dr. Amory didn't comment on Dr. Dirtbag's heinous actions; she instead, hammered me about my motives and behavior—as if I were the guilty abusive partner. I was disturbed by her accusing innuendoes and I said to her sternly, "I feel like you're picking on me—you've not said a word to David about his hurtful behavior." To my astonishment, she replied, "That's because you're the only one who is unhappy."

OMG! Dr. Dirtbag had snowed the shrink! He had used his private sessions with Dr. Amory to paint me as the irratio- nal, overbearing, demanding, money-wanton bitch.

That was our last visit to Dr. Got-Her-Head-Up-Her-Ass. That was fine with Dr. Dirtbag because he didn't want to spend the time, effort or money on fixing our relationship.

When the therapist fails to identify that he or she is dealing with a couple in which one of the partners is an abusive, antisocial, sociopathic personality, the counseling process can undermine the non-abusive partner's interests while abetting the abuser.

Conning the Counselor

Abusive, antisocial, sociopathic personalities can be effective con-artists. Those with well-developed verbal abilities charm and fool their victims, and hoodwink unquestioning or unenlightened therapists. If a couples therapist is focused on validating the feelings of both patients in a relationship, in which one partner is an abuser, or the therapist is self-absorbed in his or her abilities and desire to restore equality and harmony to the relationship, they may overlook the reality that one of the partners is an academy award-winning pathological liar who privately abuses his wife or girlfriend.

> To a psychopath [sociopath], a therapist is just one more person who must be conned, and the psychopath plays the part right until the therapist is convinced of his or her "rehabilitation."
>
> **—Michael Seto**

Abusive sociopathic men can adapt quickly to the therapy process. They appear interested and concerned. They can present an amicable façade and offer logical explanations that dupe and gain the support of naïve and uninformed therapists.

> *Dr. Wiseman, a discerning, veteran Ph.D. psychologist, was our second counselor. I prayed fervently that she would recognize David's hurtful actions and set us on a straight path. Again I tried to describe his sinister covert behavior. Again David pretended to be truthful, receptive and eager to work on our problems. I described his ruthless berating behavior; he minimized it, calling it "needling." Clearly Dr. Wiseman was perplexed.*

"I want you guys to tape record your conversations," Dr. Wiseman said. "Maybe it will give us some insight into how you interact with one another."

What a stellar idea, I thought secretly. We left her office and I immediately purchased a small digital tape recorder.

It was Sunday night and my must-see TV show "Desperate Housewives" came on at eight o'clock. David had been drinking beer for several hours while cooking our dinner. We prepared our plates and we went into the living room to watch my show. He had barely spoken a word to me all evening—suddenly, he wanted to be Chatty Cathy. He began to browbeat me about my deceased father. I pulled out the mini-digital recorder, pressed record and I placed it on the coffee table in front of us.

"Why do you hate your dad?" he asked.

"I don't hate my father. We just didn't have a close relationship," I said. And I went back to watching my show.

David persisted. "But why do you hate him?" he demanded. "You said you hated him—TELL ME WHY!" He kept hammering me about my deceased dad.

"Will you please shut the **** up and let me watch my show!" I pleaded.

David badgered me throughout the hour show while the recorder continued to tape our conversation. He knew the recorder was running… he even frowned at it … and yet couldn't control his abusive nature.

I finally gave up on watching my show. I turned off the recorder, threw my dinner in the kitchen disposal and went outside to sit on the patio. Sitting alone in the dark I reveled, believing at last I had definitive proof of Dr. Dirtbag's verbally abusive behavior.

My Head-Shrink Girlfriend Within clapped her hands, danced a small jig and poured herself a glass of Gotcha-Pinot Grigio.

The following week in our counseling session I pulled out the small recorder to play for Dr. Wiseman—only to discover that the recordings were missing. I turned to David in disbelief and I asked him, "Where are the recordings of our dinner conversation?"

With his most goofy, bewildered faked-face he replied, "I don't know. It's not there? I listened to them the other night ... I must have accidently erased it."

"What do you mean you must of accidently erased it!" I roared. "How could you do that?!?! You had to press the erase button twice to delete a recording for Chrissakes! And there were three recordings. You would have had to click the erase button six times consecutively to delete three recordings! You want me to believe that you ACCIDENTLY erased three conversations?!?! Are you insane?!?!" I screamed.

My heart plummeted. It was the only evidence I had to prove that I was not over-reacting to his insidious remarks. I was not misinterpreting his verbal abuse. I was not imagining his covert menacing behavior.

The following week I went to see Dr. Wiseman alone.

"He's a snake," Dr. Wiseman said bluntly.

Finally—someone confirmed what my head kept screaming; that I'm not crazy. He was lying to me. He was berating and punishing me. And he was conning everyone he came into contact with. It was a wrenching-sweet moment. My nightmare was validated, but with this confirmation, I had to face my reality—that the man I loved more than life itself was a cruel, abusive monster—or as Dr. Wiseman put it so succinctly—a reptile.

*My reality was: I was in love with a
cruel and abusive monster.*

Individual Therapy

In failing to expose the sociopath the uninformed therapist empowers the abuser.

"The antisocial personality disorder is notoriously difficult to treat," states Mayo Clinic. "People with this disorder may not even want treatment or think they need treatment ... when they do agree to therapy they will try to undermine the process with their denial, distortion and deception."

The abuser who is coerced to attend individual counseling will often use his private sessions to his advantage. Without his partner present to dispute him, he can easily portray her as a demanding, deceitful, hormonal lunatic. The therapist, who does not interview the abuser's partner, may unknowingly support and ill-advise the abuser making it easier for him to mistreat his partner.

I was at the end of my rope with Dr. Dirtbag. He had manipulated and deceived three counselors. He had repeatedly broken his promises to cease his abusive behavior. I left him and I told him if we were ever going to be together again he would have to attend in-depth therapy. He enrolled in a weekend couples recovery program. He asked me to go with him. I declined, telling him, "You need to do this on your own." Surprisingly, he attended the weekend recovery group several states away. When he returned home, he was a changed man—but not for the good.

Dr. Dirtbag made excellent use of his therapy weekend. He learned new and exciting psychology mumbo jumbo with which to condemn me—he was armed with allegations and deflection. He accused me of "emotional blackmail" and "false memory" and "frustration-aggression" behavior. He was brewing with hostility and resentment towards me. He called me repeatedly, berating me on the phone and hanging up on me. He was extremely mercu-

> He accused me of "emotional blackmail" and "false memory."

rial. One minute he was chirping about the new friends he had made and the personal revelations he had gained at the retreat—and the next minute he was jabbing and lashing out at me. Never had he been so irrational.

From Dr. Dirtbag's ranting and raving I deduced the following: he was incensed because I broke-up with him. He was infuriated that I had forced him to go to weekend therapy. He was indignant that he was at a couples retreat without his partner. He was seething with animosity because he couldn't get me back under his thumb.

Dr. Dirtbag had spent all weekend convincing himself, his therapist and his new recovery pals that I was the deranged She-Satan. I am certain he portrayed me as the selfish, insensitive, brow-beating absentee partner given to unpredictable mood swings, demanding behavior, drunken episodes and uncontrollable fits of rage. He gained the sympathy, support and misguided advice of his therapist and weekend buddies, while garnering state-of-the-art psychological ammo with which to fault me for our relationship failure. By the time Dr. Dirtbag had de-planed his return flight he was loaded and cocked for revenge. Dr. Dirtbag was shooting his end game.

My Special Forces Girlfriend Within puts on her ballistic helmet and bomb disposal suit. She hoists a RPG-7 rocket-propelled grenade launcher to her shoulder and she glares at her abusive boyfriend, *Bring it, you lily-livered woman-beating pond scum!*

Couples Therapy

If you cross, question or challenge an abuser, he will take it out on you.

Surprisingly couples counseling is not recommended for the abusive relationship. It is said to be inappropriate for domestic abuse for multiple reasons: (1) when the abused partner attends couples counseling it implies that she shares in the responsibility for the abuse; a belief that many abusers have; (2) it does not address the core issue—which is the abuse; (3) it helps abusers justify blaming their partners giving them more excuses for being violent, and (4) exposing the abuser in couples counseling may anger him and escalate his abuse of his partner.

In fact, evidence suggests that therapy makes some abusive personalities worse.

Dr. Dirtbag's argumentative dinnertime manners were insufferable. Dining out was his opportunity to have me as his captive audience so he could ridicule me. I drug him to a counselor to correct his pernicious behavior. The counselor gave us homework: a questionnaire asking us what we each wanted out of our relationship. Several days later Dr. Dirtbag invited me out to dinner.

"Bring the questionnaire," he instructed me. "It'll be a good time for us to discuss our answers."

I was delighted—thinking he wanted to improve our relationship. At the restaurant we were seated at a table, our cocktails were served, our dinner was ordered and Dr. Dirtbag starts his interrogation.

"Sooo," he said (in his drill sergeant demeanor) "What did you answer to question 3? Where do yooou see yourself in five years?"

I knew immediately where this was headed. Dr. Dirtbag was getting ready to serve me a heaping platter of belligerent condemnation.

"I would like to write another book, travel and maybe have a second home in the mountains. What about you?" I asked sincerely, politely.

Dr. Dirtbag reared back in his chair, slapped the table with his hand, rattling the silverware and plates, and laughed haughtily. "Ho! Ho! Ho! ... And who's going to pay for all of this?"

I felt a sharp thud in my third chakra. In a split-nanosecond Dr. Dirtbag had trampled and demoralized my self-esteem.

Our entrees arrived. I shut down. And David continued his interrogation.

"Sooo ... what was your answer to question number 5?" he quipped. He knew he had wounded me. He was setting me up for his second nasty right hook jab.

I sat at the table in silence, looking down woefully at my dinner plate, picking at my food, contemplating my options. How could David do that to me? How could he use our counseling session to berate me in public? How could he pin me down, cross examine me and humiliate me while having dinner at a nice restaurant? I lifted my eyes and I glared at him across the table and I wondered—what kind of monster was he? I folded my napkin and I placed it on the table. I picked up my purse, pushed my chair back and I stood up straight and I walked to maître d' station and requested a cab ride home.

Abusers use public humiliation to undermine their victim.

The abuser's goal is to always control and dominate his partner. He may temporarily placate his partner by participating in therapy— but his co-operation will most certainly be short-lived. They will use their counseling sessions to learn about psychological principles and they use their new information to outwit the therapist, dissect their partner's vulnerabilities, and further confound, demean and control their partner.

"Couples counseling can be a big setback for the abused woman," states Lundy Bancroft. The abuser does not seek "positive communication" or "equality." He sees couples counseling as an opportunity to justify the abuse. He accuses his partner of "pushing his buttons" and "touching him off." If the abused woman reacts in anger or stands up to her abuser she may look

like the offending partner and be told to adjust her behavior for more a "harmonious" relationship. The therapist may turn to her and say, "But he feels abused by you, too." The therapist "inadvertently echoes the abuser's attitude and the woman is forced to deal with yet another context in which she has to defend herself."

The abuser will use therapy to manipulate his way out of the doghouse and restore old leverage in the relationship. If he was kicked out of the house or barred from the home with a restraining order, he will put on the appearance of improved behavior to regain entry into the home. "I'm doing so much better," he will say, and, "My medication is helping a lot." Or he will lay a guilt trip on his abused partner, saying, "We can't work on our relationship living apart." Or a pity play, "I need your help; I can't do this alone." Once he has finagled his way back into your graces—or he feels he is giving up too much by having to alter his controlling, abusive behavior, he will concoct excuses to drop out of therapy. He'll say, "This program is too expensive." Or, "The counselor doesn't know what he is talking about. This is doing more harm than good." And, "Our problems are not that bad; we do better on our own." Or—as Dr. Dirtbag did, the abuser may pretend to have gained new insight into his hurtful behavior.

When they feel they have regained control of their victim they will resume their customary abuse.

Dr. Dirtbag came home one afternoon from a session with his individual therapist telling me he had learned a new technique that would help him control his so-called "needling" of me. He said, "Whenever I start needling you, thump me hard on my forehead with your finger," and he popped me on my forehead to demonstrate. "Do that enough times and I bet I can learn to stop," he claimed.

I was okay with that. Each time Dr. Dirtbag started "needling" me, I got in his face and I gave a sharp whack right between his beady eyes. At first I was afraid my aggression would anger him, but I soon realized it was yet another cat-and-rat game for him. He verbally abused me. I thumped him. And he got off the hook.

Mike convinced Abigail's family and friends she was the culprit in their relationship.

"She's given up on us. I guess our marriage doesn't mean anything to her anymore," he told Abigail's mother. He told their married friends, "Her girlfriends are a bad influence on her. They keep dragging her to bars." (Reality: an occasional happy hour with girlfriends at a trendy restaurant.) And, "Her job consumes her life."

Abigail had a different perspective:

No one knew the real Mike—a lying abusive asshole. He gained the sympathy of everyone, including our couples counselor. Our counselor said, "Anyone can be successfully married as long as they are committed to making it work." My mom told me I needed to examine my priorities. My girlfriend told me it was my spiritual struggle in life. Everyone persuaded me to give Mike another chance. I let him back into the house. Two weeks later he accused me of having an affair, shoved me into the wall, struck me in the face, breaking my nose, sending me to the emergency room. I kicked Mike out of the house and got a restraining order against him. My family and friends quit buying into his pity plays.

He's got a good heart. I saw it one day.

By the time the abused woman finds therapy she can be in a state of shock and hopelessness. Many victims believe their abusive partners share their reality of wanting a loving relationship. They cling to the hope that their partner will recognize his hurtful behavior, repent and return to the loving, adoring man she knew in the beginning of their relationship.

The problem is, my styling *Shoe Sistas* ...

The longer a woman is with an abuser, the more immune he becomes to your threats and tears. The less he expresses remorse for his hurtful behavior. The less he worries about losing you and the relationship—and the more destructive he becomes.

> *Yes*—your abuser's apologies and loving gestures in between his episodes of abuse make it difficult for you to leave him.
>
> *Yes*—you believe that he loves you and you are the only person who can help him.
>
> *Yes*—it's hurts like hell to live your life without him.
>
> *Yes*—it's terrifying to think about starting your life over alone.

But you will never have a caring, non-disruptive relationship with an abusive, narcissistic, sociopathic man. Not ever! Never! Ever! *Not even when skinny pigs, wearing red high heels, fly!*

The designer question is:

Do you repeatedly date or are you in a relationship with an abusive man. If so, what are your emotional issues which cause you to attract and remain loyal to this type of man? Therein lies the answer to your relationship problems.

Alcohol, Drugs and a Dirtbag

Alcohol and drugs do not a monster make.

*L*et's dispel a myth: that drinking and drugs cause a man to be belligerent, aggressive and violent. And—if he would quit drinking or drugging he would cease his verbal and physical abuse.

> **Addiction does not cause partner abuse, and recovery from addiction does not "cure" partner abuse.**
>
> —Lundy Bancroft, *Why Does He Do That?*

In a national study seventy-five percent of the instances where physical aggression occurred, no alcohol was used by either partner. Moreover, many batterers continue their violence even after "drying out."

Alcohol or drugs *does not* and *cannot* make one person abuse another. An abuser may cite alcohol as an excuse for their violence. Alcohol may escalate an abusive event. Alcohol can act as an "un-inhibitor," intensifying abusive incidents—but alcohol *DOES NOT* cause the abuse.

Dr. Dirtbag was an expert at justifying his inebriated abusive behavior. He said "wine made him crazy," so he switched to beer. It wasn't long before his "beer behavior" was equally unpredictable and offensive, so he switched to bourbon. He mixed his bourbon with ice and coke in a tinted tumbler to conceal his daytime drinking. One

Dr. Dirtbag was a closet drinker

afternoon I was baffled by his drastic change in behavior so I
secretly took a sip of his iced "coke" sitting on the kitchen coun-
ter. My eyes crossed, my nose flared and my throat screamed,
"Holy crap, Jim Beam!"

"Alcohol does not change a person's fundamental *value system,*"
says Bancroft. "People's personalities when intoxicated, even though
somewhat altered, still bear some relationship to who they are
when sober." In other words, our core values, beliefs and behaviors
already exist inside each of us. If we do not believe we should rob a
bank, then getting drunk won't abruptly turn us into bank robbers.
Nor will alcohol or drugs suddenly turn a person into a villain,
rapist or murderer. Alcohol will, however, states Bancroft, help the
abuser overcome any "shame and embarrassment" that might hold
him back, and provide him an "excuse" to unleash his innate and
pent-up anger.

What Happens When an Abuser Gets Sober?

You cannot change an abuser's behavior
by changing your behavior.
The abuser cannot change his behavior until he
gives up his denial of the abuse.

The abuser will often blame alcohol or drugs for their abusive
behavior. And they will use their sobriety to help them control and
manipulate their victims. They may threaten to drink or "dope up"
if they don't get their way. Or they may use it as a bargaining chip;
"I'll stop drinking if you'll quit spending money," or "if you'll pay
more attention to me," or "if you'll stop going out with friends."
Even when men who batter stop drinking or using drugs, their
violence most often continues," explains Bancroft. In fact, many
battered women say the "violence got worse" during substance
abuse recovery.

I thought excessive drinking was at the core of Dr. Dirtbag's erratic and abusive behavior. I thought if he would quit drinking he could cease abusing me. I threatened to leave him if he didn't stop drinking. With my belongings half-packed, he knew I was serious. He pledged to stop drinking and I told him if I ever suspected him of drinking he would have to take a breathalyzer test.

"Don't worry," he promised. "I love you and I'll do anything to keep us together." It didn't take long for Dr. Dirtbag to sneak a drink, and when he did all hell broke loose.

An alcoholic will make a "special" trip to the store to supposedly buy something for the house so he can down a quick drink or beer.

A month passed and Dr. Dirtbag remained sober. It was a beautiful, sunny Saturday afternoon. Dr. Dirtbag was outside puttering around, doing odd jobs. He went to the hardware store to get wood screws to repair a loose window shutter. When he left the house he was cheery, even-tempered and focused. When he returned he was restless, grumpy and splitting off in different directions. He said he wanted to go for a ride in his sports car. He drove. I was his passenger. His behavior was queer and his driving was jerky and careless. He began speeding 50, 60, 70 miles an hour down a narrow residential two-lane road.

"Slow down," I pleaded.

He ignored me.

"You're scaring me," I screamed.

Dr. Dirtbag slammed on the brakes bringing his car to a screeching, rubber-burning halt in the middle of the road. He turned and he glared at me, his eyes were wide-eyed and menacing. He punched the accelerator, throwing the car forward, rounding curves at alarming speeds. My heart was pounding, my white knuckles clenched the door handle and my feet bore into the floorboard as if I could forcefully stop the Maserati should a car suddenly jut out in front of us. Suddenly I realized—Dr. Dirtbag had been drinking. I don't know how or where he got the booze, but I was certain he had been drinking.

Minutes later Dr. Dirtbag pulled the Maserati into our driveway and I jumped out of his car and into mine and I sped off to the drugstore to purchase a breathalyzer test. I had to know. Had he been drinking?

Little did I know at the time that breathalyzers were not an over-the-counter retail item. I drove to three different drugstores frantically searching for the device that could register his breath's alcohol content. I went home empty-handed, upset that once again, I had been outwitted by Dr. Evil-Knievel-Dirtbag.

Several days later (when threatened by My Sword-Wielding Ninja Girlfriend Within) Dr. Dirtbag reluctantly admitted to drinking that day. He confessed to downing a beer at the corner market on the way to the hardware store. His excuse was: he thought he could handle it. Déjà vu; it was the same irrational, irresponsible drinking behavior which landed him a DUI in Charlotte when I first started dating him—a glaring red flag I choose to ignore.

Medicating a Dirtbag

Medication will not correct the harmful mindset of an abuser.

Medication or therapy may temporarily lessen the symptoms of the antisocial personality, reports the Mayo Clinic, but because "antisocial personality disorder is essentially a way of being, rather than a curable condition, affected people are likely to need close, long-term care and follow-up."

According to Lundy Bancroft, medication is not a long-term solution to correct an abuser's behavior for two important reasons:

1. No medication yet discovered will turn an abuser into a loving, considerate, appropriate partner. It will just take the edge off his absolute worst behavior—if it even does that.

2. Abusers don't like to be medicated because they tend to be too selfish to put up with the side effects and almost always quit the medication in a few months.

Dr. Dirtbag self-diagnosed himself as having a social phobia disorder characterized by anxiety in social situations (another hard-to-refute, sympathy-gaining justification for his hurtful, obnoxious public behavior). He obtained a prescription from his therapist and began taking SSRI's (selective serotonin reuptake inhibitors) to control his "mood swings" and "social anxiety." His verbal abuse seemed to subside. I thought he was making progress. But he became withdrawn, sullen and agitated as if he were tormented by angry, restless demons. When I mentioned his changed demeanor he said, "Really? The ladies in the office said they liked the new me. They said I'm so cheerful." I wasn't even sure if Dr. Dirtbag was taking his medication because he concealed his pill bottle. No matter, several weeks later Dr. Dirt-Vader was ready to rock and roll.

There are no medications that can instill honesty, compassion, guilt, remorse and empathy. Understanding that an abusive, anti-social, narcissistic, sociopathic brain is wired to inflict unhappiness and harm to others should help you avoid, or dump an abusive man in search of a healthy relationship—*if not, Shoe Sista, you need more counseling!*

His End Game

When he believes you are permanently leaving him— he will begin his end game.

Y ou play by the rules. Anti-social personalities make their own rules. You are truthful and fair-minded and you feel bad if you tell a lie or you do or say something that hurts your partner's feelings. Antisocial personalities are free of moral restraints and they can lie, cheat and pursue illicit, self-gratifying desires, and they will not feel guilt, shame or regret for their reprehensible actions.

You are held back by your conscience. Sociopaths have no conscience. They are totally devoted to self and can easily discard loved ones without a second thought. When a spouse or girlfriend no longer serves their needs they are capable of coldheartedly abandoning them without feeling, warning or logical reason.

Abandonment can happen quickly without the current victim knowing that her ASP partner was looking for someone new. There may be no warning that he was getting ready to dispose of you like the evening trash. No clues that he had already sealed the deal with a new romantic interest. And when he does dump you, there will be no apologies or expression of remorse—because he will have justified his destructive actions.

He may have another relationship lined up before he dumps you.

Remember the night Dr. Dirtbag put me in a brutal headlock? It was a setup. Unbeknownst to me he had met and slept with another woman. There was one teensy weensy problem—Dr. Dirtbag and I had not completely severed our relationship.

It was Friday night and Dr. Dirtbag slithered into town in his reptile suit with an axe. As was with his customary militant strategy he took me to dinner, instigated a vicious argument, and when we returned home he physically assaulted me. It was brilliant! During his long drive to my house he premeditated an altercation between us, he invited me to dine out, and when the suitable situation presented itself at the restaurant, he suckered me into the worst fight of our relationship. In Dr. Dirtbag's delusional screwball mind, I flirted with another man and I deserved to be punished, creating the justification he needed to trash me for his Bimbo waiting for him back home.

My Snake-Handler Girlfriend Within appears. She looks wild-eyed mad. I think she's going to make me a good-looking pair of *gen-u-wine* anaconda cowgirl boots out of Dr. Dirtbag's hide.

The ASP may not consciously know that they are deliberately abandoning their partner, but they consciously do the things that they know will run her off.

Sociopaths' end game tactics are varied. If they still see value in the relationship they may try to win you back so they can resume their control and abuse of you. They may turn nice and "promise to change," stop drinking, enter therapy or an abuser program. They may suddenly take care of the things that you have been complaining about. When I threatened to leave Dr. Dirtbag, he finally refinished my night stand and fixed my car's bumper. They may tell you "that you will be lost without him," or "no one else will want to be with you."

> He knows he used to be able to control you with charm, affection and promises. He also remembers how well intimidation or aggression worked at other times. Now both of these tools are losing their effectiveness, so he tries to increase the voltage.
>
> —Lundy Bancroft, *Why Does He Do That?*

That's when your mentally disturbed partner's end game begins to look like a *blitzkrieg*—a swift military attack.

When an abusive, narcissistic sociopathic man believes the relationship is over, or he can no longer control you, or you are seeing someone else, or he is finished with you—his behavior can change dramatically and overnight. They can become extremely unpredictable, destructive and dangerous. They will use minor issues to set you up for extreme verbal or physical abusive events. Their increased rage will seem to come out of nowhere and for no apparent reason. They will say and do new and outrageous vicious acts against you. They will set you up to anger you so they can justify abusing you, and then dump you for their next romantic target. All the while, the sociopath draws satisfaction from the drama and pain they create.

The arguments between Dr. Dirtbag and me had risen to terrifying proportion. His verbal attacks were startling and had escalated to threats of physical assault. I had stopped threatening to leave him and I began bringing boxes home to pack my possessions. After watching me pack for several days he invited me out to dinner. I still did not comprehend the sly devise of his abuse—I thought it was his last ditch attempt at reconciliation.

At the restaurant he asked for an isolated table in a far corner. This was unusual because he always wanted to sit near the bar so he could have an audience. The waiter seated us at a remote table, our drinks were served and the fight bell sounded.

My Laila Ali Girlfriend Within enters the restaurant wearing a SIC Couture little black dress. She raises her red boxing gloves. She glares at Dr. Dirtbag's sadsack face; she bobs and she weaves, contemplating—*a corkscrew punch or a crushing liver shot?*

Dr. Dirtbag dug in deep that night. Never had I been so blindsided by his verbal attack, nor had he been so vicious. He berated me through the entire meal about the money he had spent on our relationship and he blamed me for all of our relationship problems. He was determined to take me out.

I left the restaurant in a battered daze. At home I went straight to the spare bedroom and locked myself in, making Dr. Dirtbag even angrier. He banged on my door yelling at me to let him in. I knew he kept a loaded revolver in his dresser and I was terrified he would kick in the door (as he had twice before) and I would be staring down the barrel of a .40 caliber Luger. I picked up my cell phone and called his father, the only person on the planet who might calm him.

Fifteen minutes later Dr. Dirtbag's Dad was knocking on my bedroom door. "Sugar, it's me, open the door."

I swung open the door, grabbed Dad by his arm, and I pulled into my bedroom.

"He's lost it," I cried. "I'm afraid of him. You've got to talk him."

Dad looked at me somewhat confused, disbelieving that his wunderkind-doctor-son could behave so badly. He gave me a fatherly hug and he left my room to go speak to his deranged offspring.

Ten minutes later Dad again tapped on my door. "Sugar, open the door."

I cracked the door open, peering at him in the hallway. "Sugar, do you know what this is on the carpet?" he asked, pointing to the cream-colored carpet in the hallway.

I looked down at the cream-colored carpet and to my amazement I saw small pink spots starting outside my bedroom door leading down the hallway into the master bedroom. It looked like a small animal had stepped into pink paint, leaving a trail of tiny pink paw prints.

*From across the house I heard Dr. Dirtbag yell, "**Why would she do this? Why would she mark up the house like this?**"*

Dad went home. Dr. Dirtbag retreated to the far side of the house. And I locked myself in the spare bedroom with a baseball bat tucked beside me in the bed. The next morning Dr. Dirtbag was gone and so were the tiny pink paw prints. Shrugging it off, I poured myself a cup of coffee and went to my vanity to put on my makeup. I went through my cosmetics routine, I applied my foundation, eyeshadow, brow pencil, mascara and blush ... and I reached for my—lip gloss?

My Lancôme Girlfriend Within screams, ***Where the hell is my favorite lip gloss?!?!***

My lip gloss, which I always kept in the pencil tumbler on my vanity counter—was instead—in the brush tumbler. Surreal. Bizarre. Insane. The thought of what Dr. Dirtbag had done was inconceivable. Unbelievably, astonishingly Dr. Dirtbag had spotted the hallway carpet with my lip gloss to convince his father I was a hysterical, crazed lunatic. It was his most psychotic, most devious, most scheming, and yes, most creative act of trickery and deception. Three days later my belongings were moving down the highway in a moving van.

Nadine's husband Quentin was the ideal husband, father, Sunday school teacher and businessman. When she exposed his sordid secret life he began his end game.

After twenty-six years of marriage Nadine discovered that Quentin was having a long-standing affair. She began to investigate their martial finances; to her horror she discovered they were in debt tens of thousands of dollars. Quentin had maxed out their credit cards. He had taken out a second mortgage on their home, signing her name to the loan papers. He had drained their savings and retirement accounts. They owed large sums on their tax returns, to which he had also falsified her signature.

Nadine was devastated. She confronted Quentin about his infidelity, deceit and their enormous debt. Quentin, the always composed, stable partner, suddenly became irate. He denied his affair and he blamed Nadine for their indebtedness, claiming she spent too much money on clothes and decorating the house. Nadine said:

When I exposed Quentin he became this angry alien. He ransacked my dresser and closets. He threw my clothes, jewelry and personal belongings onto the bedroom floor, handed me plastic garbage bags and said, "Here, pack your shit and get the hell out. I don't want to ever see your ugly face again."

I loved Quentin and I begged him to go to a marriage counselor—but he didn't want to work things out. He demanded that I move out of the house. He insisted that our two teenage sons remain with him, and he immediately filed for a divorce. He tried to turn my sons against me, bribing them with new computers and iPods. He told them our divorce was my fault. I got a job as a retail clerk and I rented a room in a woman's home. Quentin hired an expensive divorce attorney, he maintained his comfortable lifestyle, while I was forced to ask permission to visit my sons in my own home.

My Gloria Allred Attorney Girlfriend Within appears in court wearing a Chanel pencil skirt suit and spiked red platform heels. As a litigator she strikes fear in the hearts of her opposition! She represents Nadine's divorce case pro-bono—*just because she can.*

Christine's boyfriend's end game was a retail issue.

Christine broke up with her abusive boyfriend, Ted. He helped her move her belongings out of his house. In the process he "accidently" dropped and shattered the expensive beveled glass insert to her dining room table. *"Oops, I'm sorry. It was an accident,"* he claimed. He "accidently" demolished her jewelry armoire. He "unintentionally" poked a hole in her pricey oil painting. He alleged each incident was a clumsy mishap. To further punish her, he called her while she was out of town looking for an apartment, claiming "burglars" had stolen several of her boxed belongings and an oil painting stored in his garage. It was contradicting insanity. He did things to penalize her for leaving him—knowing his actions would anger her and run her off.

When Jackie broke up with her controlling, hyper-jealous, verbally abusive boyfriend, Kenny, he became scary. In his mind if he couldn't have Jackie—*no one would have her.* Said Jackie:

Against my better judgment I let Kenny back into my home to get his things. He followed me into my bedroom and he grabbed me by my shoulders, shook me and shoved me down onto the bed, jumped on top of me and straddled me, pinning my arms down with his knees. He took his fingers and pried my eyelids open wide, he leaned into my face, his angry hot breath invading my senses and with gritted teeth he growled, "Open your eyes when I talk to you, Jackie! Do you hear me? You will never be with another man. I don't care if it's one year, two years ... if you ever think about marrying another man I will make you a widow." And then he got up, he opened my jewelry case, destroyed the jewelry he had given me, and he grabbed his things and he stormed out my front door.

Her jealous, crazy ex-boyfriend stalked her wearing a wig.

Kenny continued to stalk and terrorize Jackie. She called the police three times for his threatening behavior. The third time a female officer from the domestic violence squad responded to her call. The officer ran a background check on Kenny and found out, in addition to a DUI, he had a history of domestic violence.

The officer told Jackie, "We had a similar situation like this last year a mile from here. The woman went back and forth with her abusive boyfriend, like you're doing with Kenny. He started out being verbally abusive. He escalated to physical abuse. And then one night her boyfriend slit her throat and killed her. Your guy is capable of the same violence."

Every year, 1 in 3 women, who is a victim of homicide, is murdered by her current or former partner, states Safe Horizon victims' services agency. "Women are more likely to be killed by an intimate partner than men."

Statistics show that abusive men who kill their girlfriends or wives do so after they have been separated or divorced. Abusive men often believe they "own" their female partner or they view a woman's departure as the ultimate betrayal which, in their minds, justifies retaliation or murder. If you are in this type of situation— get out, protect yourself and seek assistance. Confide in family members, a trusted friend, a pastor and a family doctor. Get the legal and financial help you need. Seek out counseling, women's centers and join support groups. Build your skills for independent living, such as finding employment, going back to school and managing your own finances.

Abba, a celebrated 1980's Swedish pop music group, sings the song "The Winner Takes It All." It's an emotional ballad reflecting the end of a relationship in which one partner is left with a broken heart, and the other partner is unscathed and emotionally intact.

The song lyrics are:

The winner takes it all ... The loser standing small ... Beside the victory ...That's her destiny.

You will never come out on top with an abusive, narcissistic, antisocial, sociopathic man.

> Because he is sicker than you are smart, you will never "win" with him. So all of your book smarts and street smarts and relationship smarts will not out smart his ability to psychologically damage you ... Once you know this the battle is over.
>
> —Sandra L. Brown

The sociopath takes it all ... *his victim has to fall.*

Rise up strong, competent, confident Shoe Sistas. Put on your red high heels and tell that self-serving, good-for-nothin' abusive dead animal to take a one-way trip to Siberia. Establish your independence, fill you minds with thoughts of love, hope and designer shoes, and hold out for a wonderful man who will love, honor and adore you.

Part Three

Internet Dead Animals

"I like Nascar, huntin' and quiet evenings spitting
sunflower seeds off my porch ... if you need a good man
hear I am."

—ladieslove4me

Cyber Playground

You are chatting online and smitten with an attractive, charming bachelor ... when in truth a conniving, cheating scam-artist is chatting with his next victim.

Years ago women met their boyfriends and husbands at college, the workplace, church, through friends, and even night clubs. It was a small circle of influence and introduction.

Years ago single men and women who used personal ads were considered desperate, sleazy or psycho. Today, not only is internet dating an accepted, effective contemporary vehicle for single men and women to meet, date and find love—according to Dating Sites Reviews, 1 in 5 singles are currently in a committed relationship with someone they met on a dating site. I have several girlfriends who met and married the love of their lives from an online dating service.

Internet dating sets up a blind date for you.

Online dating increases your chances of finding a committed relationship or marriage. Instead of meeting a suitor every leap year, you are introduced to numerous viable candidates within a matter of months. Online dating speeds up the relationship process. I call it is fast-forward dating. Romantic connections happen more quickly with online dating. You have an opportunity to ask questions which pre-qualify your online candidate. Prior to meeting in person a mutual attraction develops through email correspondence, chats and phone conversations. When you do meet, you know in advance you are both seeking a relationship.

The downside is: the internet is an innovative playground for scammers, romance artists and married men (or women) who create a false online front. They can conceal their identity with a secret email address, a phony profile, the anonymity of a cell phone, and if necessary a post office box. Dating long distance allows the dishonest person to conceal their true activities indefinitely. They can hide a girlfriend or a wife, problems with an ex and children, a drinking problem, drug and other addictions, criminal history, a shoddy reputation, financial difficulties and a dysfunctional or abusive personality. If you have been dating a long-distance man for a while, and he hasn't asked you to visit him, you need to ask yourself—*why?* It's our responsibility, as women, to proceed cautiously on an online dating service. Meet in public. Ask lots of questions. Pay attention to your instincts. Don't be a nincompoop— do a simple background check.

James: Kathy was 40-lbs. heavier than her online photo. My God, did she think I wouldn't notice?

Kathy: I don't understand! We got along great on the phone. He loved my picture. Then we met and I never heard from him again!

Whirlwind Romeo

*Before you even think about online dating,
you must know the warning signs of dating scams.*

*Y*ou wouldn't shoot or pack a gun without first knowing gun safety and acquiring a permit—*would you?* To do so could mean tragic injury. You wouldn't use a plastic surgeon for a facelift, or a DD breast augmentation or a tummy tuck without your girlfriend's recommendation and validating his medical degree—*would you?* I certainly hope not, unless you're okay with rubber-band lips, Frankenskank eyes, paralyzed nerves and missing nipples (true story). You wouldn't post your online profile and date men from a dating site website without knowing the dangers of internet dating—*would you?*

My Judge Judy Girlfriend Within hammers her mallet, *You spent $72.00 getting your hair done? Well, you wasted your money! Now shut up and raise your right hand and swear, "No, oh hell no, I wouldn't dare post my profile on the Internet without knowing the dangers of internet dating!"*

*His internet personal ad read: "Finished mourning!
Ready to move on!"*

The no. 1 sign of an insincere suitor or con-artist is a push for quick involvement. Whirlwind Romeo comes on strong in the beginning. He's an eager-beaver to win your attention and affection. He has tons of time for you with his frequent phone calls, emails and chats. He wants to speak with you the first thing in the morning and right before you go to sleep. He will talk about falling in "love" quickly. He will tell you he has never felt like this about another woman. He's never felt so much so fast and he will say things like: you are a "God send."

Romance con-artists are experts at detecting the needy, lonely and naive woman. They will ask you about your hopes, dreams and relationship aspirations. They will size you up and they will know just what to say to steal your heart. They may tell you of their dreams and past hurts and how they once "had it all" but lost it, and they will blame their relationship failures on an ex-wife or former girlfriend so you will feel sorry for them. As the relationship progresses they may claim an unexpected illness, hospital visit or personal emergency setting you up for a loan they never intend to pay back.

Keith was 10 years older, 20 lbs. heavier and had noticeably less hair than his posted photo. When I showed up for our introductory meeting at the restaurant, he jumped in my face because he knew I wouldn't recognize him. Really? What did he hope to gain from that?

"AlwaysFaithful17" to His Wife and Two Girlfriends

Becky, an attractive 48-year-old emergency room nurse, met Ronnie on an online dating site. Becky lived in St. Louis. Ronnie, a 54-year-old software salesman, lived 300 miles away in Illinois.

Becky was flattered when Ronnie emailed her saying she had a beautiful smile and he would love to hear from her—and so she emailed him back. He told her his company was transferring him to St. Louis and he was seeking a relationship in the city where he would soon be living.

Ronnie quickly expressed his adoration for Becky with his constant emails, daily phone calls and snail-mail greeting cards. He sent her articles from magazines and newspapers he thought she would like. He sent her a picture of a Caribbean cruise with a scribbled note that said, "I've always wanted to go on a Caribbean cruise!!!" He sent her a newspaper advertisement for leopard high heels and wrote, "You would look hot in these!" He seemed to know just what to say and do to get her serious attention.

Two months went by and Ronnie continued his hot-and-heady communication with Becky. Becky had fallen in love with her phantom-cyber-lover, but he repeatedly canceled his travel plans to come to St. Louis to meet her in person, citing an unexpected emergency or a business situation. He finally made a trip to St. Louis to "search for a house" for his upcoming job relocation, and to take Becky to dinner. Said Becky:

I couldn't have been more delighted when I met Ronnie. He was handsome like his photos. He was charming and entertaining. I had already emotionally bonded with him through emails and phone conversations. Fifteen minutes after being with him I knew he was my dream man. After dinner we went to my apartment and we made passionate love.

The next morning Ronnie returned to Illinois and everything returned to normal. He continued to call and email Becky. He expressed his love for her; he even insinuated marriage. *And yet—* he didn't invite her to visit him. He rarely called at night. He failed to call her most weekends. He never answered his cell phone, her calls went to his voicemail and he didn't have a home phone.

Handsome young men on dating sites wink and flirt with older women to feed their ego.

Becky suggested that she wanted to come see him in Peoria. Ronnie said his house was a mess, and he had custody of his 12-year-old son on weekends. He said he didn't need a home phone, and he didn't call her at night, because he traveled all the time. He said he didn't answer his cell phone because it was a company phone with limited personal talk time.

Robert posted several photos of himself from the waist up on his dating profile. He had thick silver hair, a handsome chiseled face, and he was a snappy dresser. When I saw him in person my jaw hit the restaurant floor. Robert, who advertised himself as 5'10", barely stood up to my chin, and I'm 5'5".

Becky was lovesick for Ronnie but her gut was nauseated from uncertainty and mistrust. She finally googled him on the Internet. She couldn't find him through the typical people search websites, like Anywho.com, BeenVerified.com and Intelius.com, nor was he listed in the white pages. A light bulb went off in her head. She met Ronnie on the online dating site PlentyofFish.com. She began searching for him on PlentyofFish.com in neighboring states—and she found him. AlwaysFaithful17 was using the same photo and sappy online name in three other states.

Oh, dude . . . you are so busted!

Becky was proactive: she posted a phony woman's profile on the PlentyofFish site. She posed as a fun-loving 39-year-old redhead, named "Lady4u," looking for romance. Lady4u contacted Ronnie and he bit like a largemouth cyber-bass and he poured on the same syrupy crap to Lady4u that he also told Becky. He told Lady4u that he was moving to her city and he would love to meet her. Becky responded to his intimate chats and emails and then she nailed him, posting his photo and profile on www.romancescams.

com, the largest online resource of photos and profiles of known romance scammers around the world. Thus the saying: Hell hath no fury like a cyber-woman scorned.

Internet Red Flags

It's easy to spot online scam artists if you know what to look for. Ask yourself these questions:

- Does he push for an exclusive dating relationship early on?
- Does he send cards, gifts and trinkets from the get-go?
- Does he talk about intimacy or sex right away?
- Does he constantly call, email and text you, to the point you wonder if he's checking on you?
- Does he want you to get a web cam or a Skype account?
- Are his answers evasive and sketchy?
- Does he ask questions about your financial status or does he reveal his quickly?
- Does he boast of financial assets, future wealth or possessions?
- Does he constantly have excuses for everything?
- Is he taking too long to meet you in person?

Married Men Hunting

Eighty percent of married men cheat in America. The rest cheat in Europe.

—Jackie Mason

*L*arry Lizard, a married man, slithered onto to the Internet, paid $70 for an online dating site membership, posted a phony photo and a hyped-up profile, and then—*click!* He presented himself to thousands of single women as a loving, successful, divorced man looking for the last love of his life. A woman's best defense against these lowlife belly-crawling Gila Monsters is to be aware of the distinct warning signs of married men who use the internet to cheat.

An MSNBC survey states that 30% of the men using an online dating service are married. Alas, women rank slightly less!

I received the following email from a Match.com suitor:

> Wow where have you been hiding. I saw your pictures and profile and they took my breath away. My name is James Bond. Yes Im a few minor zip codes away and yes I am a tad older but I am far from old and planes do fly to Tenn. If you would like to talk to a kind, caring, gentle, loving, educated, romantic, successful stockbroker who is honest and ethical and who loves kids dogs bright woman and laughter then Im your man.You truly take my breathaway
>
> James Bond [grammar and typos belong to Mr. Bond]

James Bond was handsome enough in his two headshot photos. He was in his late nifty fifties. He had a pleasant smile, a stocky build with a "Terry-Bradshaw-power-donut" hairdo. And even though he lived 600 miles away, his flattering message got my attention—and so I emailed him. He emailed me back with a complimentary message and his phone number. I took that as an invitation to call him. I called him two evenings later (I wanted to see if he would answer an unexpected phone call at night.) When he answered he sounded a wee bit startled and uncomfortable. We talked for 15 minutes and then he said he would call me back. Mr. Bond didn't call back ... he instead began texting me a series of schmaltzy, mindless messages every evening at bedtime:

"Hey beautiful how r u?" And, "I can't wait 2 meet u." After a week of his cheesy, late-night lip homage, I texted him saying, *"Sorry, 007, I'm not interested in a text relationship."*

Summary: James Bond's (assuming that's his real agent name) interest in me was strictly ego-boosting flirtation. If he had been serious about seeing me he would have called me for a conversation and booked a flight to come see me. But, my guess is, his wife wouldn't let him.

A Match.com email sent to me from TeeUp4Us:

> HI Smiling Lady
>
> I am in the process of moving to northern alabama from Pittsburgh ...I do not have a picture posted but would be pleased to forward recent pictures if you would be interested ...I am divorced and looking for a new start in the south ...I spent the majority of my business career on Wall Street so I am very financially secure ...you made me smile just looking at your picture ...I would love to meet you.
>
> Jim [Typos belong to Jim]

I didn't respond to Jim because he did not post a photo. A week later I received a second message from TeeUp4Us, which read:

> Hi, Jim is married. I am his wife in Pennsylvania. He is not moving to Alabama. He just goes there during the week to work. We have been married for 3 months. We are newlyweds.

My Fiona Shackleton (divorce attorney to the stars) Girlfriend Within: *Seriously? And she is still with him why?*

I wrote her back:

> Dear Wife,
>
> I hope you get this message.
>
> I suspected that Jim was married because (a) he didn't post a photo and he wanted to send it to me on the sly in an email, (b) he wants to date out of state, and (c) he dangled the "Wall Street" bait in front of me. All red flags!
>
> You are married to a pathological liar and consummate cheater, and regardless of what he tells you he is NOT going to change. My guess is he is also verbally abusive; if he's not now he will be and he will make you feel like the crazy one. My advice to you is cut your losses, get out now and don't let that sleazebucket back into your life, because if you do, you will sink deeper into his control and he will repeatedly break your heart.
>
> Jim, if you're reading this, you're a no-good cheating snake!
>
> (And I recommended several self-help books for her to read about abusive, anti-social personalities.)
>
> Good luck—Nancy

Married men are more likely to initiate the first contact. They search the Internet for needy, naïve women they can manipulate. They will immediately ask you personal questions, but they are hesitant to talk about themselves. Married men do not want to post their pictures on dating websites for everyone to see. They instead offer to email a picture to your personal email account.

When in doubt ask yourself these questions:

- Does he not post a photo? Does he post a picture that is dark or blurry? (He doesn't want anyone to recognize him.)

- Does he post only one photo or is he unwilling to trade additional photos? (His online photo may not be his.)

- Do you only get a cell phone number because he claims to have no home phone?

- Are you able to reach him by phone at night and weekends?

- Do you call but constantly go to voicemail? (An indication that he has a girlfriend, wife or family and it is inconvenient to talk.)

- Are his calls and responses back to you irregular or at set times? (He calls when he is driving or at work, away from his wife or girlfriend.)

- Does he call from a "private number" or block your number to keep you from calling his number?

- Does he say that he travels a lot and that's why you can't reach him by phone? Or he's frequently out of the service area; his battery died or he was with a client?

- Will he not share his last name with you? (Maybe he gave you a phony name—the reason he doesn't show up when you Google or research him.)

- Does he avoid conversations about himself, his family or upbringing? (Some men say they've lead a boring life, or they change the subject and they focus the conversation on you to avoid divulging the details of their lives.)

- Is he secretive about where he lives? Or you can't come to his house because it's inconvenient, it's messy or he's not ready for company?

- Do you get the chance to meet his friends or family? (If not, odds are you are a secret in his life.)

- Does he have an excuse for not spending a holiday, his birthday or other celebrations with you?

My Ballsy Woman Within takes matters into her own hands. She googles her online suitor, she finds out where he works, and she shows up unexpectedly at his office. Sitting on his desk is a framed family portrait of him, his lovely wife and two young children and their puppy dog.

The Sweetheart Scam

Con-artists are known for their intelligence, creative imagination, charm and persuasive powers.

y Psychic Sylvia Brown Girlfriend Within gazes into her crystal ball: *I see danger ahead. An exquisite, charming, irresistible man ... his name is ... Monolo, Christian or Louis ... oh, my bad—that's my closet!*

Things aren't always what they appear to be on internet dating sites. A person's photo may or may not be their own. Anonymous email accounts are effortlessly created. A person's true identity and whereabouts can be concealed with a throwaway phone. You think you are conversing with a sweet and sensitive man who is looking for a relationship or marriage, just as you are. In reality you're talking to a criminal sitting in an internet cafe using a well-rehearsed script. He's hunting through chat rooms, dating and social networking sites searching for victims to dupe and cash in on. If you are over 40, recently divorced, a widow, elderly or disabled—all the better for the online predator.

Scammers are adept at psychological profiling and they use a woman's weakness to their advantage.

The Nigerian romance scam is one of the most popular scams of all times. The Internet provides an effective vehicle for these scammers who live in the foreign countries of Nigeria, Ghana, Ivory

Coast, Senegal, Malaysia and others. They establish phony profiles in chat rooms and dating and social websites. They list false gender, race, age, location and sexual orientation. They post photos stolen from modeling sites or social networks such as MySpace, Tagged or Facebook, and they scan the Internet for potential victims. In their correspondence they pose themselves as engineers, construction workers and other professionals working job assignments in faraway countries. Once email communication is established with you they promote romance and intimate conversations. When they are confident they have gained your affection and trust they will ask you for money for studies, sick relatives, emergencies and misfortune. They may pretend to finally be coming to see you, but something happens to them—they have a car accident, or they get robbed and beaten and are hospitalized and they contact you to ask for financial help. Or they will use the re-shipping scam. The scammer asks you to re-ship goods for them. Unknown to you, the goods are purchased with stolen credit cards and if you assist them you are an accessory to a crime. Or they use the Nigerian Advance Fee Fraud, also called the 419 scam. They tell you they have won millions in a lottery and they offer to transfer large sums of money into your bank account, but you must provide up-front fees for various taxes, attorney fees or transaction costs. After you send the money you never hear from them again.

Jenny received an email from a man on a free online dating site. In his photo he was the handsome, ash-blonde, smiling 40-year-old man-next-door. *Or was he ... ?*

My Skeptical Girlfriend Within purses her lips and smiles cynically, *Free? Quality? ... I'm just saying!*

Jenny tells her story:

> *Thomas popped up on my computer screen on a dating site one night, wanting to know if I wanted to chat. We chatted back and forth for a week and then we switched to emails. He told*

me he was a construction worker and when the economy took a nosedive he accepted a six-month contract in Nigeria building a hospital.

At first Thomas's emails were cordial—but they quickly escalated to intimate conversations, poems and love letters. *He was adoring, caring and sensitive. He sent me perfume and a teddy bear on my birthday all the way from Nigeria. He said he had fallen in love with me. I thought I had found the man of my dreams. Within two months he was talking of marriage. A month later he emailed me about a money problem; he said his boss had paid him in money orders which he was having trouble cashing. He asked me to cash his money orders at my bank and wire the money to him in Nigeria.*

Con-artists know how to tell a good "sob" story.

Jenny felt okay about Thomas's request and over the following weeks she cashed two (2) $800 money orders and forwarded the funds to him in Nigeria. A month later Thomas said he was ready to come back to the States but he was running short of money and he needed $500 to pay his final apartment bill; otherwise the landlord would have him incarcerated—plus he needed $800 for a plane ticket. He pledged to pay her back when he got to the States.

Thomas told me he was desperate to be with me, said Jenny. He said he bought me a 2-karat diamond engagement ring. At that point I would have paid anything to get him home.

Jenny sent Thomas another $1300. Then her bank called, telling her that the money orders she cashed were counterfeit. The altered money orders were purchased for $20 but had been "washed" and "doctored" to read $800. Jenny was flabbergasted. Said Jenny:

I was certain the bank was in error. I emailed Thomas repeatedly about the money orders but he wouldn't respond. Then my friend told me about a Nigerian scam website. I read the scam reports on the website and I realized I had been a victim.

Jenny never heard from Thomas again and she had to take out a second mortgage on her home to pay back the $2900 to the bank. Jenny later admitted:

I allowed my loneliness, my longing to be with a man, and my soft heart to interfere with my common sense and intuition. It was a costly mistake I'll never make again.

If a man sends you a message of love before a face-to-face meeting—put on your Louboutin Leopard tennies, grab your Gucci leather wallet and run for your life! Genuine, stable people do not fall head over heels in love, sight unseen.

Warning Signs of Nigerian Scammers

- Be suspicious of any potential suitor who communicates only by email and ignores your requests to talk by phone.

- Be skeptical of anyone who deals in money orders, cashier checks, wire transfers, escrow services or online payment methods.

- Beware of long distance transactions that involve receiving or shipping merchandise.

- Be cautious of real estate deals, investments offering high returns, joint ventures and clearing house letters.

- Do not rent housing without seeing the interior, or purchase expensive items from unreliable sources sight unseen (the housing unit or merchandise may be below advertised quality or not even exist).

- Do not submit to credit checks or background checks for a job or housing until you have met the interviewer, or the landlord or agent in person at the property.

- Never give out any personal information regarding your social security, savings, checking, credit, or other financial accounts, or your eBay or PayPal information.

Facebook Predator

Becoming friends with someone on Facebook can provide a motherload of private and personal information.

Depending on what you post on Facebook someone can see your location or address, statistics, interests, comments, activities, employment and photos, as well as gain personal information about your associates, friends and family. There is even an option called "Facebook Places" which allows you to share your real-time whereabouts with onlookers; for example a time-stamped Facebook post reports: *"Nancy just checked into Boscos."* I mean, do you really want to let an angry ex know where you are so he can harass you; or a stalker so he can molest you, or a robber so he can burglarize your home while you are downing a peach martini at Boscos? Even the Navy and the Air Force realize the precarious implications of internet posts and have reportedly asked their personnel to rid their mobile devices of this tell-all Facebook application.

My Astronaut Dr. Sally Ride Girlfriend Within, first American woman in space on the Space Shuttle Challenger, looks at her iPhone, stares at her Facebook wall and seriously contemplates: *Could it be internet douchebags know something NASA doesn't?* Sally Ride died July 23, 2012.

Anyone with a cell phone can snap an unflattering or compromising photo of you and instantly post it to Facebook for the world to see. Until recently, they could "tag" and post an embarrassing photo to your Facebook wall without your permission.

I have become guarded about others haphazardly snapping my picture with their iPhones and then posting it to Facebook as they see fit. You must first ask my permission, giving me time to put down my wine glass, un-cross my blurred eyes and reapply my lipstick before capturing my image.

My girlfriend Reba had an innocent, yet awkward photo taken of her and posted on Facebook. Reba attended a singles mixer at Valentino's Italian restaurant. A guy friend was snapping random pictures of everyone. She posed for a photograph next to a Greek goddess statue holding a large pitcher, supposedly pouring wine from the pitcher. In jest Reba laughingly stooped down in front of the Goddess, tilted her head backward under the pitcher and opened her mouth wide as if the wine were flowing into her mouth.

Visualize erotic. Now—get your mind out the gutter!

Needless to say, Reba was embarrassed by the posting and she asked the guy to delete the photo from Facebook; which he did with an apology. But not before many of her friends, family, business associates and unknown onlookers saw her compromising pose.

Facebook Hustler

Vivian met Kurt on an online dating service. Her profile and photos revealed her as a tall, slender, attractive 54-year-old blonde artist living in Dallas. Kurt posted himself as a 44-year-old home builder living in Canada.

Kurt contacted Vivian through the dating website. He requested her personal email address. Their emails volleyed back and forth for several days. He sent her his phone number and he asked for her phone number. He called her and he immediately sent her a Facebook friend request, which she accepted, giving him full access to her photos and personal information.

Vivian tells her story:

The first time Kurt called me we talked on the phone for five hours. He told me I was stunning and beautiful. The following morning he sent me a good morning email. He sent numerous emails throughout the day. He called me that evening and we talked for two hours. He was open and sharing and he said he had found his "match." The next day he sent more adoring emails and we had another two-hour nighttime phone conversation. He told me I was the woman of his dreams. On the fourth evening Kurt said to me, "I saw your pictures on Facebook. You look like you have a size 5 ½ ring finger."

My heart leaped because I did wear a size 5 ½ ring. How could he know that? I thought. I asked him, "What are you talking about?"

He said, "Vivian, I'm flying to Dallas in two months and the only thing I want to change about you is your last name. I am going to put a ring on your finger. I am going to build you a magnificent house in Canada with panoramic windows facing the mountains to inspire your painting. You can lease your house and bring your clothes because you won't need anything else." And then he sent me an image of a meadow with blooming wild flowers at the base of a snow-capped mountain range.

I was dumbstruck by Kurt's outlandish suggestion. I said, "Whoa! This is too fast. You're scaring me."

He replied, "Vivian, I know why you're scared; you're falling in love with me. Don't worry. I'm going to make you my bride and I'm never going to let you go."

At first I laughed because I thought he was kidding—and then a sense of trepidation struck me. I instinctively felt this man was a threat to my safety. A person does not fall in love and commit to that level in four days. I blocked Kurt's phone calls and emails, and I removed him from my Facebook account.

Mr. Canada combed the dating and social sites for naive and vulnerable women looking for love. His goal was to gain as much personal information as fast as he could, and then he morphed into a knight in shining armor. In a very short time he had skill-fully acquired a dangerous amount of personal information from Vivian. He got her personal email address so he could receive and send more photos. He got her phone number so he could talk in-timately with her. And he became friends with her on Facebook, giving him unlimited access to her personal and business informa-tion and activities. As her Facebook friend he could also befriend her friends and family, social and business connections, as well as, gain information about complete strangers who casually accept his friend request.

Sybil received an email from a male acquaintance (a non-Facebook friend) asking her to fix him up with two of her Facebook girlfriends. Sybil said:

> *He had scanned my Facebook friends looking for attractive women to date. His request felt creepy and invasive. Not to mention he was a recovering alcohol and sex addict, not some-one my two girlfriends would be interested in dating.*

My Cyber Girlfriend Within runs to her computer, she turns down an email marriage proposal from her Arabian Oil Sheikh (whom she has never met), she hides her Facebook profile and she closes her online dating membership.

Protect Yourself

Being cyber informed is being cyber forewarned.

orty percent of all Facebook profiles are fake, according to a CBS News study. If you have 500 Facebook friends it is likely you don't know a large percentage of these people—and you are sharing information with unscrupulous people misrepresenting themselves.

Facebook Precautions:

1. Never post your address, phone number, full birth date, social security number, financial information, making you vulnerable to identity thieves, scams, burglars, or worse.

2. Never reveal when you are on vacation or out-of-town, or your schedule. It is wise to keep your children's and grand-children's names and locations private.

3. Check your privacy settings periodically. Every time Face-book redesigns the site, which happens occasionally, it puts your privacy settings back to default in which, essentially, all of your information is made public. It is up to you to reset your privacy settings.

4. Think twice about approving a friend request who appears to have mutual friends. Email the mutual friend to validate his or her true identity.

5. Be cautious of odd-sounding emails from your friends. Hackers frequently assume the identity of a known friend.

They send you an email claiming to be on vacation abroad and robbed of all their money; they plead for money, promising to pay you back when they return to the States.

Online Dating Safeguards:

Nowadays it is an accepted practice, for both women and men, to check out an online suitor. My girlfriend told her online dream man she performed two background checks on him. It didn't stop him from marrying her.

- Check out an online man through public records, research websites and connections. A simple Google search can reveal basic information. If you are serious about a suitor I suggest you pay for an in-depth online investigation. Just do it—it will be worth the money you spend.

- Save all emails and chat logs, and pay close attention to details. As time passes you may pick up on discrepancies. Rereading old emails can validate your gut intuition of man's questionable behavior.

- Arrange your first meeting in a public place like a coffee shop, book store or restaurant. Don't invite him to your home or accept a lift home until you know the person well.

- Tell a friend who, when and where you are meeting an online man. Send a friend his phone number(s), his email correspondence and his photos and other identifying information. Ask a friend to call you in the middle of your date to check on you.

- Ask to see his driver's license. Take out your license and play the "I'll show you mine if you'll show me yours." If he balks, he's probably not who he says he is.

- Ask for his home phone number and home address. When you decide you can trust him insist on an invitation to his house. If he declines, something's wrong.

- Ask him questions about his family, friends and past. A con-artist tends to be vague or tight-lipped about personal matters. If you meet his family and friends, don't be afraid to ask personal questions about him.

- Make note of the car he is driving and the license plate. Run a make on it if you have the resources.

- Most importantly, always trust your gut instincts. If you feel suspicious or uncomfortable about a man, there's probably a good reason you feel the way you do.

My Girlfriend Within is meeting a Match.com guy at Starbucks. Before leaving her house she forwarded his email correspondence, dating profile, photos and cell number to her girlfriend, priest and attorney; she updated her will and she dropped a can of mace and a fingerprint kit in her purse. As instructed, her girlfriend called her 30 minutes into the introductory meet-up. *"Is he cute,"* her girlfriend asked exuberantly. *Dunno,* My Girlfriend Within groaned, *He didn't show up!*

For a few dollars you find out a person's age, current address and phone number, previous marriages and divorces, complete address history, current and previous jobs, known aliases, date and state of SSN issue, average income; relatives, associates and neighbors; family tree, driver's license, FAA certifications, hunting and fishing permits, concealed weapons permits and professional licenses; properties owned and sold with sale date and price; vehicle, airplane and boat registrations; corporate affiliations and bankruptcies; criminal history; sexual offenses and accidents.

Part Four

Hall of Shame

"Listen to what a man says ... watch closer what a man does."

—Nancy Nichols

Soul-mate? Think Again!

I don't miss him. I miss who I thought he was.

—Anonymous

oul-mate? Are you kidding me? Why then does he lie to you; demean, control and manipulate you, hit on your best girlfriend, verbally abuse you, threaten you, and even slug you, and repeatedly rip out your heart?

I've known plenty of women who have fallen in love with their soul-mates—*including me.*

In the beginning a soul-mate is the most wonderful, understanding, attentive, affectionate man you'll ever know. You feel an instant, magnetic, ignited connection with your soul-mate. It is a feeling of deep and natural affinity, intimacy, intellectual, spiritual and sexual compatibility. You feel acceptance in his presence. You find solace in his words. You are lost in the depth of his eyes. You melt at the touch of his hand. You entrust your life to your soul-mate, quickly, passionately and completely—only to find out later—*he is really the man-from-hell.*

Monica and Jamie fell hopelessly in love with their soul-mates.

Monica tells her story:

George wasn't the most handsome man in the world—but there was an immediate magical attraction between us. He was charming, thoughtful and generous. He quickly professed his love for me and he immediately became an important part of my life. He did everything for me. He washed my car, he fixed my leaky faucet and he cooked dinner for us. Our relationship was effortless. We talked for hours. We laughed continuously. In our moments of silence we felt an unspoken connection. But he was jealous of other men talking to me and he resented the time I spent with my girlfriends and family. I ignored it because I thought it was a declaration of his love for me. But he began to hyper-criticize and berate me. Seven months into our relationship he lost his temper and struck me across the face. That was the beginning of his verbal and physical abuse. Two months later I left George wondering where my dream man went.

Kitty shares a similar soul-mate story:

When Patrick and I met there was a powerful mental and physical connection. He was the best lover I've ever had. His body scent was intoxicating. When we kissed his breath was like an aphrodisiac. Our love-making seemed sacred. We believed ourselves to be God-mates. A year later I caught Patrick cheating on me. I forgave him and gave him another chance. Two months later my soul-mate dumped me for my best girlfriend.

*In the beginning my soul-mate made me feel like the most cherished woman in the world.
In the end he made me feel stupid, insecure and sexually undesirable.*

There was an undeniable, instant affinity between David and me—two physical energy bodies magnetically drawn to one another. I had never felt such an overwhelming mental and emotional connection with a man. He had never felt such strong feelings for a woman. We believed fate had brought us together. Every weekend he drove two hours to see me, or I would drive to see him. In eight months we never missed a weekend being together. When we were together nothing else seemed to matter. We shut out the outside world and we melted into one another. I told my girlfriend, "I'm going underground. I'll talk to you Monday"—meaning: David's here. I'm totally immersed in him. I won't be taking calls. Truly, I thought I had met my destined sacred partner. In reality he was a throwback to my dysfunctional, hurtful past. The man I called my soul-mate was, instead, the most deceptive, psychotic, abusive man who had ever crossed my path.

Corrupt Soul-Mates Roam the Planet Earth

A soul-mate will tell you he's never known anyone like you before—that you are the most wonderful, beautiful woman that's ever been in his life. That you are God's gift to him, an angel, and he will love you until the day he dies—and if he ever lost you he would never get over you. Six months later, maybe a year, an abusing, raging, lying alien emerges from the body of the sweetest, most loving man you've ever known. So abrupt is his transformation, it's as if you went to bed one night and you awoke with a total stranger the next morning.

How can this be? You've never met a man with whom you felt such an overpowering emotional and physical connection. He felt like your brother, your father, your best friend, your boyfriend or husband and lover all rolled into one person. It's as if you had known him in another life. You see past his surface feelings. You embrace his inner soul—and he does you. The emotional bond is profound. The physical intimacy is rapturous. You feel blessed and complete with your soul-mate. It feels too good to be true.

Listen, Shoe Sistas! A soul-mate doesn't mean he is capable of a long-term, caring, supportive, honest relationship. He may be the best lover you've ever had. He may be an excellent provider, a generous giver, the most endearing personality and greatest communicator that's ever crossed your path—that's why it's so hard to comprehend how he can hyper-criticize you, cheat on you, blame and manipulate you, verbally abuse you, and even physically assault you.

If you have met your true soul-mate there are no games. There is no pretending. No deception. No maltreatment. There is no reprisal because honesty, selflessness and unconditional love are the foundation upon which your relationship is built.

- A true soul-mate respects your ideas, thoughts and feelings.

- A true soul-mate supports your efforts and empowers your dreams.

- A true soul-mate encourages your independence and personal growth.

- A true soul-mate accepts your imperfections and personality quirks.

- A true soul-mate sympathizes with your heartbreak, struggles and fears.

- A true soul-mate is forgiving and trustworthy.

A true soul-mate *does not* hyper-criticize, demean, berate, control, manipulate or lie to you. Nor does he make you jealous or cheat on you. No matter how intense your feelings are for your partner, a true soul-mate DOES NOT verbally or physically abuse you! *Never! No way! No how!*

My Hopeless-Romantic Girlfriend Within picks up John Keats's book of poetry. Keats wrote a love letter to his beloved Fanny Brawne, "I cannot exist without you—I am forgetful of every thing but seeing you again—my life seems to stop there—I see no further. You have absorb'd me. I have a sensation at the present moment as though I were dissolving ..."

Love Hurts

I believe that a man and woman connect at the soul-mate level (a bonding which transcends a normal relationship) because of sui generis—"in a class of its own," a unique and special emotional attraction. This kindred magnetism evolves from our upbringing, societal background, varied relationships and life's experiences, all of which affect our innate personality, character and beliefs, and form distinct emotional traits within each of us. Combine a man's and a woman's compatible emotional traits with harmonious combustible pheromones and—*kaboom!*—soul-mates are born!

The problem is: a kindred spirit may possess dysfunctional traits from our hurtful past. He may represent an emotionally detached or abusive father—or a hypercritical, controlling mother. Our kindred spirit may, in fact, be an unfaithful, alcoholic boyfriend or a domineering, abusive husband. The larger problem of loving a malfunctioning kindred spirit is—it's hard, if not sometimes impossible, to permanently walk away from the man who has held your heart in his hand—because you are *soul-tied.*

Better to pay attention to the red flags of a dysfunctional man on the front end so you'll be sane, alive and available when your true soul-mate comes along.

The Lying, Seducing Scumbag Didn't Call Back

One of the most frequent questions single women ask is: Why does a man not call back?

It happened again! Kitty went out with a wonderful man. She had a stupendous time, and then, for no apparent reason—she never heard from him again. But this was no ordinary date. *No sir-ree!* This handsome man was her previous boss whom she had not seen in fifteen years. A man she respected for his exceptional business skills and adored for his delightful personality.

Kitty shares her story:

I was walking by two men sitting at the bar at Fleming's restaurant when this attractive gray-haired man said, "Hey, young lady, don't I know you?" My immediate knee-jerk reaction was: this cute man is hitting on me. My eyes didn't recognize the guy—but my ears said, I know this raspy voice from somewhere! "OMG!" I shrilled. "Bernie! ... It's you!" Slowly I began to identify Bernie. His face was older. His hair had turned silver and he wore updated eyeglasses. At fifty-something he was more handsome than ever and divorced after twenty-six years of marriage.

Several weeks later Bernie called Kitty to invite her to his home for dinner. They cooked, and they laughed, they caught up on old times and they drank two bottles of wine. After dinner Bernie popped some nostalgic tunes into his CD player and they began to dance in his living room. And then, in the midst of a bebop twirl, he kissed Kitty (*Holy red stilettos! She didn't see that coming!*) and he kissed her and he kissed her. An hour later she thanked Bernie for a wonderful evening, gave him a call-me-later goodnight kiss and she drove herself home.

Bernie never called again.

My Rejected Girlfriend Within presses her lips into a hard line and frowns, *That dog!*

Kitty said: I was stunned and I was hurt. I questioned myself. Did I drink too much and act stupid? Was I not pretty enough, not smart enough or too old? Did I bruise his male ego when I politely turned down his offer to stay for a serious make-out session? Or was he embarrassed because my sophisticated ex-boss got smashed and turned into a lecherous old man? No, I looked hot in my tight black jeans, starched white shirt, gray houndstooth vest and long pearls. I was affable, conversational and engaging—and I acted like a lady. I was certain Bernie was totally into me. Sooo ... what the heck happened?

It'll take one bottle of wine to get over that scumbag. Bartender! Set er' up!

Two months later Bernie finally called Kitty.

"I've been meaning to call you," Bernie said, "but my Dad got sick ... my kids were here for the holidays ... I had problems at work ... blah, blah, blah ..."

Bernie—talk to the hand!

Red Flags:

There were no warning signs that Bernie would be a one-date-wonder. However, the night Kitty had dinner with him he did *casually* mention that he had recently quit dating *"some girl."* My guess is: Bernie had broken up with his girlfriend, the holidays were in front of him, he was alone, and the lure of a familiar intimate companion pulled him back into a failing relationship. In other words—*it was easy!* Bernie temporarily went back to his old sweetheart, and after the holidays, he called Kitty—*thinking he would give her another go-at-it.*

Don't Fret It, Girl!

It is my strong opinion, based on my long-standing, expert personal experience, that if a man expresses a strong interest in a woman, and then he suddenly and unexpectedly evaporates, more times than not, there is a fresh ex-girlfriend or lingering flame hovering in the background. The problem is, as women we don't know about it, we are confounded by his abrupt rejection, and we therefore cope with our hurt feelings. Foul ball, guys!

It's Not Always About You!

Minnie met Darren while visiting her girlfriend Penny in Hilton Head Island. They were sitting at the bar at Wise Guys having drinks when Darren magically appeared. The mental and physical connection between Minnie and Darren was extraordinary. They looked like brother and sister; they were both fair-skinned, flaxen blondes, resembling cute Golden Retriever puppies. Darren was trim, 5-feet-8, wearing faded designer jeans and a white filigree embroidered shirt, his long sleeves casually rolled up. Minnie was petite, 5-feet-4, wearing a white spaghetti-strap sundress, her soft pale hair fell off her tan shoulders. Sitting at the bar, Darren was all smiles and white teeth, ordering cocktails for everyone—Minnie beamed, drinking in his presence.

Minnie followed Darren to his oceanfront home for a late night drink. He was considerate and gentlemanly. They talked and they kissed into the wee hours. Minnie didn't want to drive home and risk a DUI, and so they passed out fully clothed on his king-size bed. The next morning Minnie left Darren asleep in bed and began her three-hour drive back home to Georgia.

Darren called and texted Minnie the following weeks—clearly he was smitten with her. The fourth week he made plans to visit her. Minnie cleaned her house, went to the grocery and liquor store and she arranged for her teenage son to stay with his Dad for the weekend. Friday afternoon Darren texted Minnie saying he had a problem at work and he couldn't leave until the next morning. Saturday morning came and went and she never heard from him again. Minnie was, to say the least, crushed.

Two months later Minnie again visited her girlfriend Penny in Hilton Head Island. She texted Darren saying she was in town. He met her for a late dinner at a beachside bar and grill. Sitting at a remote table, he smiled at her sweetly, caringly touched her hand and said, "You've cut your hair. It's looks nice." Minnie looked into his chocolate puppy-dog eyes and melted. The waitress asked for their drink orders. Minnie ordered a vodka and tonic. Darren ordered a glass of ice water with a lemon.

You never know what someone else is going through ...

Darren was a handsome, successful, sweet-natured man, who, unbeknownst to Minnie, had been wrestling for months with his alcoholic demons. Sitting in the restaurant he told Minnie he was arrested for a DUI, he quit drinking and he was attending regular A.A. meetings. Part of his recovery process was to alter his social activities. What he didn't say was—he also had to re-evaluate his friendships. Darren realized it was time for him to get sober, and even though he adored Minnie, it was a bad time for him to start a new out-of-town relationship which involved drinking.

Red Flags:

When a man doesn't call you back—remind yourself—it's not always about you.

If a man doesn't call you back, and you're sure you did nothing wrong, like: trying too hard, talking negatively in general, talking too much, bad-mouthing your ex's, displaying anxious, jealous or mistrusting behavior, putting emphasis on money, drinking too much, answering or checking your phone, or caving in for sex on the first date—*whew!* If you're sure you did not exhibit any of these man-repellant traits—don't waste your time and energy trying to figure him out.

If a man doesn't call you back, don't immediately assume that there is something wrong with you. Maybe his work is a priority and he is bogged down at work. Maybe the chemistry wasn't mutual; it was there for you, but not for him—not a good reason to beat yourself up. Maybe he's coping with personal issues, he has lingering feelings for an old flame, or he's healing from a recent breakup (do you really want to be his sloppy rebound?). Maybe he's looking for a fling, and he senses that you're not. *Maybe* he has a girlfriend—or a wife. Maybe there's something wrong with him and not *you!*

My friend Michael says men don't call back because, "We have a change of heart, or a relationship appears complicated and we don't want to start something that we can't or don't want to finish."

Whatever!

Bottom line—if a man is not calling you, it's because he's not interested in you—which means, Shoe Sistas, he's not thinking about you. Stop thinking about him and get on with your life.

Now put on your lipstick, your kick-ass red high heels and get back out there—because men are like buses—a better ride will be along in five minutes.

My Girlfriend Within applies her Wet n Wild lip gloss, puts on her sky-high red platform shoes and starts out her front door to go stand at the bus stop. Hearing thunder she grabs her umbrella, *Holy cow, it's raining men!*

Bible Sexting Snake

The snake lied to Eve in the Garden of Eden and then he slithered onto the Internet to deceive and bed women.

Wendy, an attractive 51-year-old, met Kevin on a Christian dating website. Wendy lived in Scranton, N.Y. Kevin, a surgical instruments representative, lived in Pittsburgh. Kevin emailed Wendy. She checked out his online profile. He was handsome, smiling and well-groomed. He described himself as a 48-year-old Christian man looking for a Christian woman who would be his best friend and partner in life. Wendy replied to Kevin's email. He responded, asking for her phone number. He called her once—and then he switched to frequent text messages.

Wendy tells her story:

I went to Pittsburgh on business; Kevin and I arranged to meet for dinner. I didn't recognize him when I walked into the lobby of the restaurant. He looked ten years older than his online photos, twenty pounds heavier and his hair was thinner. But he was still handsome and there was instant chemistry between us—so I dismissed it. Kevin's story was, he was married for 23 years, his wife had an affair and so he divorced her. He presented himself as a devout Christian, interjecting scriptures in our conversation to back up a moral point. He talked about doing his "personal work" after his divorce. He taught a divorce recovery program for men and women at his church for the past eight years.

I returned to Scranton and Kevin stepped up his pursuit. Every morning he would text me, "Good morning, precious, have a blessed day." He texted sweet nothings throughout the day and he called me every night before I went to bed. He said he couldn't wait for me to meet his children and take me to church with him. He told me he was closing his dating profile. Within two weeks he had verbally said, "I love you," and he jokingly inferred marriage. I knew his proclamations of love were happening way too fast. But he truly seemed genuine and I was falling in love with him.

I met Kevin in Pittsburgh again. We enjoyed a romantic dinner. After dinner he walked me to my car, he pressed me up against my car door, gave me a passionate kiss and his hand found my breast. The next morning I drove home. He continued to call me nightly. "When are you going to marry me," he cooed over the phone. He texted me daily, saying, "I want to be with you." Then he jacked up his game. He texted, "When are we going to make love?" And he wrote, "Dreamed of u last nite, got excited." I shirked it off and replied, "Take a cold shower." He phoned me at bedtime and he asked me, "What are you wearing," knowing that the answer was a "nightie" or "nothing." And then he began sexting, "I get hard thinkin about u." "I hope u get wet when u think of me," and finally, "I want 2 feel myself n side u."

My 50-Shades Girlfriend Within drops her vibrator, *Holy fricken crap! What did he just text?!?!*

I was shocked and I was uncertain of how to respond to him. He made it sound like he was kinda-sorta joking. I wondered … should I be a sport and text-flirt back with him? But my core felt oddly violated by his lewd assertions. I texted him back, saying I was uncomfortable talking like that. He apologized and he became withdrawn in the following days.

The following week Kevin resumed his pursuit; he booked a hotel in Scranton and he drove three hours to take me to dinner. After dinner we went back to my place. He sat in the big club chair in my living room and he motioned for me to sit on his lap. I sat sideways on his lap, my arm around his shoulder, my body leaning against his broad chest, and my legs dangling off the side of his thighs. He put his arm around my waist and he quizzed me about my relationship failures.

Kevin thought of himself as a spiritual relationship guru. He dissected my personal problems. He told me what it took to have a healthy relationship. He said he wasn't ready to have sex with me. And then he began kissing me and rubbing his hands up and down and all around my body. Thirty minutes later we were in my bed making love. The next day Kevin returned home.

I asked myself: How would Jesus reply to a Bible sexting snake?

For weeks Kevin texted me every morning at eight o'clock, saying, "Good morning precious, have a blessed day." After our conjugal visit, he didn't call or text me for two days. The third day he texted, "Good morning, have a nice day."

The batteries died on My 50 Shades Girlfriend Within's rabbit. *Crap!* She screws her face and glares at me, *So WTF happened to "Precious"?*

In my heart I knew Kevin had pulled back—and so I didn't reply to his text. The next day his text accusations began:

Kevin: I don't play games.

Wendy: You haven't called me. Ur playing games now.

Kevin: Ur a hypocrite. You asked me to lay w you n bed.

Wendy: Ur sex texting was a precursor to everything that happened.

Kevin: Ur not who I thought you were.

Wendy: U teach a dating class. U need to rethink your Christian walk.

Kevin: U need 2 complete ur personal work. Don't call me again!

Wendy: Don't worry—I don't call sex predators.

My last text didn't get through to Kevin because in a matter of seconds he had blocked my cell phone—I mean, how many people know how to instantly block phone numbers? This told me this was not the first time this had happened.

A month later I had dinner with my girlfriend Teresa who lived Pittsburgh. I showed her Kevin's online dating profile and she screamed, "Oh my God, I know that guy, he dated my girl-friend Sandy. You have to talk to her—he did the same thing to her. She met him on a dating site. He professed to be a big-time Christian. They dated for several weeks. He sent her vulgar messages. He groped her on a date. She scolded him—and then she never heard from him again."

Red Flags:

The snake pushed the sexual envelope and when she took a bite of the forbidden fruit—he condemned her for sexual immorality.

Short and sweet—beware of good-looking men quoting scripture. Kevin was a scripture-spouting, sanctimonious fraud. He presented himself as a devout Christian looking for a virtuous woman—and then he seduced women with his obscene, pornographic text messages. If a woman reprimanded him for his offensive behavior he tucked his spear-tipped tail and fled into darkness. If a woman submitted to his lascivious overtures he condemned her as the wanton tramp, thus cleansing his self-righteous conscious of any wrongdoing. In other words, it was okay for him to seduce, but it was not okay for a woman to succumb.

Kevin attended church every Sunday morning. He led a weekly Christian divorce recovery group in which he taught appropriate dating behavior to newly divorced men and women. Surely his class included honesty, respect and decency. Nevertheless, Kevin posted outdated photos and falsified his age on an online dating site, he sought out single women—and then he exploited them with his lewd and degrading text messages.

It was okay for the sexting snake to seduce, but it wasn't okay for her to succumb.

My Joyce Meyers Girlfriend Within ogles her Jimmy Choo red platform heels as she cautiously steps across the stage to the microphone, *I ask ya, Could this jerk be any more of a lowlife hypocrite?*

Let's take this Christian hypocrite one step further: I seriously doubt Kevin became an unprincipled sexting-slimeball overnight. I suspect that he was the adulterous partner in his marriage. I suspect that he surfs porn sites and he reads smutty x-rated magazines. One can only imagine what he is doing with his spare hand while texting vulgar messages to women.

My 50 Shades Girlfriend Within hides her vibrator before her boyfriend comes home. She knells beside her bed, folds her hands and bows her head in prayer, *Please Dear Lord, can I be a fly on an iCloud on this Bible-sexting snake's judgment day?*

Jack-Ass Busted on Facebook

It's not okay to break off a relationship with a boyfriend or girlfriend with an email or text message— that's FUBB (fouled up beyond belief).

I'm not interested in the hunks because they require too much work with their inflated egos and roving eyes. My motto is: I want to be cuter than my man because (1) he will appreciate me more, and (2) he will more likely remain true-blue.

Too bad Betsy didn't employ my dating philosophy.

Jack, a handsome 57-year-old eHarmony hookup, was the first man that gave Betsy goose bumps since her breakup with her boyfriend two years ago.

It was a steamy summer in Baton Rouge. Betsy met Jack for an introductory drink at Mansurs Bar and Grill. She was immediately smitten by his 6-foot-2 bronze, muscular frame, charcoal twinkling eyes, mischievous Creole-French dialect and slightly thinning silver hair. He was equally intrigued by her toned curves, bubbly personality and flirtatious blonde bangs and long ponytail.

Jack eagerly pursued Betsy. Betsy slept with her amorous Cajun on the third date. But several weeks into dating him she couldn't seem to connect with him at an emotional level. Their conversations were trivial and shallow. He never called her by name. He asked her few questions about herself. He rarely gave her a compliment. And he was exceedingly tight-lipped about his personal matters.

Blonde Betsy tells her story:

Physically speaking Jack was my perfect man. I loved the way he looked, the way he handled himself, the way he dressed, the way he smelled and I especially loved his playful nature—and he was a fantastic lover.

Fun-wise Jack was an enthusiastic partner. Cooking in the kitchen with him was magic. We practically lived in my pool. We downloaded old songs from iTunes, laughed, sang and danced to the music. We cuddled on the sofa watching TV. It was the most laid-back fun I had had with a man in years.

Wallet-wise Jack was a challenge. He never asked me out; he instead invited himself over for dinner, occasionally bringing food and his beer. He never chipped in for the pricey iTunes songs I downloaded and burned to my DVD's for his car. He said his money was tight because of the bad economy—I understood.

Emotionally she was drawing a blank.

Relationship-wise Jack was dependable, agreeable and affectionate. He texted me throughout the day, he called me almost every night and he was eager to see me several times a week. But I found myself questioning his motives. I accused him of being a "player." I asked him, "Is there another woman in the background?" He swore he wasn't involved with anyone. He said he had been dumped twice in the past three years, and he didn't want to get hurt again.

All in all, Jack felt like my ideal man, except for one vital detail—emotionally I was drawing a blank. Against my better judgment I continued to date him.

Dating a man for four weeks is long enough for a girl to ask a guy for help with small tasks. It's how we test a man to see if he is willing to give of himself and his time.

I asked Jack to help me clean my .38 snubbie. His wimpy response was, "Oh, it's not hard, just get yourself a cleaning kit at WalMart." When my grill ran out of gas after cooking his "free" steaks, chicken and shrimp, I casually mentioned, "Oh, by the way, honey, the grill is out of gas." He responded with an "hmm" and "okay"—but he never offered to refuel the gas container. And when I asked him to help me fix the itty-bitty switch on my lamp he mumbled an inept, lazy excuse. He did, however, clean my pool several times right before popping a beer and jumping onto a water float.

I struggled through the weeks with Jack's aloof communicating style. Our phone conversations were brief, trifling and quasi-dutiful. His text messages were childish and sexual. He spent the night regularly but he never spoke of wanting a relationship with me. Every time he kissed me goodnight and went home, I was left wondering, What are we doing? Are we in a relationship? Or am I merely a sexual commodity?

It was an extremely hot August and week five of dating Jack. I flew to Philadelphia to visit my son. Jack pledged to water my outdoor plants and clean my pool while I was away. My first day in Philly I felt something was different between us. He barely texted me. He didn't return my phone call. When he did answer the phone he was distant. Four days later I returned home. I texted him saying, "I'm home," and I went to bed. Early the next morning I received an email from him. Jack finally had something to say.

His email was titled, "Confused." It read:

I am having a very difficult time writing this. Everything is so great with you. We laugh, we sing, we dance, we cook, we enjoy each other's company so much and I find myself having feelings for you, but everything is happening so fast and it scares me. I feel there are times when you want to hear me say something really meaningful ... something you can hang your hat on so to speak. I want to share my feelings but I'm being very guarded and it's holding me

back. You are everything a man could dream of and I do want to love again but I just can't at this time and I need to say good-bye.
XOXO ... Jack

WTC?!?!
My Rock Star Pink Girlfriend Within rides up on her Triumph Bonneville motorcycle wearing Elisanero black leather buckle boots, singing, *So what? I'm still a rock star!"*
Moaned Betsy, *"Truly, I did not see this coming."*
The following week Betsy visited Jack's Facebook page looking for answers.

Three days after Jack broke up with me his out-of-town niece posted a message on his Facebook wall: "Hi, Uncle Jack. Can't wait to see you and Jill next week."
*Are you (bleeping) kidding me?!?!" Who the (bleep! *!?#? bleep!) is Jill?*
I scrolled down Jack's Facebook wall, looking for clues from the previous months. Seven months earlier there was a December photo of Jack and Jill sitting on a sofa, she glazing at him with love-sick eyes while they ate reindeer cake with their friends and family. The pieces of Jack's relationship puzzle came together—Jill was the ex-girlfriend who dumped him and broke his heart six months before I met him. It was crystal clear—Jack dumped me in a cryptic internet message and went back to Jill.

She wanted Shallow-Jack to say something that felt like the truth.

Red Flags:

Red Flag No. 1: Jack was a handsome man at fifty-seven—*and he knew it.* He often spoke about other women in the flirtatious sense; a sign that he needed admiration from more than one woman.

Red Flag No. 2: Jack was sexually aggressive, but he was emotionally withholding—a strong indicator that his interest in Betsy was sexually motivated.

Red Flag No. 3: Jack played the "I'm-scared-of-being-hurt" sympathy card. When a man senses a woman's desire to commit, he uses his past issues to remain emotionally detached while enjoying the intimate benefits of a relationship.

Red Flag No. 4: Jack continued to send Betsy insincere text messages after he went back to Jill, for instance, *"Wanted to say hi before I went to bed."* It was his attempt to keep Betsy in the wings in case things didn't work out with Jill.

Here's what you need to understand about a man:

1. When a man tells you he is not ready for a relationship—*believe him.* He is not going to fall deeply in love and want to marry you because you are super-caring, super-affectionate, super-loving, super-patient, super-sexy, and most of all—super available. If he is not totally into you, you are a convenient girlfriend until the woman-who-rocks-his-world comes along.

2. When a man truly wants an honest, meaningful relationship he will let you know in his actions and his words. He will ask you questions about yourself. He will compliment you and call you endearing names. He will call you regularly and take you to dinner and outings. He will introduce you to his friends and family and he will want to meet your family and friends. He will express interest in your life and goals. He will refer to his future plans with you in it. He will gladly help you with the small jobs and repairs around your home. He will look for ways to win your heart and commitment.

3. When a quality man is truly interested in you, your gut won't churn, your heart won't ache and you won't constantly worry if he is sincere about being in a relationship with you (well,

you might because of your own self-doubt). You will, instead, feel a sense of contentment and peace because you know he loves and wants to be with you—and only you.

Footnote:

A year later Jack emailed Betsy in a weak attempt to renew his booty-call relationship. Betsy asked him about Jill; he told her Jill broke up with him.

Ya gotta believe Jill knew something Betsy didn't. Delete. Delete. Delete. Erase. Erase. Erase. End of Jackass story.

Douglas Dug His Grave

Don't fall prey to the influence of a dead animal's charm, for the moment he gets you, he will reveal his nasty, bad-natured self.

Douglas, a large 6-foot-4, 57-year-old man, was comfortable towering over everyone. As a former ex-military officer and public figure he was accustomed to barking out orders without being challenged.

I was introduced to Doug through a mutual Facebook friend. His first email included his photo and professional biography. I was impressed—not only because of his business-like relationship approach, but because his email glowed with politeness and southern charm. We spoke by phone and then we began dating.

Doug was a take-charge gentleman who planned our outings with finesse. He recommended what nights to go out, where to dine and the best movies to see. He chose Saturday as our weekend date night. We went to evening church service and dinner afterwards. I didn't have to think about a thing. It was an extreme treat for a woman consumed with business matters.

Doug knew the path to my heart. He texted me throughout the day. He called me at lunch and every night. He opened every door for me. He kissed me gently and he held my hand in public. He bragged openly to his friends about the beautiful, intelligent woman who had come into his life. He professed to want a loving, committed Christian relationship. He said he didn't want to have sex until the time was right. He wanted someone to grow old with and travel with in retirement. But what got my attention most was how he admired and supported my work.

"I'll be your chauffeur, valet, travel guide and business assistant," Doug said. "You tell me what you need, babe. I've got your back." He even wanted me to introduce him to my friends as my "garde du corps," French for "body guard." I thought I had found my dream man.

Conversations with Doug were one-sided, long-winded and cerebral. He fancied himself a relationship guru, talking incessantly about what constituted a meaningful relationship. He gave me his favorite motivational book to read. He wanted to discuss the book's life-altering philosophies. But when I tried to express my thoughts about the book he cut me short with his dialogue and he rejected my opinions. Talking with him became tedious, constricting and exhausting. I became stingy with my viewpoints and I learned to just say, *"Uh, huh."*

Doug always opted for a Saturday night date. Four weeks into dating him I had to work on a Sunday morning so I requested a Friday night date, to which he replied, *"We'll see."*

My Menopausal Girlfriend Within has a severe hot flash. She pops Prozac, Nuerontin and Premarin pills, she checks her HRT arm patch and she screams, *We'll see? We'll see? What kind of ego-tripping, lamebrain response is "we'll see"?!?*

It was the Friday in question and Doug continued his controlling behavior. He did not address whether or not we were going out that evening. He didn't call me all day. He quit texting me at noon. He was waiting for me to call him to ask if we were going out. I didn't call him because I *guaran-damn-tee* you—he was going to say *"no."*

I didn't text or call Doug. I instead went out with a girlfriend. Later that evening, while I was enjoying drinks and dinner at Elfo's, his text messages started rolling in.

7:15 p.m.

> Doug: U going?

7:28 p.m.

> Me: What do u mean, u going?

Doug didn't reply to my text ... and I am beginning to reconsider, thinking: *It's Friday night, I'm probably being too hard on him—and I miss him*—so I break down and I call him on his home phone. *No answer.* I call him on his mobile phone. *Again—* no answer.

Asshole!

At 8:05 p.m. a text came in from Doug:

> Doug: Hope ur ok, haven't heard from u. Sent couple of texts, hope u had a great day and ur having nice evening. Luv ya. Miss you babe. Doug

WHAT?!?! my brain cells screamed. *Is he smoking rancid broccoli? How can he dare say that? I responded to his morning text and I called him twice that evening.*

Men are such morons!

An hour later Doug resends the same message:

9:05 p.m.

> Doug: Hope ur ok, haven't heard from u. Sent couple of texts, hope u had a great day and ur having nice evening. Luv ya. Miss you babe. Doug

Whatever! I did not respond.

Doug texts again.

9:10 p.m.

> Doug: Don't want 2 interrupt ur evening, never sure if text gets thru. Sorry, didn't hear from u. Nite

Doug called me the following evening. He acted like everything was hunky dory. I noticed that he was slurring his words; no doubt, he'd been at the watering hole with his beer-soaked buddies. He said he didn't remember me asking him to go out on Friday night and he claimed he didn't receive my text messages or phone calls. And then he projected the blame onto me, saying, "When I didn't hear from you I thought you were blowing me off."

The jury is in: Doug was a manipulating, controlling, punishing dead animal.

A man may rule an army, but he can't maintain a relationship with a woman using control and domination.

Red Flags:

Doug seemed too good to be true—*because he wasn't.* I was extremely flattered by the full-court press dating approach of a handsome, strong, accomplished man like Doug. But in reality his sweet talk, constant attention and emotionally contrived conversations were an elaborate formula to influence, manipulate and eventually control me.

Red Flag No. 1: Doug was extremely jealous; the foremost sign of a controlling, abusive man. He was suspicious when a male friend telephoned me. He was annoyed if a strange man spoke to me, and he chastised me when I casually mentioned any man.

Red Flag No. 2: Doug quickly professed his devotion to me. The second week of dating Doug he told me wasn't dating anyone else and that he would prefer that I didn't—a tactic to cut me off from the dating pool and monopolize my time. He talked incessantly about our relationship—a ploy to create quick and intense involvement. When I confided a past hurtful relationship, he said, "You have a strong man here who wants to love and take care of you if you'll let him"—sappy verbiage to gain my trust. Doug's statements were designed to break down my independence and gain control over me.

Red Flag No. 3: Doug kept tabs on me with his constant texting and phone calls. He texted me relentlessly throughout the day and he became irritated if I didn't acknowledge every one of his text messages—or if my reply was not equally saccharine.

Phone conversations with Doug were equally exasperating. One evening, after listening to forty-five minutes of his pretentious, ego-driven, psychological babble, I felt drained and depressed.

At bedtime Doug and I would have our final phone conversation, I would say "goodnight," hang up the phone, turn out the light and roll over to go to sleep. Five minutes later *A controller will try to establish co-dependency in his victims.* he called back for no reason other than to invade my privacy. It was as if he was monitoring me and I began to resent his constant interruptions.

Red Flag No. 4: Doug was a consummate controller. I was talking to him on the telephone one evening when he told me to turn down my TV. A minute later he said, "What that's beeping noise in the background; can you stop whatever it is?" It was my microwave in the adjoining room alerting that my tea was ready. *Who can hear something like that!* He even controlled the intimacy level of our relationship by saying he didn't want to sleep with me until it was "right." My guess was, he was concealing an ED issue.

Red Flag No. 5: Doug had been divorced for twenty years. He was flippant about his marriage; as if it held little or no value to him. He blamed his ex-girlfriends for his other relationship failures. There's a reason some people stay single for two decades.

Red Flag No. 6: In the end Doug confirmed my suspicions that he was an all-out controlling batterer. When I withdrew from Doug he bombarded me with text messages, pleading that I see him. When I ignored his messages he besieged me with late night phone calls and left me cajoling voice mails that quickly escalated to criticism and blame. When I texted him, *"Please leave me alone,"* his messages became insulting and caustic. When he finally realized he wasn't going win me back, he became vulgar, demoralizing and verbally abusive, giving me a fast-forward preview of what a relationship with him would be like—punishing and scary.

Doug felt out of control because he couldn't control me.

In the beginning Doug was drawn to my confidence and self-assured presence. In the end he couldn't stand it because he couldn't "power over" me.

How do you communicate with a controller? You don't. You erase his text messages without reading them. You delete his voice mails without listening to them. And you block his future communication attempts. Open the door to a manipulating controller and he will (1) pull you back into his brow-beating world with his smooth-talk and worthless apologies—and when he knows he has you, (2) he will stab you with a parting scathing insult.

Delete. Delete. Delete. Don't give an asshole the chance to do his dirty work.

Texting Gigolos

He kept texting me after we broke up.
I thought it meant he still loved me and missed me.

It's ten o'clock at night and you're cozy in bed, watching TV. You're waiting to hear from your sweetie. Your iPhone vibrates. It's him, text messaging you, "tired, going 2 zzz, OXOX LUMU cm 2MORO." (SMS, short message service for: tired, going to bed, hugs and kisses, love you miss you, call me tomorrow.)

Now that your beloved has said goodnight you're content to turn off your bedside lamp, close your eyes and fall sleep because you believe he is doing the same—when in reality, your snookums is at a late night party hitting on one hot chick. Or maybe he is telling the truth; he is home in bed—with the size-4 hussy-skank from the office. You'll never know ... because text messaging provides him the shroud of secrecy, while saddling you with the burden of proof.

Let's get this out of the way; women are
equally guilty of misusing text messaging.

The Pros of Text Messaging

How does anyone live without wine, a really nice purse, red high heels and text messaging?

Text messaging is the modern, succinct, efficient mode of communication. It enables us to sneak mini-messages to the ones we love. It relays important information quickly and discreetly without annoying, lengthy conversations. It allows us to receive communication, yet ignore the sender. Many people have a "text before you talk" policy; meaning, text me what you want first; I'll decide if I want to talk to you. With text messaging you are unencumbered and in control of your communication.

As long as your mobile phone has a signal, you can stay in touch with anyone, anywhere, at anytime.

It's your first date with Mr. Hunkalicious. You're driving to meet him at a restaurant, traffic is bumper to bumper and you're running horribly late.

"B there n 10," you text-message him.

"K, no prob," he texts back.

Instantly everything is peachy.

You're stuck in a boring, all-day business meeting when all of sudden it hits you—today is your sister's birthday! You're mobile phone is in your lap, the conference table conceals your hands and you can text practically blindfolded. You quickly peck out a message, "H-BDAY sis, love u." You hit send and your boss is none the wiser.

Perhaps you received news that your early morning sales meeting has been moved up an hour. You're co-worker-girlfriend needs this update but she's at a movie with her boyfriend. You text her, "Meeting moved 2 8am." Thirty minutes later she texts you back, "thx u saved my a**."

Lastly, you're out-of-town on business, you're eating

It's not okay to answer or reply to a text message while you're in a conversation with someone, especially if you're dining. Dude, that's rude!

alone in a restaurant and you miss your sweetheart. Suddenly your phone signals an incoming text message. You look at the screen and read, "thinking about u, miss & love u, Pookie."

Awww, how does anyone subsist without text messaging?

The Cons of Text Messaging

Text messaging has been said to be an addictive, compulsive activity which eliminates personal interaction. The bigger problem is, text messaging in the wrong hands has become a tool of deception, lip service and head games.

It's no secret that the phone is not man's best friend. Some men say texting is the easiest way to ask a girl out. "Who cares if you get a text rejection; it's virtually painless," said one guy. Another man said texting gives him time to think of a witty comeback. "It's like playing chess: I don't have to respond instantly; I can strategize my reply." Other men, I am sorry to report, use text messaging to conceal their whereabouts, mask their infidelity, and send insincere flirtations that mislead and dupe women.

Texting is not an acceptable substitution for conversation.

It is up to us, as women, to debunk a man's textcrap.

Spineless Texters

It's not okay to text insincere, misleading flirtations that toy with a woman's emotions.

Megan met Nathan at happy hour. They hit it off, exchanged cell numbers and he texted her the next day, *"Great 2 meet u, want 2 c u again."* Megan texted Nathan back, *"Great meeting u, let's get 2gether."*

Nathan continued texting Megan for two weeks. He finally texted a cyber invitation, *"Movies, food, Sunday?"* Megan texted him back, *"Sure, call me."* Nathan never called nor did he text Megan back. *Why?* Because Megan's affirmative answer required this texting-gutless-wonder to date in real time—something he never intended to do.

The no. 1 lie men tell for disappearing off the face of the Earth: He dropped his phone in water causing him to lose his phone numbers.

My daughter Krissy has the funniest, quirkiest humor of any woman I know. We were laughing one night about guys sending their textcrap.

"I think guys try to evoke emotion out us," Krissy said. "I call them my 'Boos.' They boo-text us wanting to get together. Our natural tendency is to say *yes.* They get their ego stroked—and then they blow us off. It makes me believe they do it to a lot of women."

The next night my long-distance boasting Maserati-Pilot boo-texted me.

My Maserati-Boo had been calling and texting me sporadically for two years. On and off. Off and on. One night I got fed up with his boo-texting and I erased him from my phone contact list. Months passed and late one night my iPhone buzzed an unknown incoming text: it read, "Hey, babe, whatcha doing?"

Confused, I texted back, "Who is this?"

A text came back, "Seriously—u don't know?"

A couple of stabs later, I realized it was Maserati–Boo.

"How's the love of my life?" he texted.

I had obliviously injured his Boo-ego. I texted, "If I were love of ur life u'd be on a plane to c me." It was a boo-test.

"I'll book a ticket 2morrow, c u this weekend," Boo texted.

Yeah, right! My Girlfriend Within ran out the door to Dillard's to buy a new BCBG black knit dress and red python pumps so she could hold her breath for 72 hours!

Maserati-Boo did not text or call me back and I reentered his number in my contact list so I could ignore his babbling boo-texting—which, incidentally, he texted one month later.

Is he putting in face time?

My girlfriend Katie met Stephen on eHarmony. They chatted online for a while, exchanged phone numbers and then he texted her on and off for a year—but he never asked her out. He would text her, saying, *"Whatcha doin this weekend?"* but he wouldn't extend an invitation. He would text her on a Friday afternoon, saying, *"Margaritas???"* and then she wouldn't hear from him again for two weeks.

"He acts like he likes me," Katie said. (She meant to say: he texts like he likes me). Katie asked me, *"What do you think?"* (She was really asking: do you think he's going to ask me out?)

I said, "Katie, if you enjoy having a text relationship with this cyber-dude, then text away—but if you're hoping that he is eventually going to ask you out—sorry, hon, *that hound don't hunt.*"

Cheating Texters

Yvonne met Trent, a CEO banker in his late fifties, while having cocktails with her girlfriends at a trendy Boston restaurant. Trent, a charming, stout, balding, suit-and-tie man, sought a sexual relationship with Yvonne. Trent courted Yvonne for several weeks in high style, and as tempting as it was to enjoy his lavish lifestyle of dining, travel and retail perks, Yvonne passed on his "friends with benefits" offer. He quickly dropped his pursuit of her and he immediately became involved with another woman.

OMGYG2BK Did that scumbag just text me, "R U horny?"

Yvonne saw Trent two weeks later at happy hour with his new squeeze. Squeeze was seated at the bar. He was standing next to her like a lovesick rhino, with his hand on her thigh, rubbing his lower body up against her, hanging onto to her every word.

It's not okay to text a booty call unless a woman shares your relationship sentiments.

"It didn't make sense," Yvonne said. "I knew he was involved with this woman, but he was still texting me, 'Hey beautiful, what u doing? miss u.'" That's when I realized he was sending me his lascivious, insincere messages whenever he had a 45-minute drive home.

Drunk Texters

Helen met Sterling at the annual September SOS (Society of Standers) beach club event in Myrtle Beach.

Sterling was a real GQ, a mixture of boyish charm and super-sexy. Helen spotted him at the bar. He was tall and lanky, with tousled blonde hair, wearing a crisp white shirt and distressed designer jeans hanging slightly off his hips. She was drawn to his sophistication, wit and obvious success. After enjoying a fun weekend together they talked long-distance several times and then they began to commute to see one another; he driving to Knoxville and she flying to Raleigh. Helen frowns as she tells her story:

From the beginning Sterling's preferred method of communication was text messaging. He texted me to ask me out for a date. He texted me trip details. When he traveled he texted me constantly during the day with endearing notes, "I miss u" and "Can't wait to c u." But his communication was frustrating. I kept asking myself, why doesn't he pick up the phone and call me? His texting was undependable. Some weekends I wouldn't hear from him at all—his excuse was he took his young sons to his cabin in the mountains and he didn't have a cell signal. But when I visited his cabin my phone service worked fine. Another time he was traveling on business. He told me he would call me when he arrived at his destination—I never heard from him. I quizzed him—he said he texted me and he left a voice message. I checked and I rechecked but there were no text or voice messages. He blamed the phone carrier, claim-

> It's not okay to "text flirt" with a woman if you're involved with someone else.

ing, "That damn phone service is so unreliable, I'm going to change companies."

I felt like Sterling was hiding something or someone three hundred miles away. Then one night he screwed up. He texted me at nine o'clock, saying he was at home and he was going to bed. Something didn't feel right. I called him forty-five minutes later. To my surprise (thinking he was asleep) he answered his phone on the first ring. He was drunk and talking gibberish—and then I heard a distinct sound in the background: "click-click click-click click-click." It was his car's turn signal blinking. Sterling was driving home from a night of drinking.

Debbie texted her boyfriend Sam late one night:

> Debbie: Hi babe, what are you doing?

> Sam: Nothing much, 'em really tired. Just going to sleep now babe. And you?

> Debbie: In the club standing behind you.

Traveling Texters

Some men use meaningless text flirtations as a source of entertainment, like listening to the radio while driving down the street.

Janine knew when her New Jersey guy was traveling because he started texting her throughout the day and night.

I wouldn't hear from Adam for a month and then all of a sudden I would start getting text messages from him. He would text, "hi gorgeous, what r u doin?" I know he's texting because he's bored driving from city to city, staying in hotels. He texted me last night at eleven o'clock saying, "are you still beautiful?" What the crap is that about? He thinks I'm beautiful but he doesn't ask me out!

"He's amusing himself and stringing you along," I told Janine. "If he were truly interested in you, he would pick up the phone, call you at a decent hour and ask to see you."

Listen up, Shoe Sistas! When a man texts flirts, but he rarely or never calls you on the phone, or he never asks you out—it is because:

1. He is involved with someone else, or ...

2. He's not looking for a relationship—or, at least, not with you.

Abusive Texters

Some men use text messaging to stalk, browbeat, intimidate, and even threaten women.

Trudy had a penchant for successful, good-looking men who wanted to control and dominate women. Jim was no exception. He was a tall, dark and handsome, affluent financial executive with an arrogant, narcissistic personality.

It's not okay to use text messaging as an instrument of harassment, intimidation and verbal abuse.

Jim romanced, bedded and dumped Trudy in four short weeks. But that wasn't enough to satiate his abusive relationship appetite. He wanted to continue to bully Trudy with his berating text messages.

It had been three weeks since Jim trashed Trudy, when he walked into a popular happy hour and saw her talking with her girlfriends at the bar. Trudy was unaware of Jim's presence across the room. He texted her, watching her intently as she held her phone up to read his incoming message.

"U dress like a hi school whore. I'm embarrassed 2 know u," his message said.

Trudy was beyond stunned. Her head jerked up and she saw Jim smirking at her from across the room. Fear and mortification struck her and she fled the restaurant humiliated and crying. Mission accomplished. Jim was openly smug.

Disappearing Text Messages

Men know that it is difficult for a woman to disprove an undelivered email, text message or missing voice mail—because it's possible, *but highly unlikely,* that a text or voice message can be sent to the wrong address, accidentally erased, or mysteriously disappear into cyberspace.

Patty lived in Atlanta. He quasi-boyfriend Robert lived 350 miles away. He texted her saying he missed her and he wanted to come see her. They texted back and forth for a week making plans for the weekend. The day of his departure Patty texted him asking him for his arrival time. He never texted back, he wouldn't answer his phone, nor did he arrive in Atlanta. The following week she texted him, "What happened 2 u?!?" He texted back, "Didn't u get my text?? weather was terrible ... had 2 cancel my trip!!"

After standing me up on a Friday night Douglas argued for days that he did not receive my text or voice mail messages. Little did he know that I had graduated summa cum laude from Dr. Dirtbag's School of Smoke and Mirrors.

Dougie boy was determined to control me. A week after I shut him down he was still texting me his hypocritical babble, "Please talk 2 me," "u have plans 2nite baby?" And, "I still miss U and U me. Let's resolve." For him it was a contrived game of cat and mouse, control and conquer.

It was nine o'clock at night. I was lying in bed reading a self-improvement book when Doug's annoying text messages began rolling in.

> We missed u tonite. R u up, pls call me.

He was letting me know he had been out drinking with his buddies.

My Girlfriend Within rolls her emerald green eyes, *Moron!*

I decided to give Doug a taste of his own textcrap. I picked up my iPhone and I texted him:

> On my way to ur house 2 talk.

And then I slid deeper beneath my Martha Stewart over-stuffed comforter and I went back to reading "The Power of Positive Thinking."

Ten minutes passed.

I had never been to Doug's home. It made it easy for me to pretend I was lost. I put my book aside and I texted him again:

> Driving around ur neighborhood, can't find u!

Dougie immediately texted me back:

> WRU?? I'm standing outside so u can c me.

Thirty minutes passed.

I finished my chamomile tea, brushed my teeth, fluffed my feather down pillows, read another think-positive chapter and I texted Doug:

> Driving round n circles, can't find u!

Doug texted me repeatedly, beseechingly:

> Call me, where r u, don't c ur car!

I wasn't about to call that abusive asshole. My final text read:

> Can't find u, going home, nite.

I placed my iPhone on my bedside table, closed my book, turned off my bedside lamp and I rolled over to go to sleep, smiling in naughty satisfaction, envisioning Chicken Douglas Little running around his neighborhood for an hour frantically looking for me. The next morning I blocked Doug from calling me and sending me his nasty messages.

My Girlfriend Within pulled out her iPhone. Erase. Erase. Erase. Delete. Delete. Delete. *Now, don't you feel better?*

Bucket of Bolts

27

Dump a man and you'll see his true colors.

I met Bart, an attractive Austin businessman, the night I was hosting a women's social mixer at a popular Houston restaurant. He was sitting at the bar, near my group of women, having dinner and wine while watching the overhead TV. He looked intriguing, respectable and approachable. I casually perched myself on a bar chair next to him to rest my red high heels. *Well, okay ... to flirt with him.* He was congenial and fun to talk to. He said he was seeking work in Houston as a profitability analyst consultant. He asked for my phone number, and he called the following week and asked me out.

I met Bart for dinner at The Capital Grill. He was courteous and he had the air of a well-bred man. He was an excellent conversationalist, he spoke fluent French and he was knowledgeable about wines and food. He was a skydiver, tennis player and he was well-traveled abroad. We shared an interest in cooking and we talked in length about recipes, culinary techniques and which grocery stores carried the hard-to-find ingredients. After dinner, he walked me to my car, we said goodnight, and we went our separate ways. The next week Bart again invited me to dinner.

I met Bart for our second date at an eclectic Montrose bistro he had selected. He didn't offer to pick me up at my home—*and I soon found out why.*

I arrived early at the restaurant. I was sitting in my car in the parking lot, touching up my lipstick, when I saw Bart drive up in an old beat-up BMW. I was shocked to see such a polished, articulate businessman driving such a rattletrap. He got out of his car, saw me,

190

and looking slightly embarrassed, he walked over to me, greeted me with a hug and handed me a large sack brimming with bags of organic snacks he had purchased at the natural foods store we discussed on our first date.

Inside the restaurant he greeted the hostess and she escorted us to the far side of the building to a quaint wine chamber. Inside the small, narrow room was a single table for two, bedecked with white linen cloth and a crystal vase of long-stemmed red-orange Gerbera daisies. Dozens of lit tea candles glimmered on the rustic wooden shelves that housed hundreds of bottles of wine.

My Girlfriend Within swoons—she is duly impressed!

Bart had given much thought to our dinner date. He presented me with a sackful of goodies. He reserved a unique and intimate dining setting. He pre-selected a fine bottle of Sauvignon Blanc for us to drink. During our dinner conversation he told me he found a new recipe he thought I would enjoy—dates stuffed with cheese, and he invited me to go to the IMAX theatre with him on Saturday. I was caught up in his flattery and before I considered what I was doing, I invited him to my home for cheese-stuffed dates after the IMAX show.

An hour and a half later Bart walked me to my car, gave me a restrained kiss, and seeing his dilapidated Bemmer again, I wondered why such a smooth act was riding around in a bucket of bolts.

He kept asking me if I liked the restaurant. He needed to know he was making made a good impression on me.

I was not yet comfortable with Bart coming to my home. There were nebulous aspects about him I had yet to discern; for instance: The night I met Bart he told me he was "out" of business cards. *That's strange*—a fastidious professional man comes to town to seek a major consulting position—*but he doesn't have any business cards?* His phone had a Houston area code—*that's odd*—he doesn't live here. He was vague about his past marriage and where he lived in Austin. He dodged my questions about his current relationship status—saying, it was complicated. He was evasive about his consulting work in Houston—he said his client was confidential. He was renting a room in a pilot's crash pad. I asked myself: why did an accomplished, sophisticated Austin businessman live in a flophouse, have a Houston cellular area code and drive a junkyard clunker?

I got an uneasy feeling I was being set up.

Something didn't feel right. *Yes*, Bart was charming and gentlemanly—but his courtship seemed contrived. He was guarded with his answers. He chose his words carefully and his conversations felt mechanical and emotionless.

I felt like Bart had finagled an invitation into my home with his cheese-stuffed dates. I called him to withdraw my invitation. He didn't answer his phone and I left him a voice message telling him I couldn't go to the IMAX with him because my out-of-town girlfriend was unexpectedly coming to visit me—in fact (to avoid future dates with Bart) she had left her husband and she would be staying with me *indefinitely*.

Bart called me several days later; I didn't answer the phone and he didn't leave a message. The following week he called me three times; again, he didn't leave a message. The next week he called every other day and then twice a day. In all he called me over a dozen times—not once leaving a message.

Red Flags: Bart was throwing out warning signals like a first string pitcher.

Red Flag No. 1: He tried too hard to impress me.

Red Flag No. 2: His answers were vague and evasive.

Red Flag No. 3: His professional status and polished attire did not match his lifestyle.

Red Flag No. 4: There's something fishy about a man who calls you with bulldog persistence—but he won't leave a message.

I concluded that Bart had a shady past, financial difficulties and either a girlfriend or a wife. I surmised that Bart moved from city to city, not only to find work, but a woman he could bilk. He would look for a suitable target, romance his way into her heart, pose a phony business venture or personal emergency and then he would leave them with an empty bank account, racked up credit cards and a broken heart.

The final tipoff was his stalking phone behavior, leaving me to surmise he was a controlling, conniving, and possibly narcissistic man.

A month passed. I thought I had exaggerated, over-reacted, and even imagined Bart's queer behavior ... and then I ran into my ball-buster girlfriend Lisa. She also spoke with Bart the night we were at the restaurant.

"He's married! And he lives in Chicago, not Austin," Lisa laughed out loud.

My eyes widened. *"How do you know that?"* I asked, shocked and amazed.

"I asked him and he told me." She smirked.

Wow, My Girlfriend Within awed—*the gut is a powerful source of supernatural knowing.*

God Bless Mrs. Robinson

28

He makes you believe something is real when you know perfectly well it isn't.

Molly's new boyfriend, Travis, also had car issues.

*A*fter twenty-two years of marriage, Molly's husband left her for another woman. Molly got a substantial divorce settlement and enrolled in a recovery group where she met Travis, a smooth-talking Longhorn. Travis was a handsome, witty, intelligent, well-dressed 55-year-old oil industry consultant. He was open about his personal life. He shared the hurtful details of his divorce and he talked openly about his wife's infidelity. He consoled Molly about her divorce.

Molly relates her story:

Travis told me that he sold his panhandle ranch for $8 million dollars, and he moved to Dallas to venture out as an independent oil and gas consultant. Travis was incredibly knowledgeable. He was like a walking USA-Today-Wall-Street-Journal-People-Magazine. He could talk to anyone about anything. He was always saying, "Did you hear this?" or "Did you know that?" He didn't spend a lot of money on dating but he made it entertaining. We played cards in someone's home or we went to a matinee movie. One night he said, "You know what would be fun, I'll bring over a cookbook, we'll pick out a recipe, go to the grocery store and cook at home." He cooked dinner for me in his nicely decorated condo. He was always surprising me. One weekday he showed up unexpectedly at my door with a tray of Impatiens flowers.

He said, "I was impatient all day to see you; I bought flowers for us to plant in your yard." Another afternoon he came by unannounced with a bottle of wine and said, "Let's go to the park and lay on a blanket, drink wine and enjoy the afternoon." Travis was sexually gifted; sex with him was erotic and gratifying. But something kept nagging at my gut. I couldn't understand how a man of his profession could constantly goof off during the middle of the day. One day I asked him, "What are you doing here? You told me you had an important appointment this morning with a major client."

"Oh, that," he shrugged, "The guy cancelled at the last minute." And then he stayed at my house the rest of the afternoon without making or receiving a single phone call.

Travis drove an old model car in need of repair. I said, "Don't you need to get your taillight fixed?" "I'll get around to it," he said. When the back window wouldn't go up, he said apathetically, "Don't worry about it—just don't put it down." It didn't make sense. Travis was a factitious, immaculately dressed man who could fix anything—and yet—he wouldn't replace a burnt-out ninety-nine cent taillight.

Nine months passed and Travis' stories became more and more conflicting. I caught him in several small lies. He didn't call when he said he would. He showed up two hours late without plausible explanation. I couldn't deal with his undependable behavior and so I broke up with him. A month later a strange woman called me.

"You need to be careful," the woman said. "Travis is not who he says he is. He seduces rich divorcees and widows for their money." I felt a hard thud in my stomach. She told me she had dated Travis for two years. She gave him money to help him through a financial rough patch. When he asked her to marry him she hired a private investigator and she learned that he had been repeatedly fired from jobs, he had served felony time for misallocating government farm grants and the government seized and auctioned off his ranch to satisfy his debt—and then his wife divorced him.

But there's more ...

The entire time Travis was wooing and dating Molly, he was also conning a 61-year-old widow who lived in his condominium complex. Travis did not have a job and he did not own an automobile. The widow Mrs. Robinson gave him money for living expenses while he also drove her car in need of a new taillight and back window repair.

Every morning Travis would dress in his fancy suits, drive Mrs. Robinson to work in her car, drop her off and then go to the library to read newspapers and magazines for several hours. He goofed off in the afternoons and then at five o'clock he would pick up Mrs. Robinson at work and take her home. At night he would use her car to go out with friends, go on a date, or go to Molly's house.

My Sharon Stone Girlfriend Within turns off *The Quick and the Dead*, puts on her black felt Stetson and straps on her Colt 45 single action revolver, *I'm going to tar that varmint's hide if I have to ride all the way to hell to do it.*

Red Flags:

Molly was a trusting and inexperienced divorcee—and yet, her gut worked overtime to warn her that Travis was a Texas-size scumbag. Looking back she realized the warning signs.

Red Flag No. 1: Gaps in his work history; irresponsible work habits, too much time on his hands.

Molly said:

No wonder Travis was a dazzling conversationalist. He spent all day at the library reading every newspaper and magazine on finance, politics, sports stats and the latest Hollywood gossip. No wonder he was a super-duper-lover having read every handbook in the library on a woman's anatomy, arousal and orgasms. When he got bored reading he showed up at my house to plant flowers, drink wine and cook recipes.

Red Flag No. 2: He doesn't introduce you to his family and close friends.

Travis wouldn't let me meet his family because he said they were "hyper-critical" and "dysfunctional." I should have demanded to meet them.

Red Flag No. 3: Ask others who may know about him.

I found out later that several friends in my recovery group knew about Travis' shady past but they didn't say anything because they said they didn't want to "pry." Had I asked questions I would have gotten an earful.

The reality was, every time Travis took me on a date he was using the widow's money and car. What baffled me was— what was this poor woman thinking when Travis was gone at night and on weekends with her car? I guess some women just don't want to know the truth.

My Sharon Stone Girlfriend Within hands Mrs. Robinson a double shot of whiskey and a loaded six-shooter.

The Dangling Golden Carrot

He placed a candy jar in front of her, spoiled her with the goodies, and when he knew he had her—he slammed the Mr. Goodbar jar shut.

A male friend once told me, "There are two dominant sources of power in the world. One is wealth. The other is sex." Throughout history men typically use wealth to get the things they want in life. While women—*knowingly* or *unknowingly*—use sex as their tool of manipulation and control.

Let's talk about money.

Abusive men will use money to influence and charm women during the courtship phase, and once the relationship is cemented, they will use money to manipulate and control their partner.

Ivan, a 56-year-old divorcee and successful commercial land developer, wasn't much to look at; he was balding, his facial features were ordinary, he wore wire spectacles, and his hump-backed body was that of a much older man. But Ivan was an intriguing Renaissance man. He was knowledgeable about period furniture and fine art. He was an experienced auction bidder. He wore expensive clothing and jewelry. He boasted of a second home in the mountains, he drove a late model convertible Jaguar, and he kept a four-seat single-engine Cessna at the airport hangar. He loved to cook and travel. His hobby was painting but his art was juvenile and disturbing with his images of contorted blood-dripping creatures. He said he was a "shock" artist. He compared himself to the surrealism of the Black Dahlia and the eccentric artists Marcel

Duchamp and Salvador Dali. Ivan wrote his own music, marched to his own band and he got Susan's attention.

Susan was an attractive, twice-divorced, 45-year-old real estate agent. Susan was weary of the single life and she was ready to remarry. She had seen Ivan at several social functions over the past year. One night at a charity event they made a romantic connection. Susan tells her story:

Ivan and I went to the casino on our first date. We were standing amid the slot machines, he reached into his pants pocket, pulled out a thick wad of folded one hundred-dollar bills, peeled off five of them, handed it to me—as if it were an everyday occurrence, and said, "Here, go have fun!"

I was unaccustomed to free money and while Ivan referred to the five hundred as "chunk change," I considered it a car note.

I gambled with Ivan's money at the blackjack table and dollar slot machines. I lost one hundred dollars and I stopped gambling—hating to lose my money or anyone's money. At the end of the evening I handed Ivan the remaining $400.

"Keep it," he said. "I'll just toss it in a jar and the kids will get it."

I thought he was testing me to see if I was a gold-digger and I insisted that he take his money back.

In the following months Ivan continued to wine, dine and pamper me. He took me on his business trips. We stayed at the best hotels, we ate and drank like fat cats, and we shopped at the nearby boutiques. He was quick to pull out his wallet when I found a pair of shoes, a purse or an outfit I wanted, and he was delighted to buy me sexy lingerie. When I tried to pay for my purchases he would push my credit card back at me and say, "Put your money up; you don't pay when you're with me."

Everything that Ivan said and did made me believe he felt it was his "job" to take care of me.

Ivan was constantly showing up at my house with unexpected gifts, nothing expensive—it was the thought that mattered. In the fourth month of dating him he surprised me with a stunning engagement ring. He painted a life of having a beautiful home, lavish

His presentation was the "golden carrot" for a security-driven woman

vacations, money to buy whatever we wanted and security in retirement. Nine months into dating him I sold my home and moved into his house 300 hundred miles away. I was certain I had found the man of my dreams.

Within months of moving in with Ivan our relationship began to change.

When we were dating Ivan portrayed himself as someone who enjoyed nice things and he had the ability to afford them. I thought that meant I would have nice things too. But when I asked for a new outfit to wear to his corporate conference, he snarled at me

He used money as a weapon to control, punish and power over me.

and said, "You've got a closet full of clothes to wear." Ivan wanted to invite the neighbors over for an outdoor dinner. His patio table and chairs was an embarrassing dilapidated, weather-wore rattan set. When I asked him to buy a new patio suite he got irate and bellowed, "What's wrong with you? There are plenty of people who have much less than we do." When I requested a nice watch for Christmas he condemned me like I had asked for the Hope Diamond. And when I went shopping and purchased two throw pillows, a cutting board and candles for the house, all for under one hundred dollars, he punished me for two days with his disapproving, sullen silence.

Ivan contrived a scheme to control my spending. He complained of a downed economy, he said his business was slow and he lied about his income, claiming obscenely low earnings.

He gave me a credit card with limited spending. When the credit card bill came he would open it in front of me, scrutinize it, frown as he wrote a check and then walk away in an irritated huff. It was his way of reminding me that (1) he was taking care of me, and (2) he was in control of my spending.

Red Flags:

An abuser's goal is to **control** his partner—and he will **use money** to do so.

Susan's relationship with Ivan was a setup. She talks about the warning signs:

From the beginning Ivan saw me as the prize to be won. He knew that I had a good job and I was accustomed to buying nice things. It was no secret that I wanted a man with intelligence, ambition and financial security. So he set out to seduce me with his boast of money and display of possessions.

Red Flag No. 1: He will ingratiate you with his generosity.

Ivan's courtship was methodical and calculating. I tried to be an equal partner in our developing relationship. I offered to ante up for dinner and event tickets—but he was adamant about paying for everything. A year later, when I conformed to his boasted lifestyle, he made me feel unreasonable and greedy for asking for the things that he could easily afford. He changed the relationship rules so he could manipulate, dominate and control me.

Red Flag No. 2: Braggarts are often astute liars. They will embellish their stories and inflate their financial worth to impress you. Listen carefully to what a man's friends and family say about him—they will unconsciously reveal the truth.

Ivan earned a substantial income as a commercial land developer, and yet he complained incessantly about the money he spent on his family. He complained about the clothes his former wife bought for their two children. He condemned her for her "exorbitant" shoe collection. He carped about the money she spent decorating their new house. He made his 18-year-old daughter grovel for college tuition and textbooks. He seemed to enjoy making his daughter squirm by withholding his emotional, intellectual and financial assistance. She tried to warn me one evening (while in her beer-loosened-tongue state) of his controlling nature. She said, "Dad never does what he says he will—you'll see." His brother said to me, while also imbibing, "Ivan has never needed anyone in his life. Good luck with that one,"—referring to our relationship. His sister-in-law said, "It's all about money for Ivan." I dismissed it as family rivalry, telling myself, "Ivan would never treat me that way—because he loves me."

Dishonorable Mention

Brett and Laurel dated for a month and he took her on a 5-day cruise for her birthday. They had not yet slept together; when Laurel refused to put out sex, Brett presented her with a bill on the last day of the cruise for half of the vacation expenses.

Red Flag No. 3: Money is the "great equalizer" for the older and less attractive man.

Ivan once told me he knew he wasn't good-looking and he realized early on to get attractive woman he would have to be successful. He spent his whole life acquiring success and money—it boosted his sagging ego and it became his god. Not a red flag—but a confirmation that Ivan the Terrible knew what he was doing.

Susan eventually broke up with Ivan and she accepted the truth about him—that he was an abusive pathological liar whose worth was a fraction of his boast. His automobiles and plane were in bad need of repair. He bought his jewelry and expensive clothes on eBay. His bank accounts were whacked in half by his ex-wife. And Susan's diamond engagement ring and the Bulgari Assioma watch he gave her for Christmas—*counterfeit*—*just like Ivan!*

My Paris Hilton Girlfriend Within asks, *What's a soup kitchen?*

Dining with Chef Evil

It's ingenious the methods men use to manipulate and punish women.

*D*ining out with Dr. Dirtbag was an adventure. He was familiar with unusual offerings on a restaurant menu. He didn't mind spending money to enjoy a good meal. He would order a variety of appetizers and entrees so we could experience different foods. He introduced me to foie gras, an exquisite, delicate duck liver—and gnocchi, tender little potato dumplings—and tapas, a Spanish dining custom of small plates of various finger foods. He studied the wine list and he ordered one or more bottles. But the longer I dated Dr. Dirtbag I realized that dining in a restaurant was his favorite time to imbibe, boast and embellish his knowledge of foods and wine. *"What vin number is this Bordeaux?"* he arrogantly asked our waiter while dining at a high-end restaurant. It was a complete misuse of a wine term. The waiter stared at him like he had a snout and hooves, realizing that Dr. Dirtbag was a supercilious fool. I was embarrassed by his brainless braggadocio.

Dinnertime, in general, was Dr. Dirtbag's chance to hurt my feelings and ruin my meal.

Dr. Dirtbag was a culinary virtuoso. His kitchen sported the finest cooking utensils, cutlery, gadgets and electrical equipment. In the dining room he arranged a beautiful formal dinner setting with gold-leaf chargers, multiple goblets, linen napkins and proper silverware placement. At the grocery story he would opt for oxtails, Alaskan King Crab Legs, haricot verts and fresh tomatillos to make his homemade salsa verde. He snipped fresh basil, cilantro, rosemary, thyme and Serrano peppers from his patio garden to create the perfect culinary flavor. He selected the perfect wine to accompany his finely prepared curried lamb chops or Steak Diane. When we were dating he prepared Lobster Thermidore for me from memory—*I think that's when I fell in love with him.*

Dr. Dirtbag insisted on cooking every meal. It was how he controlled our environment at home. He would come home from work, and around six o'clock he would pour himself a glass of wine and then Chef Evil (his alternate schizoid-manic personality) would start cooking our dinner. Chef Evil would chop onions and drink. He would braise pork chops and drink. He would sauté a cream sauce and drink. He would let the food simmer and drink. When the food was finally done he would turn off the stove, tell me the food needed to cool down and, *you guessed it*, he would continue to drink. Most nights we didn't eat until nine or ten o'clock. By that time I was hungry, cranky and sometimes drunk. I finally told him if he didn't serve dinner by seven I would send out for a pizza. He begrudgingly served dinner at a slightly earlier hour.

The more Chef Evil drank the more pungent his cooking became. He would add a little of this and more of that. He threw in overcooked leftovers and superfluous spices and condiments. There were times I couldn't eat my over-seasoned, ill-flavored dinner—and that, of course, created his displeasure and criticism. One night he defiled a potentially delicious beef stroganoff by adding excess merlot and refrigerated week-old Tupperware does-it-pass-the-smell-test vegetables. The stroganoff looked gross and it tasted worse.

Chef Evil saw me fidgeting with my food. He frowned at me and jeered, *"I cooked on this all night for you. Aren't you going to eat it?"*

"I can't," I complained, "It tastes peculiar."

He took his untouched plate to the kitchen sink, scraped his food into the disposal and stormed outside to smoke a cigarette. It was a grand performance of his unfair punishment.

Cooking in the kitchen with Chef Evil took on another sinister presence.

I loved to cook just as much as Chef Evil did, but he wanted the kitchen all to himself. One evening I insisted that he let me help him prepare dinner. Chef Evil furrowed his brow, eyeballed me, mumbled the f-bomb and barked, *"Here, chop the garlic."*

Great, I thought. I didn't care—I just wanted to sip my wine, enjoy the music from the stereo and play in the kitchen. And then I made the mistake of sticking a

Badger. Berate. Belittle. That was Chef Evil's relationship recipe.

spatula into a saucepan to sample his simmering asparagus soup.

"What are you doing?!?!" he screamed at me. *"STOP THAT! Do you know how insulting it is to taste a chef's food before it is formally served to you?"*

OMG! Chef Evil flambeed a blood vessel.

I left the kitchen without saying a word to Chef Evil. He had ruined my evening and my desire to cook with him in the kitchen ever again.

Red Flags:

I should have paid attention to the first time David ridiculed me about my weight. We were eating dinner in front of the TV and out-of-the-clear-blue-yonder, he said, *"Ya know, the reason fat people are fat is they don't know when to stop eating. Your plate is so clean when you get through eating I don't even have to wash it."* He could see the hurt in my eyes. Instead of apologizing he feigned innocence, saying, *"Oh, did I say something wrong?"* He knew I wanted to lose five pounds. His sole purpose was to shock and wound me with his spiteful put-down.

Gut check.

The first time is forgivable. The second time is a loud warning. The third offense is cause to report bad food, bad behavior and change restaurants and boyfriend.

Red Flag No. 1: He never takes responsibility for his hurtful comments.

I called Dr. Dirtbag out repeatedly for his upsetting dinnertime behavior. He never apologized, he instead blamed me, saying, "You're overreacting." And, "I can't say anything to you. I'll just keep my mouth shut." Or he swore he didn't mean it, claiming his hurtful comment was a Freudian slip. He blamed outside influences, "It was the coffee. You know I can't handle caffeine." He faulted a bad day at work, his ex-wife screamed at him on the phone, traffic sucked or the dog pooped on the carpet—blah, blah, blah, blah. Nothing was ever Dr. Dirtbag's fault.

Red Flag No. 2: Understanding the dynamics of his mealtime assaults.

It was my first Thanksgiving dinner with David's family. His mom, dad, sister and grown children were present for the traditional turkey and dressing. We were all seated around the formal dining table, sipping champagne, enjoying light-hearted conversation and eating our lovely dinner. His mother was complaining, cynical and rude. She cast her negative presence onto everyone sitting at the table. She hurled a senseless, uncalled-for insulting remark at me. I was stunned and I was hurt. No one said a word about her offensive behavior because they were accustomed to her nasty, spiteful personality.

Dr. Dirtbag learned his mealtime behavior from his mother. He pretended that dinner was a time to enjoy delicious food and socialize. He began his evening with a glass of wine to unwind with conversation. He spent hours preparing us dinner—or he would take us to a nice restaurant. Everything seemed okay ... there were no indications that our relationship wasn't completely harmonious.

But the minute I had food in front of me, he set out to sabotage my evening. He used dinnertime to express a lifetime of unhappiness.

My Paula Dean Girlfriend Within hates uppity food and uppity men. She narrows her steel-blue eyes and points her wooden spoon at Chef Evil, *Mister, ya'll need a tall glass of shut the hell up!*

Jealousy the Monster

> What the ego calls love is possessiveness and addictive clinging that can turn into hate within a second.
>
> —Eckhart Tolle

I once mistook a man's jealous, possessive behavior as a declaration of his passion and love for me. I found out the hard way it was, instead, the earliest signs of a controlling, abusive man.

No man had ever shown me such adoration with his phone calls, gifts, attention and affection. David called me constantly throughout the day, every evening and right before I fell asleep. In public he would grasp my hand and put his arm around me. At a party he catered to me, bringing me my drinks and appetizers. But his public display of affection was often uncouth and embarrassing. When we were at a party or restaurant, sitting at a table he would grab my chair and drag me closer to him. One night at a 5-star restaurant he drug my chair so close to him I was practically sitting in his lap. A group of men gawked at me as if I were a hooker. Another evening we were walking out of a restaurant, he put his arm around my shoulder, forcibly pulled me into him and gave me an aggressive tongue-probing X-rated kiss. A man walking behind us sneered, "Get a room, will ya?" I asked him to curb his public display of affection. He said, "Why? You don't want people to know we're together?"

His PDA demonstrated to everyone that I was Dr. Dirtbag's property.

Janis' boyfriend was crazy, delusional jealous. Janis said:

> *Perry was insanely jealous. It didn't matter where we were; the grocery store, the gym, a restaurant, the gas station, and even at church, he imagined I was flirting or conspiring or cheating with a another man. He was psychoneurotic. He rummaged through my wastebaskets and outside trash looking for evidence of where I had been and what I had been doing. He pieced together torn restaurant receipts and demanded to know who I ate with at each restaurant. When I got home from work or going out with my girlfriends he would grab my arm, pull me into him and sniff my hair and my clothes to see if he could smell a man's scent on me. He kept track of my menstrual cycles and birth control pills. When I shaved my legs and underarms he accused me of primping to have sex with another man. He checked the mileage on my car. If I drove further than my work or the grocery store he drilled me about my whereabouts. He called the names and numbers in my phone's call history. If a man answered he asked them why they were talking to me, how they knew me, and he accused them of trying to "get in my pants." He destroyed or hid anything he thought another man gave to me. One night we got into a fight; on his way out my back door he poured my back pain medicine down the sink disposal and he said, "I want you to feel bad so you won't feel like going out to meet some man." When we broke up he stole my favorite perfume, jewelry, clothes and shoes so I couldn't wear them around another man.*

He sat on the hood of my car in the garage to keep me from going out with my girlfriends.

Black and Blue Boyfriend

Why do men hit women? Said one abuser:

> *"I get enraged when I see her talk to another man."*

My Tina Turner Girlfriend Within shakes her tail feather and she gets a restraining order against her face-bashing, stomach-punching boyfriend.

Carrie was lonely and struggling financially when she met Shawn. Shawn was a nice-looking, divorced 53-year-old man. His life had taken a nose dive after he was convicted for a DUI, and consequently, was fired from a six-figure job. He got a job selling cellular phones where he met Carrie, a bubbly 49-year-old redhead with a petite hour-glass figure. Shawn was immediately smitten with Carrie. Against her better instincts she began dating Shawn and became sexually involved with him. Carrie was financially struggling. Shawn lent her money to pay her rent. A month later he became belligerent and accusing.

A male clothing clerk gave Marge a compliment in front of her husband. Driving home he slugged her, giving her a nasty black eye.

Soon their relationship became a volatile cycle of arguments and breakups. Shawn repeatedly drew Carrie back into the relationship with the lure of intense sex. Then one night Shawn did the unthinkable—he cold-cocked Carrie.

It was a Friday night. Carrie went out with her girlfriends to listen to a band at the Windjammer bar and grill. Shawn was watching a football game with his buddies. They planned to rendezvous at his place at 10 o'clock. Carrie was leaving the club to go meet Shawn when a guy friend asked her to dance. She agreed to one dance. One dance turned into three and now she was thirty minutes late meeting Shawn. She said goodbye to her dance partner and she turned to leave—when suddenly, Shawn appeared out of nowhere and in a micro-second he slugged Carrie in the jaw dropping her to the floor out cold—and he fled out the door before anyone realized what had happened.

Carrie lay lifeless on the Windjammer dance floor. Gathering patrons gawked down at her in disbelief. A long minute passed and Carrie's eyes slowly opened. Knocked half-senseless and dazed, she looked up at her dance-partner knelling beside her, his eyes wide-eyed and his face strained, and she wondered—*why she was laying on the dirty Windjammer floor?* And then she remembered seeing a split-second sideways glimpse of Shawn's clenched, angry face ... followed by twinkling white stars—and then her world went dark. The reality of what had happened to her was too shocking. Shawn had walked into the nightclub, saw her dancing with a man, and he viciously decked her in the middle of a crowded restaurant.

The police were summoned and Carrie filed assault charges against Shawn. An hour later Carrie arrived at the townhouse she shared with her roommate, Betty. Carrie walked through the front door and she saw Betty; Betty's face was blanched with fright. Carrie was also horrified at what had happened only minutes before she arrived home.

After Shawn's attack on Carrie, he made a beeline to Carrie's townhouse. Betty, unaware of the assault, allowed Shawn into their home. Shawn stormed through their house, ransacked Carrie's bedroom, ripped her bras, panties and lingerie to shreds, stole the jewelry and trinkets he had given her and then he demolished the massive potted flowers on her patio. The police were again summoned. They apprehended Shawn in the early morning hours cruising suspiciously by Carrie's townhouse. He was drunk—and no doubt still looking for revenge. He spent the night in jail and got his second DUI.

I laugh out loud thinking of the obvious warning signs of Dr. Dirtbag's outrageous, unabashed possessive behavior. The second week of dating him he blitzed me with a series of babbling late night phone calls. His calls felt strange. I passed it off, telling myself he missed me—in truth he was trying to control me from afar. Months passed, I was having dinner with my girlfriend and he kept calling me. I answered his first two calls, reminding him that I was having dinner with my girlfriend and I told him I would call him on my way home. He continued to call and text me. Exhausted and embarrassed by his intrusions I turned my phone off. Later that night I counted twelve missed calls and texts from him within 3 hours.

Red Flags:

Some women are flattered by jealousy from their boyfriend or husband because it makes them feel cherished. *Think again!* Down the road you will feel controlled, suffocated and violated.

Top Signs of a Jealous Man

He pushes you for an exclusive commitment. He seduces you with flattery, gifts, constant attention and dining at expensive restaurants. He may offer to pay a debt of yours. He says it is because he loves you. He may position himself as a "father figure." His goal is to feel superior to you, ingratiate you and make you dependent on him for his support and approval.

He overreacts when a man looks at you or talks to you. He may get angry at you and lash out at you. He may have a sudden mood shift and act weird. He may become distant and give you the silent treatment for the rest of the day. He may create a fight for no reason and he uses the incident as ammo against you.

He is paranoid and overly suspicious. He accuses you of flirting with other men when you're not. It's not unusual for a controlling, jealous boyfriend or husband to get angry over something as simple as a clerk or waiter smiling at you—he thinks the man is hitting on you. He may accuse you of flirting or even having affair.

He wants to control every aspect of your life. He wants to know where you are, where you've been and who you were with. He calls you incessantly when you are out with your friends. He insists on

knowing when you will be home. If you are late he may be accusing
and angry, or he is sullen and he punishes you by withdrawing his
love.

He calls you constantly during the day. He calls you ten times a
day just to "see how you are doing." He shows up at your work or at
your home unexpectedly. He's keeping tabs on you. He may call or
text you late at night, when he knows that you have gone to sleep.

He monitors your contact with others. He stands next to you
to eavesdrop on your phone conversations and he interrupts you
to pull you away from the phone. When you hang up he drills
you about your conversation. When you get a phone call from a
friend or co-worker his mood changes; he becomes distant, sullen
or upset. He may secretly check your caller ID, voice mail and text
history. He may want the passwords to your email account, saying:
it wouldn't bother you if you had nothing to hide.

He claims you are the focus of his life. He seems to put you above
everybody; in truth, he wants your life to revolve around him. If
you want to go somewhere without him he says you are neglecting
him and harming the relationship.

He may try to isolate you from the outside world. He gets upset
when you want to go out with your girlfriends—he gives you the
guilt trip accusing you of choosing your friends over him. He is
threatened by your single friends because an unattached man might
try to seduce you. He may want you to quit work or have a baby.

He criticizes your friends and family. He undermines your
friendships. He'll try to convince you, you don't need "people like
that" in your life. He resents the time you spend with your relatives.
He finds excuses to keep you from visiting them. He says your
parents are trying to turn you against him. He wants to put a wedge
between you and your loved ones because he's afraid they will point
out his controlling behavior.

He wants to know exactly how you know a guy. If you casually mention or speak to a man he becomes agitated and upset. He will drill you; how and where did you know him, did you ever date him, did you sleep with him, is he married or in a committed relationship, does he call you? Whatever you tell him he probably won't believe you.

He tells you what to wear; how to fix your makeup and hair. Some men want their girlfriends or wives to wear revealing clothing because they want other guys to envy them. When a man does check you out, he gets mad and he batters you. Other controlling men insist that you dress conservatively. They will point out that your skirt is too short, your pants are too tight and your blouse is too low-cut. They may demand that they help you shop for your clothes. They may even insist that you get rid of clothes they consider too revealing.

He wants to be the center of attention. He is jealous of your success or attractiveness. He will downplay and discredit your experiences, ideas, career, hobbies and friendships. He may criticize and create arguments about your achievements. When he is not the center of attention he loses interest in the conversation, clams up and leaves the room.

He tears you down; then he picks you up. He says something hurtful to make you feel bad about yourself—and then he re-establishes his control over you by showering you with compliments, kindness and affection. He tries to make himself look like a hero and you gradually become dependent on his approval.

Remember:

- Dating a man to fill the void in your heart will bite you in the ass.

- Sleeping with an abusive man bonds you to him at an intimate level.

- Accepting a man's financial support can trigger your co-dependence issues and ingratiate you.
- All of which can cause you to tolerate a man's hurtful behavior.

Better to get two jobs and a roommate than have one drunken abusive man beating the happiness, joy and life out of you.

The Water Torturer

32

The most insidious of abusers is the "Water Torturer."

rip. Drip. Drip ...
He fails to keep his promises to you, claiming an oversight, or he says he "forgot."

Drip. Drip. Drip ... He harshly criticizes you and then he tells you he was only trying to help.

Drip. Drip. Drip ... He insults and ridicules you and he says he was joking and you're too sensitive.

Drip. Drip. Drip ... He instigates a menacing argument and then he denies his hurtful actions.

Drip. Drip. Drip ... He contradicts your opinions. He trivializes your feelings. He blocks your communication. He counters your every thought. He undermines your efforts. And when you tell him to *"stop it"* he turns on you and says you're "overreacting."

Author Lundy Bancroft presents the "Water Torturer" in his book *Why Does He Do That?* He states that the Water Torturer is the most insidious of abusers, he is difficult to identify and the psychological effects of living with the Water Torturer can be severe and sink in deeply. Describing the Water Torturer's abuse tactics he says:

> *He assaults his victim without even raising his voice. He uses conversational tactics at low-volume, including sarcasm and derision; he openly laughs at his partner, mimicking her voice and he uses cruel and cutting remarks. He will often have a*

superior or contemptuous grin on his face, is smug and self-assured. He tends to stay calm in arguments, using his own evenness as a weapon to push his partner over the edge. If she yells in frustration, leaves the room crying, or sinks into silence he tells his victim, "See, you're the abusive one, not me. You're the one who's yelling and refusing to talk things out rationally. I wasn't even raising my voice. It's impossible to reason with you." The victim may then feel stupid and inferior, doubt her reality and even blame herself for his hurtful behavior.

Drip. Drip. Drip ... The Water Torturer makes you feel incompetent and inferior. No matter what you do or say, you can never do or say anything right.

Phoebe: Robert methodically set me up for his verbal assaults. He asked me where I wanted to go eat. I suggested the restaurant he took me to on our first date. He grumbled and said "okay." When we got to the restaurant he wouldn't order dinner. He complained, saying he didn't like their food. He finally ordered a small green salad and then he sulked like it was my fault he was eating rabbit food. I asked him what was wrong. He scowled and said, "Nothing." I felt like I had done something wrong and I was miserable the entire meal. When we got in our car he immediately started battering me. "That was terrible! Why did you choose such a crappy restaurant? The food was awful and it was so loud I couldn't hear myself think." It didn't make sense. We had enjoyed dining at this restaurant on many occasions. I asked him, "Why didn't you tell me you didn't want to go there." He shot me a "go-to-hell" look and said, "Because ... you ... wanted ... to go there." It wouldn't have mattered what restaurant I suggested because his intent was to abuse me.

> *He blasts her with his angry accusations— and he describes himself as easy-going.*

Cassie: I could never do anything right around Henry. I was damned if I did and I was damned if I didn't. It was October, we had just moved into a new house with a swimming pool. Henry worked out of town all week. Hard rains had dumped bushels of leaves into the pool. It was Friday afternoon; Henry was due home. I was standing outside looking at the pool, wondering what to do about the submerged leaves, when Henry suddenly walked into the backyard. He immediately started yelling at me, "What's wrong with you! Why haven't you skimmed the leaves out of the pool?" He grabbed the skimmer net and thrust it angrily into the water and he snapped at me, "I can't do everything."

I was thrown off balance by his unexpected harsh criticism. I struggled to explain myself. I had never owned a pool. It never occurred to me to skim the floating leaves before they sunk to the bottom of the pool. I tried to explain that he had hurt my feelings, but my words fell on cold, deaf ears. The dirty pool was another excuse for him to berate and demean me.

The goal of the Water Torturer's abuse is to tear his victim down to make her feel weak, insecure and co-dependent.

He Convinces Everyone that You're the One Who is Crazy

Drip. Drip. Drip ...

> The central attitudes driving the Water Torturer are:
> You are crazy. You fly off the handle over nothing. I can
> easily convince other people that you're the one who is
> messed up. As long as I'm calm, you can't call anything I
> do abusive, no matter how cruel. I know exactly how to
> get under your skin.
>
> —Lundy Bancroft, *Why Does He Do That?*

Ashlee's fiance Jeff convinced everyone she was an argumentive, hormonal alcoholic.

My mother and teenage daughters adored my fiancé Jeff. He was constantly pampering my girls, giving them money to go shopping, and treating them and their friends to pizza and basketball tickets. He called my mom his "favorite girlfriend." She was smitten by his compliments and attention. My mom thought he could do no wrong. But in privacy my life was a hurtful put-down. If I expressed a thought or an opinion he would argue against me. He criticized me about the way I spent my money, how I managed my time, how I disciplined my daughters and how I kept house. If I objected he would say I was unappreciative and unreasonable. If I cried he would mock me, saying, "Are you crying?" If I tried to discuss a problem with him he would say, "You are your own worst enemy. All your problems are in your head." I began to wonder if something was wrong with me. I became withdrawn and I isolated myself from my friends and family. Instead of supporting me, Jeff began driving nails in my coffin. He told my mother I was unreasonable, I had uncontrollable fits of anger and I was drinking too much. My mother cornered me and said, "You're going to run Jeff off with your drinking and your temper." Even my oldest daughter accused me, saying, "What's wrong with you, Mom? He's doing everything he can to please you." It was the worst kind of betrayal. He initiated the conflict. He enjoyed the fight. He blamed me for my depression and unhappiness. And he turned my mom and daughters against me.

Batter Up!

Drip. Drip. Drip ...

The Water Torturer harasses and persecutes you until you finally erupt into a fit of anger and tears. If you verbally retaliate he will point his blistering finger at you and scream, *"Have you lost your mind? What's wrong with you?"*

*Depriving me of my sleep was yet another way Dr. Dirtbag
tortured me. After an abusive argument I would take refuge in
to the guest bedroom to sleep. He would barge into the bedroom,
flip on the lights, wake me up and stand over me while I lay in
bed and berate me for thirty minutes. I lay there cringing at his
aggressive anger, hoping if I kept my mouth shut he would give
up and go away.*

 *I learned to lock the bedroom door—but that didn't stop Dr.
Dirtbag. He jimmied the door lock open with a credit card—
and in he came. It was after a particularly nasty argument
that I was prepared for his forced intrusion with a baseball bat.
He stood outside my locked bedroom door cajoling me to open
the door. When I refused he jimmied the lock and he swung
the door open. My pent-up rage detonated and I slammed my
baseball bat into the back of the door shattering the attached
full-length mirror. Dr. Dirtbag turned ghoulish white, his
eyes swelled to the size of Frisbees, he jumped backwards and
he slammed the door shut and stormed off to the other side of
the house. The next morning I found a piece of paper taped to
the outside on my bedroom door listing my angry words and
actions, condemning me for our altercation.*

I Found His Wife's Goodbye Letter

Drip. Drip. Drip …

> **If you are involved with a Water Torturer, you
> may struggle for years trying to figure out what is
> happening.**
>   —Lundy Bancroft, *Why Does He Do That?*

 The Water Torturer is unrelenting with his ridicule, criticisms
and blaming. You recoil to get away from his cruelty. You lick your
wounds and try to regain your equilibrium after his latest verbal
attack. You may wonder what you did wrong and you try to salvage
your positive outlook on life. And just when you think you are

starting to recover from his latest battering—he knocks you down again with yet another unexpected verbal assault. Until one day you decide it's easier to stay in bed.

I finally understood why Dr. Dirtbag's wife stayed in bed for three years. He told me she was severely depressed and medicated because of a hormonal imbalance and emotional issues. After enduring eight months of his abusive onslaughts I realized he had mentally beaten her into submission—her mind had shut down, she lay in bed numb, enveloped in despair and hopelessness. I know, because he did the same thing to me. He battered me with his cruel, unrelenting accusations and snide remarks, driving me to the edge of insanity. When I became unhinged and lost my temper, he became indignant and accusing and screamed at me, "What's wrong with you? Haven't I given you everything? Haven't I supported you? Am I not patient and forgiving?" And then I doubted the validity of my anger, pushing me closer to a mental meltdown. I couldn't concentrate. I had migraine headaches. I was listless. I lost weight. I went to bed for days to anesthetize my depression and hopelessness. Occasionally he would walk by my bed where I laid in Zombieland and inquire, "Can I get you anything?" If I had not eaten for 24 hours he would say, "What would you like for dinner?" Preparing my dinner made him believe he was a standup, caring partner—when in truth, he was waiting for me to suck up my hurt feelings, crawl out of bed and resume my life. That was his green light to resume his cycle of abuse.

Dr. Dirtbag's abuse had taken its ugly toll on me. His eyes projected resentment and rage and I wondered if he was capable of physically harming me. My internal voice screamed, get out before he destroys you—but my heart wouldn't let me leave. And then the unexpected happened—I found his wife's goodbye letter. She wrote that his drinking and abuse had destroyed their family and she and the children could no longer

stand to live with him. "I will love you till the day I die," she
wrote. I realized then, if I stayed with him, he would destroy
me too. The next day I was in my car driving ten hours to stay
indefinitely with my girlfriend.

Grief-stricken tears pour from My Girlfriend Within's eyes—
driving down the highway she can barely see the road. She wipes the
waterworks from her eyes, reaches into her Céline Nano handbag,
pulls out her pink iPhone and she changes David's name to *Dr.
Dirtbag* so she can screen his calls. I give her hug and I tell her, *Your
heart will thank you later.*

Vanishing Kielbasa

Eighty percent of married men cheat in America.
The rest cheat in Europe.

—Jackie Mason

Victor, a 51-year-old Chicago marketing consultant, was a schmoozing, boasting, Polish hot dog. He was on assignment in San Antonio revamping a large furniture wholesaler. His sole purpose was to impress everyone around him. His intention was to score sexually with Louise on their first date.

Every Wednesday night a large group of singles gather on the patio of a San Antonio bar and grill to hear local musicians jam old tunes. Louise, an attractive, divorced 52-year-old, was standing with her friends, listening to the music when Victor positioned himself next to her. He was handsome, tall and well-built, his dark hair combed back with a twinge of gray at his temples. He struck up a conversation with Louise. He got her phone number and he called her later that night to ask her out to dinner the following night—a heady compliment to a woman.

Louise tells her story:

When Victor picked me up for our first date he was dressed to the nines, wearing a silk herringbone jacket, white shirt, flowing black slacks sporting an expensive silver belt buckle. His agenda for the evening was to bedazzle me. The minute we walked into the restaurant he took the lead. He escorted me on his arm into the bar for before-dinner drinks. He joked with the bartender and he struck up conversations with the customers sitting nearby. As we were being seated for dinner he strutted around the patrons' tables to see what everyone

*was eating, smiling and greeting others as he strolled by. He
ordered two bottles of my favorite wine. He laughingly told
everyone within earshot that we were celebrating our twenti-
eth anniversary. He eyeballed me at dinner like I was dessert.*

*During dinner Victor told me he had been divorced for
eight years. He said his wife cheated on him, saying he came
home early from a business trip one day and he caught her
in bed with another man. "I know what did wrong in my
marriage," he said somewhat apologetically. "I traveled too
much." I respected him for taking responsibility for his part in
his failed marriage.*

*Victor boasted of past and current business ventures. He
told me he was a senior partner of a marketing firm and he
lived in a hi-rise apartment suite in the heart of downtown
Chicago and he owned a 68-ft Ferretti yacht that was docked
in a Tampa Bay marina. He said he was an avid golfer, a
big gambler and he frequently flew to Las Vegas to gamble
with his buddies. He said he was on a six-month consulting
assignment in San Antonio and he lived nearby in a leased
apartment.*

*Victor let me know that his job afforded him a nice income
and travel opportunities. He asked me, "Wouldn't you like to
have a great guy like me in your life to dine with and travel?"*

"Of course," I replied—thinking he was already "into me."

*The night was going great. After dinner we went to my
place, sat on my sofa, drank more wine and we talked. We
had intellectual and physical chemistry. Victor began kissing
me and said, "Lou, you're the whole package. You're beautiful. You're smart. You're classy. When you walk into a room
every guy is looking at you on my arm." It was one of the most
flattering compliments a man had ever given me. And then
his hands began to wander.*

*I pushed Victor's hands away. He smirked and for thirty
minutes he tried to convince me to take him upstairs to my
bedroom—and for thirty minutes I said, "No!" And then suddenly, he grabbed his silk herringbone jacket and he stormed*

out my front door without a goodnight peck or kiss my ass. I was stunned and I was hurt by his rude departure—but I was also smitten by Victor's extraversion, pursuit and flattery. Victor didn't call back and I carried a torch for him in the following weeks.

Six weeks later I ran into Victor at Swig Martini Bar. He saw me across the bar and he immediately sent me a glass of Pinot Noir. He came over to me and began a friendly conversation. The chemistry between us was undeniable. He again asked me out, I accepted, he wined and dined me, he accompanied me to my home afterwards, and he again wanted to jump my bones. I stood my ground. He got miffed and he again abruptly took flight.

This pattern repeated itself several more times over the next five months—and then one Friday night we broke the seduction cycle and I slept with him.

The next morning Victor woke up in my bed and he stayed with me the rest of the weekend. He began his Saturday with a Bloody Mary. We went to the grocery and liquor stores and he stocked my kitchen with wine, booze and food for us to enjoy the upcoming week. "The Bears game is Monday night," he said. "I'll make my famous chili and cornbread." The following two weeks Victor brought me bottles of wine, double bunches of flowers and his special-cut steaks from Chicago. He made himself comfortable in my home. He voluntarily made small repairs; he fixed the patio sliding door, he took out the trash and he cleaned my pool and hot tub. Our conversations were stimulating, sex was exciting, and he continued to court me in style. In my mind we were a happy couple playing house. I had fallen for Victor and I was certain he was falling in love with me.

And then Victor unexplainably vanished for two weeks.

I was angry and I was hurt by Victor's insensitive, puzzling behavior. I visited my married friends, Janet and John, whining to them about my Vanishing Kielbasa.

"Are you sure he's not married?" Janet quizzed. John's eyes narrowed, he took a sip of his vodka Cape Cod, looked at me, grimaced and nodded in agreement.

"No! How could he?" I protested. "He's here all week and almost every weekend."

"I think it's worth checking out." Janet insisted. John stared at me, his face somber, and again, he nodded.

The next day I did an internet search.

My Diane Sawyer Girlfriend Within sits at her computer and googles: Vanishing Victor Kielbasa, *Holy Zuckerberg! You can find a ton of online crap without paying for a background check.*

Victor said he had owned a successful wholesale automotive parts warehouse that he sold for millions. I googled it—and he did. He said he once co-owned a restaurant and lounge on the Chicago River in downtown Chicago. I googled it—that was also true. I found his name repeatedly linked to a 50-year-old woman through an online people search—his wife, I wondered? I googled the woman's name. It took two minutes and a dozen clicks for her to pop up as a Chicago real estate agent complete with head shot, business address, office and mobile phone numbers. Not a good day for V.

I called the Chicago real estate woman, posing myself as another woman I knew Victor had dated.

"No, he's not divorced," Mrs. Kielbasa said dejectedly. "We've been married for 25 years. He's a consultant. He travels a lot. He tries to get home when he can."

His wife sounded bewildered, as if she were trying to rationalize Victor's cheating behavior. No doubt this was not the first time one of Kielbasa's girlfriends has contacted her.

My Lorena Bobbitt Girlfriend Within walks through door holding a Wolfgang Puck serrated butcher knife.

Victor called me later than day, asking me to meet him for a drink. (I was certain his wife had called him.) I let him squirm for an hour while I drank and ate his free drinks and appetizers—and then I blasted him for his cheating, despicable behavior.

That was the last time I saw the Vanishing Kielbasa. Four months later I learned he was hanging out in a different part of San Antonio still parading as a single man.

Don't Go There Girl!

The top excuses cheating men give women for not getting a divorce: His wife is sick and he can't leave her. He fears financial ruin. He's waiting for his children to grow up and get out of school.

Red Flags:

It's the same naïve song with a different verse: Louise craved having a man in her life, so much that, she closed her eyes to Victor's dysfunctional, hurtful behavior and succumbed to her emotional and sexual longings.

Never assume. Ask, "Are ya married, Tiger Woods?"

Most married men who cheat don't intend to leave their wives. They may talk as if they want to—but why would they? Many wives are oblivious to their husband's infidelity. Or they turn a blind eye to their husband's cheating because they don't want a divorce. Either way, his wife keeps the night light burning at home, and he knows if he loses you, he has his wife to go home to.

Red Flag No. 1: Louise blatantly ignored Victor's most obvious problem—alcoholism.

I knew Victor had a drinking problem. He sucked down his drinks in a restaurant, he always brought two magnums of wine to my house, and he kept a backup in the trunk of his car. He began drinking Bloody Marys on a Saturday morning and on Sunday he got drunk while cleaning my pool. I shrugged it off, thinking he was entitled to some weekend fun.

Red Flag No. 2: Louise was overly smitten by Victor's flattery, exciting lifestyle, social savvy and intense pursuit.

I didn't investigate Victor's relationship status because he didn't act like or talk like a married man. He rarely went home to Chicago. He repeatedly told me the details of his divorce and how his wife cheated on him ... I mean, what kind of person does that?

Thinking back Louise realized that Victor did frequently disappear. He was gone for Thanksgiving, Christmas, Easter, his grown daughter's birthday, golf and gambling trips, and he supposedly worked several weekends out of town helping his partner with assignments. He didn't call or text Louise those weekends. In retrospect, she believes he was, in fact, with his wife in Chicago.

Red Flag No. 3: Louise underplayed Victor's hit-and-run dating behavior.

Most women would have written Victor off after his first boorish disappearing act. Louise condoned his rude behavior by going out with him again and again. And each time she went out with him, she adjusted to his untrustworthy behavior.

I called Victor out for his hurtful, disappearing behavior. He blamed me, saying he didn't call me back because I rejected him sexually. After I slept with him his justification was, "You got all these walls up and I'm just protecting myself." When I took down the so-called walls he ran out of excuses and he would evaporate without explanation.

Red Flag No. 4: Victor minimized and ignored Louise's requests to take her to Chicago.

For the zillionth time, don't get serious about a guy until you see his home setting. If an out-of-town man wants sexual intimacy, he had better be willing to fork up a plane trip to his city to visit his home—*first!*

Had Louise done her homework, before she gave her heart away, she would have discovered, in addition to Victor being married, his yacht was corporate property (still not a bad deal), his downtown Chicago apartment was his business office, and he lived in the burbs with his lovely, head-in-the-sand wife.

Want to find out if a guy is married?

Website WomanSavers.com offers a surplus of tips on how to catch a cheater, including but not limited to: tracer services that identify ownership of automobiles, boats and real estate, as well as, locate Canada and off shore bank accounts; DNA testing kits (aka: infidelity test that detects traces of semen left behind in undergarments after sex—*ewwww!*); spy equipment (e.g., video and audio surveillance, peephole spy, scramblers, night vision and your very own police badge); GPS tracking systems for real-time location of vehicles and cellular phones; plus internet monitoring and computer key logger software.

Lawd, Shoe Sista! Wouldn't it just be easier to ask a man for his driver's license, social security number, birth certificate, dental records, last five years' tax returns and pay $39.99 for a simple background check?

Don't Go There Girl!

If a man cheats on his wife, and he divorces and marries you, when the stars line up just right, we will also cheat on you.

Liar, Liar, Pants on Fire!

A man of such obvious and exemplary charm must be a liar.

—Anita Brookner

Gregarious, dramatic, shrewd, seductive, self-serving and shameless—pathological liars will tell elaborate and fantastic stories and claim it to be their life story.

Pathological liars are said to differ from compulsive liars. Compulsive liars typically deceive out of habit to avoid situations, confrontation, accountability and responsibilities—they are not viewed as overly manipulative. Pathological liars live in their own reality most of the time. They are seen as manipulative, cunning and egotistical. They deceive to get their way. They lie to get sympathy. They do not value truth. They don't admit they lie. They have no remorse for lying. They do not worry about the consequences of lying. They are sometimes delusional in that they believe their own lies.

The naïve and unsuspecting woman can be duped by the pathological liar's grandiosity and superficial charm.

Pathological liars tend to be intelligent. They can be charismatic and are exceedingly convincing when spinning their tales of wealth, possessions and accomplishments. They will present themselves as highly successful, impressively educated, well traveled, amazingly brave and they will cite connections to the influential and famous.

Their lies can be complex, impulsive, irrational and escalating and can drag on for years. Pathological liars love to one-up; whatever you say, do or have—they will have to do better. Their deceit sometimes seems to serve no obvious purpose other than to seek attention and feel superior. They exploit and deceive to get their way with little regard for the rights and feelings of others. They tell so many lies they forget their lies and contradict themselves. And when they're caught in a lie they become defensive and angry— or they will fabricate another lie to mask the first lie. If they no longer value a relationship they may not even bother to deny their deception.

Their lies become a reality to them.

Dr. Dirtbag's lying made no sense. He was successful and he had plenty of money—and yet, he claimed he won a million-dollar lawsuit that never happened. He boasted of real estate property, exorbitant bank accounts and investments that didn't exist. He bragged of trips abroad and speaking engage-ments that never took place. He fabricated conversations that were never spoken.

Dr. Dirtbag and I broke up. A month later he called me in the pre-dawn hours saying he was accosted by three men try-ing to rob him in the parking lot of a late night diner. He said one of the men struck him on the side of his head. Dr. Dirt-bag retaliated with a Taekwondo move, he thrust his knuckles into his attacker's throat, the man fell to the ground and then he side-kicked a second guy. Startled by Dr. Dirtbag's forceful defense the two standing men fled while the felled man lay on the pavement out cold. He said he feared that he had crushed the unconscious man's trachea—but he didn't stick around to find out.

I told my girlfriend about Dr. Dirtbag's close encounter. She burst into laughter and said, "Surely you don't believe his crap! He's making it up to get your sympathy."

It Sounds Like the Truth—But It Doesn't Feel Like the Truth

Don't dismiss your gut feeling.

A pathological liar's greatest talent is wrapping an extraordinary lie around microscopic bits of fact making it difficult for you to unravel his twisted stories.

Charles was an enterprising pathological liar. He surprised Gloria, his girlfriend of four months, with a stunning 4-carat brilliant cut diamond engagement ring. He told her, and he bragged to everyone, that it was a rare GIA certified "FL" flawless, white diamond mined in Siberia. Eventually Gloria had it appraised. It was Moissanite—a dazzling silicon carbide gemstone worn often by celebrities—but worth a smidgen of a genuine diamond.

He told Gloria he was an investor in a patented medical product that was being acquired by a major corporation—his share of the windfall was to be $10 million dollars. She stumbled across a statement from his alleged golden goose investment; his monthly dividend was $13.65.

He kept a 2-inch stack of rubber-banded $100 dollar bills in his briefcase. When he gambled he pulled out his bankroll to impress everyone. Gloria sneaked a peek at his stack of bills one day. It was five or so $100 dollar bills padded with one-dollar bills.

What made him so convincing was he believed his own bullshit.

He told people he owned a second home; he was referring to the family home he lost to his ex-wife in his divorce. He even told acquaintances he co-owned Gloria's 5-bedroom house. On and on and on ... Charles' property, jewelry, automobiles, business deals and money was something he once owned and lost, something he never had, or he had it but it was worth a thousand times less than his boast. Eventually Gloria realized that Charles' half-truths were designed to keep her guessing and locked into an abusive relationship.

Dr. Dirtbag was a genius at misrepresentation, diversion, illusion and trickery. I knew in my gut he was lying to me—but how could I expose a cunning liar who constantly said, "I don't remember," "I don't understand," or "You misunderstood?" More infuriating was when I presented him the undeniable truth that exposed his lies, he would blatantly deny his actions, fabricate more lies and expect me to buy into his craziness—and I began to doubt my sanity.

What made Dr. Dirtbag so believable was that he embellished and distorted small pieces of the truth leaving me wondering what was fact—and what was fiction. He once owned a 35-foot cruiser he kept at a nearby river marina. One evening I overheard him boasting to his golf buddy (and only friend) that he harbored a 70-foot yacht in Italy. His buddy must have smelled a swamp rat because he later asked me, "Does he really have a yacht in Italy?" I looked at him, rolled my eyes and said, "He's your friend—ask him!"

Lairs Bring Out the Worst in a Woman

There is something about a liar which causes a woman to resort to equally bad behavior.

Meryl had never spied on a man's privacy but her fiancé's behavior was evasive, conflicting and suspicious. She found herself waiting until he was in the shower to rummage through his wallet. She snooped through his credit card statements looking for suspicious charges. She stood silently outside the doorway to eavesdrop on his phone conversations. One day, when he went fishing, she ransacked his desk and she found his internet passwords scribbled on a small piece of yellow pa-per folded and tucked in the back of his top desk drawer. She entered his password into his email account and within mo-ments she learned he was corresponding with multiple women on a dating website. When she confronted him he blasted her, saying she had no right to spy on him and she had violated his trust. Point taken—but the fact remains he was a lying, cheating lizard.

Bethany was married to a pathological liar. Bethany tells her story of lies and betrayal:

Allen lied to me when we were dating. He told me he was divorced—but he was, instead, separated. I continued to date him. He finally got a divorce, we got married and he man-aged our joint checking account. A year after we were married a bill collector called about an unpaid credit card. I asked Al-len about it. He said his check must have gotten lost in the mail and he would take care of it. Several months later our electricity was cut off at our house. Allen swore on his Dodge Ram truck that he mailed the check. He paid the bill and our electricity was turned back on.

Allen was an independent contractor. He seemed to always drive by our house and get the mail before I got home from work. I was a mom with a fulltime career—I was too busy to balance our checking account and pay bills. It was a Saturday, Allen was working and I retrieved our mail from the mailbox. My heart stopped—there were numerous letters of severe past due notices. Allen arrived home and I stormed out the front door to his truck, I dug under his truck seat and in his glove compartment and I pulled out envelope after envelope of un-paid bills and late notices that he had opened and then hidden. One of the envelopes was our home mortgage statement which he had not paid in three months. I called the bank but they said our house had already gone into foreclosure. I threatened Allen with a divorce if he didn't file a Chapter 13 to protect our home. He filed wage earner bankruptcy (and I didn't), our house was saved from foreclosure and I divorced my no-good husband. The bankruptcy court garnished Allen's paychecks for eight years. At the end of eight years our house was released from bankruptcy, we sold the house, split the equity and Allen went on to marry and lie to his third and fourth wives.

Once you've realized he has lied, you can then question the validity of everything he says and has said.

—Patricia Evans, *The Verbally Abusive Relationship*

Pay Attention to Details

When dating a man ask lots of questions.

Gut instincts don't always make sense. You feel something is not right—but you have no logical evidence to cause you to mistrust a man. Asking questions can clear up your doubts—or confirm your mistrust. A seemingly innocent piece of information could be the very thing you need to expose a man's deception.

Louise unknowingly exposed out-of-towner Vanishing-Victor-Kielbasa as a married man by asking to see a snapshot of his children. He showed her a wallet photo of his children, as youngsters standing beside their mom. He claimed it was his ex-wife. Louise became suspicious of his unreliable behavior and so she did an Internet search on him; the search associated him with a woman his age. She googled the woman, and out of hundreds of thousands of possibilities, the woman popped up as a Chicago real estate agent complete with head shot and contact information. "She was older than the photo, but I could see it was the same woman, giving me the gumption to call her," said Louise. "She confirmed positively Victor was her husband. Had I not asked to see a photo of his children, he would have gotten away with posing as a single man."

Lisa met Ray, a swimming pool builder, at an ATM Machine. He flirted with her; he got her phone number, he asked her out and they began to date. Lisa quizzed him about his past; where did he grow up? What was his career background? He boasted of once being a chef at a 5-star hotel in Detroit. But when Lisa asked him to help her make a cheesecake, "He could barely butter a pan!" she exclaimed. She paid for an internet background check. She discovered, not only was Ray dishonorably discharged from the military and he had two DUI's, he had spent a year and a half in jail for embezzlement. Lisa confronted Ray about the embezzlement. He told Lisa he and his ex-girlfriend worked together at a jewelry store; she was the store's accountant, she stole $100,000.00 and he took the rap because she had a young son and he didn't want her to go to jail. Whatever! Ray—you're excused!

⚓

Tanya's fiancé Larry always kept his cell phone on silent in his pants pocket. "I never heard his phone ring," Tanya said. "He would pull it out of his pocket, answer it and walk off to talk in private. A couple of times he left his cell phone on the kitchen counter; the screen lit up with a call from a man named "Ken," he looked at it and he pushed the "ignore" button. I asked him who Ken was. He said it was a guy from work and he would call him back later. After that he took his phone with him whenever he left the room, even when he went to bathroom. He stopped charging his phone at home; he charged it in his car or at work. He stopped using his cell phone alarm to wake him up in the mornings and he bought an alarm clock. He said the vibrating emails alerts disturbed his sleep; he turned his phone off at bedtime and he placed it under his pillow. Early one morning Larry's pit bull got out of

> *He kept his cell phone on vibrate with the screen lying face down.*

the backyard. Larry threw on his gym shorts and ran out the front door after his dog, leaving his cell phone under his pillow. I grabbed it, turned it on and I scanned his call log. There were a dozen incoming and outgoing calls from "Ken." I hit redial, my heart pounded, fearing the truth. A woman answered, cooing, "Hey baby, I thought about you last night!" I said, "This is Larry's fiancé." The woman immediately hung up on me. I wrote Larry a note on the bathroom mirror, saying, "Ken called." Ken's real name was Kendra.

Red Flags:

If you're listening to details and you're evaluating with your brain, and not your emotions, you will begin to recognize a pathological liar's illogical, contradictory, deceptive bologna.

Pathological liars are notorious for exaggeration and far-fetched stories. They lie so much they will forget the small details they told you previously. If you suspect a person is lying, pay attention to the inconsistencies in their stories. Jot down notes to validate your instincts. Later, when he tries to make you doubt your memory or cognition, and he claims he didn't do or say something—you will have your notes to confirm the truth.

Remember—intelligent, confident, successful men are slow to toot their own horns. Insecure people will exhibit exaggerated self-importance to mask their feelings of low self-worth. If a man comes out of the gate bragging of riches, possessions and accomplishments—you may be dealing with a pathological liar.

Tight-Lipped Zombie

35

*She wanted a man who was as excited about
her, as she was about him.*

One of the most difficult of relationships is to be involved
with an emotionally unavailable partner—also referred to
as EUM (emotionally unavailable man).

Emotionally unavailable men are not necessarily bad boys.
They can be stable, caring and considerate and we fall in love with
their endearing qualities. But we are perplexed and frustrated by
their ambiguous behavior. In the beginning an EUM may pursue
you hard. He may be affectionate and attentive—but he is often
difficult to read. You feel like he likes you, but conversation with
him is shallow and confusing. You never quite know where you
stand with an EUM.

Sex with an emotionally unavailable man leaves you feeling
empty and longing for a meaningful connection. Living with him
can be lonely and oppressing. When once he was seemingly alive
and passionate about you, he slid into a state of non-emotions and
non-communication. You feel like your relationship is one-sided.
You feel like you express more love, care and commitment than you
receive. You work overtime to understand his brooding, withdrawn
personality. You struggle to connect with him at an intimate level.

Experts say that many emotionally unavailable people want
a serious relationship but their emotional baggage prevents them
from making an intimate connection. Some are untrusting; they
fear rejection or they have a fear of being controlled. Men especially

are afraid of "losing" themselves in a relationship and they will subconsciously, or even knowingly, erect barriers to avoid emotional intimacy—or sabotage a relationship.

Trying to fix the dysfunctional mindset of an emotionally unavailable man is improbable—if not impossible. Said one male online blogger:

> *Unavailable men are not actually emotionally unavailable, they are emotionally handicapped. They have emotions, just not the ones you're looking for. They may be passionate about sports, cars, music, and politics—just not about you.*

If you are married to an emotionally unavailable man—my sincere condolences. If you are single woman, heed the warning signs of the EUM and avoid a relationship with him.

Dating a Zombie

The courtship of an emotionally unavailable man can be baffling, deflating and hurtful. A seemingly great guy pursues you. He calls you, he asks you out and he says and does things to pull you into a relationship. He is courteous and attentive, and he wants to sleep with you. And when you give yourself to him—he withdraws his affection and his pursuit. He may even cease dating you altogether. You are bewildered and devastated by his sudden change of heart. You may even blame yourself ... wondering what you did to run him off.

Sabrina, an attractive 45-year-old guitarist and singer, moved to Nashville. She was excited about living in a vibrant new city that could advance her musical dreams. Her girlfriend Mary Ann introduced her to her guy friend, Jerry, a successful 53-year-old hotel entrepreneur. Sabrina thought her life was finally coming together. Sabrina tells her story.

I met Mary Ann, her boyfriend and Jerry for happy hour at the Palm in downtown Nashville. We sat at the bar drinking and talking. I thought Jerry was okay; he was moderately nice-looking but a bit uptight. Our drinks turned into dinner and Jerry warmed up to me. He buttered my bread. He held my hand under the table. He stared at me admiringly as I talked and he politely picked up my check. He asked me out for that weekend and he began calling me every morning and night. The chemistry between us was strong. I slept with him on the third date and in the heat of the moment he accidentally murmured, "I love you."

Jerry was the sweetest, most gentlemanly man I had ever met. He took me wherever I wanted to go. We dined in nice restaurants. We went to an outdoor festival. He held my hand in public, he pulled my chair out to seat me, and he was quick to pour my wine. He opened my car door and he walked on the outside of the sidewalk—something many men don't know to do. In my home he was caring and thoughtful. He worked beside me in the kitchen washing the dishes as I cooked. He instinctively set the table and he took out the trash. When he spent the night I would awake the next morning to the smell of fresh I always kissed and hugged him first. *coffee. I would find him sitting patiently in front of the TV waiting to pour me a cup. He spoke in relationship terms; he said he told his friends and mother about me, making me think we were moving forward as a couple. Jerry was not an exciting man but I was slowly falling in love with him. Several weeks later—Jerry disappeared.*

Jerry called me two weeks after his vanishing act. I questioned him and I asked him if he was "okay." He blamed his rude behavior on stress caused by a pending legal matter and an upcoming hand operation. "I'm sorry; it's my fault," he said. "I'm not at a good place right now."

I accepted his explanation and we resumed our intimate relationship. A week later he disappeared again.

Another week passed. Thinking Jerry was again in one of his funks, I texted him a flirty message, saying: "Sitting by fireplace w glass wine." He texted me back and he came over to my place. We had drinks. I cooked dinner and we had sex. But sex with Jerry was unsatisfying. His foreplay was half-ass and his after-play was non-existent. Lying in bed with him he wouldn't cuddle or touch me. I felt dejected sleeping next to him. He stopped talking about us in relationship terms. I withdrew to my place of protection and indifference. And he quit calling me altogether.

His detached behavior made me feel empty inside.

My Rejected Girlfriend Within is filling out a Cosmo relationship quiz, "Is He Only After Your Bod?" She contemplates question No. 1: *Does he dial you the same night and say, "Hey, wanna come over?"* She grimaces and checks "yes."

Women crave the emotionally-detached man.

During the following months Sabrina missed Jerry and she would occasionally call or text him. She convinced herself she could be content to have a boyfriend who never took her out—but could get an erection. They would meet for drinks, dinner and sex—and he would again—evaporate. One night she drunk texted him—said Sabrina:

I had several glasses of wine at happy hour with my girlfriends. Driving home I longed to see Jerry. I tested the waters with a text: "On the way over." He didn't reply. I called him and I said, "Did you get my text?" He replied, "Yeaaah ... I unlocked the door," as if to say apathetically, "Whataya want from me?" I didn't bother going to Jerry's that evening and I quit texting him.

Sabrina was determined to leave Jerry alone; she even ignored one of his rare phone calls. Months passed, it was the holidays, and Sabrina was rebounding from a brief and disappointing relationship. She texted Jerry. They met for drinks. Drinks turned into dinner, and dessert was, of course, sex. But this time was different. Jerry seemed to have a change of heart. They spent the whole weekend together. He insinuated that he had strong feelings for Sabrina and that he was ready for a relationship. "Truly I thought this time was different," Sabrina said, "and so I allowed myself to have feelings for Jerry."

The weekend ended. Jerry went out of town on business. He called Sabrina Monday evening like the dutiful boyfriend. They made plans to be together that Wednesday night—and then, like every time before, Jerry fell off the face of the Earth.

Red Flags:

Dating Jerry was an upsetting, demoralizing cycle for Sabrina. She enjoyed the warm and fuzzy feelings of his companionship—but she was repeatedly dumbfounded and hurt by his unexpected withdrawal. She kept trying to revive their original relationship of when he was the attentive suitor and she was the happy responder. Sometimes Jerry would reciprocate to her hinted invitations—sometimes he wouldn't. When he didn't Sabrina felt diminished. When he did, it was a one-night stand, and she felt debased. Eventually she quit texting and calling Jerry, and he silently went away, because a relationship required him to be emotionally involved.

Red Flag No. 1: The first night Sabrina met Jerry she thought he had a negative edge.

When I first met Jerry his conversation was laced with pes-
simism. His answers were smart-alecky, he said things like,
"Why would I want to do that," and a drawn-out, "Yeaaah,"
meaning, "Duh!" I thought he was jerk but after a couple of
drinks he was doting and attentive—so I let it pass. Several
weeks into our relationship his negativity became apparent
and it was irritating and depressing. But I was already sleep-
ing with him and I downplayed it.

Red Flag No. 2: Disparaging comments about his ex-girlfriend.

Jerry constantly bad-mouthed his previous girlfriend of
twelve years. He boasted that she was twenty years younger
than him. He said she was emotionally dysfunctional, hooked
on prescriptive drugs and she dated him for his money and
sex. He described their relationship as sexually addictive and
volatile with constant breakups and make-ups. He said she re-
peatedly broke up with him, dated other men, and even mar-
ried another man—but she kept coming back to him because
"he" gave her mind-blowing orgasms.

My 50 Shades Girlfriend Within sits straight up in her bed,
glares at her snoring boyfriend passed out after his huge orgasm.
She whacks him upside the head, *Hey, Cowboy! Wake up! My turn!*

Conclusion: Jerry's relationship with the younger woman was a
tumultuous tug-of-war. He was the older man—he held the power
and the money. She was the younger woman—she had the hot body.
He was insensitive and emotionally withholding; consequently she
was starved for emotional validation—and when she didn't get it
she sought out the company of other men.

It's hard to recognize an emotionally unavailable man, when he
is ardently pursuing you, because we misread his pulsing penis for
a beating heart. And when his blood flows back to his main brain,
and he becomes his normal detached, impersonal self, we think we
did something wrong to alienate him.

Married to a Zombie

*There's nothing more lonely than being
lonely in your marriage.*

Some EUMs will court you, romance you and even marry you.
But once the knot is tied he will turn on a dime and withdraw his
communication and affection.

> *I was once married to an emotionally unavailable, non-
> communicating man. He was a good man, but he was extremely
> introverted, tight-lipped and unfeeling. When we were dating
> he pursued me with ardor and purpose. When we married
> he was physically present and predictable. We socialized, we
> traveled and we did things together. To the outside world
> our marriage seemed idealistic. He appeared to be the perfect
> husband and I put up the front of being happily married. But
> in privacy our conversations were shallow or non-existent. Sex
> was a quickie-get-his-rocks-off. He was rigid and unsympathetic
> to my feelings. I felt unloved and unwanted. He refused to work
> on our relationship and I craved a man's emotional support and
> intimate companionship. When I divorced him our married
> friends shunned me. I knew what they were thinking—how
> could she do that to such a wonderful man? I divorced my
> husband because I was dying inside.*

Darlene, a divorcee, was forty-four when she married Chuck, a
58-year-old retired fireman. Darlene was attractive, outgoing and
professional. She enjoyed her career and her social outings with
her girlfriends. Chuck was gregarious and fun-loving in public; in
private he was an insensitive recluse. Darlene relates her story:

> *When Chuck and I dated I knew he wasn't much of a talker.
> But he was persistent in pursuing me. After we slept together
> sex became our intimate communication. We married after*

dating for only eight months. He was honest, dependable and stable. He never forgot my birthday or our anniversary. He was considerate to my children, family and friends. Six months after we married he went into a dark cave.

Having a conversation with Chuck was like talking to a zombie. When I tried to have a casual conversation with him I got no response. If I tried to talk to him about our problems he would shut down. If I got upset and expressed my hurt feelings he made me feel bad about myself.

Chuck was brooding and withdrawn at home—but when we went to a party or social event he magically came alive. Chuck was a handsome black-tie escort. He was charming, witty and friendly and he would dance all night with other women. When the final song of the night was announced, as the respectful husband, he would seek me out for the last dance. Party after party he abandoned me to socialize, flirt and dance with other women. I resented his neglect, and when I saw him looking for me for the last dance I would hide from him to punish him.

Daily life with Chuck was like living with a lifeless deaf-mute roommate. His favorite companion was our German Sheppard. His outside interests were bowling once a week with his buddies and fishing alone on

He petted the dog more than he stroked me

the weekends. At night I cooked dinner while he watched TV in the living room. We ate dinner in silence in front of the TV. I washed the dishes while he remained in a TV-coma. Every night at 10 o'clock he got up from the sofa, walked to the bedroom, brushed his teeth, got into bed, patted the mattress for the dog to jump up and lie down between him and me ... and then he stroked the dog and watched the news and Jay Leno until he fell asleep.

Sex with Chuck was a sixty-second rodeo. His foreplay was predictable and unpleasant. Once a week he would take his little blue pill and thirty minutes later, when Jay Leno signed off, he would reach under the sheets, touch my sex and wiggle his fingers, signaling that he wanted to (in his words) "fuck." I would pretend to be aroused. He hopped on, got his jolly—and then hopped off. I resented his crude, degrading attitude about sex. Eventually I quit wanting to have sex with him altogether—and he, of course, went deeper into his cave.

I tried to be content with my life without Chuck in it. I went out with my girlfriends for fun and mental stimulation. I threw myself into an exciting career with a great salary and frequent travel. I invited Chuck to travel with me. I pleaded with him to go to couples counseling to work on our problems. He said, "Okay," and then he went back to doing whatever it was he was doing. My career satisfied my emotional void for years—but I was alone on the road all week and I was alone again when I returned home. Then one Friday afternoon, after a week-long business trip, I pulled onto my street and when I saw my house I was engulfed with a gripping, sickening, empty feeling. I pulled my car to the curb and with tears rolling down my cheek, I called my guy friend and he met me for drinks. That's when I knew my marriage was over. I divorced Chuck because I didn't want to cheat on him.

Red Flags:

Darlene married her father figure. Chuck married his trophy wife. After they were married Chuck felt he no longer had to romance Darlene, and he set her on his mantle and resumed his normal personality—a non-communicating, emotionally unavailable corpse.

Red Flag No. 1: Pay attention to your first impressions about a man. Darlene recognized her husband's introvert personality on the first two dates.

From the beginning Chuck was closemouthed and quiet. Having a conversation with him was like pulling teeth. I told

myself I didn't want to go out with him again, but I was flat-
tered by his strong pursuit of me. When I slept with him I also
gave him my heart.

Red Flag No. 2: Pay attention to what his family and friends say
about him.

Chuck's friends, co-workers and grown children made re-
marks about his aloof and sullen behavior. His friends said,
"You're so good for Chuck. I've never seen him like this. He's
really come out of his shell," and, "Chuck never talks to any-
one." His daughter told me, "When we were teenagers and
company came to our house Dad would clam up and leave the
room." His son-in-law added, "Yeah, I was afraid of him."
Time and time again people remarked on his anti-social be-
havior. I thought I was special because I made him a better
man—and so I married him. The problem was his rejecting,
brooding behavior turned me into an angry, resentful wife.

We Are Our Worst Enemy

Women tend to blame and punish themselves for a man's
sudden and unexplainable withdrawal. We ask ourselves,
"What did I do wrong?" "Am I too nice?" "Am I not pretty
enough?" "Was I too available?" When in truth, there's
nothing wrong with us—the problem is we are involved
with a self-interested, non-communicating emotionally
withholding man.

Warning! Warning! Signs of Mr. Unavailable

Read and heed ...

- He comes on strong in the beginning, but after he gets
  your attention, or you sleep with him, he backs off with
  his affection, phone calls and pursuit. When you question
  him about it he gives you an excuse; he blames "timing." He

tells you "if only things were different, you'd be the perfect girlfriend." "It's not you," he says. "It's me."

- He admits to being commitment-phobic. He acts like he's totally into you—but he claims "he's not over his last girlfriend or recent divorce." He says, "I'm not ready for a relationship." If you continue seeing him, you have accepted his "sleep-over-non-relationship" terms.

- He's angry at his ex-wife or ex-girlfriend because she left him, or she nailed him financially. Or he still loves her. Either way—he still has strong feelings for his ex, making him emotionally unsuitable for a relationship.

- He is rigid about his schedule (a sign he may be seeing someone else). He determines the momentum of the relationship; he sets up when and where he will see you.

- He takes the relationship too slow; after months of sleeping with him he doesn't take the relationship forward. You're not sure if you are "couple" or you're just hanging out.

- He is resistant to involving himself in your life. He ignores your requests to participate in the things you want to do. He never takes you around his friends and he doesn't introduce you to his family.

- He relies on text messages, instant messaging and email for the majority of his communication with you. Most of his messaging is idle chatter. You keep thinking he will ask you out—maybe he will; more likely he won't.

He is shallow ...

- Your conversations are trifling and superficial. You are vulnerable with your thoughts and feelings. He tells you just enough to keep you in a go-no-where relationship. When you try to talk to him about the status of your relationship, he tells you what you want to hear or he skirts the issue. You constantly wonder *where you stand with him*.

- Phone conversations with him are frustrating and trivial. He may call semi-regularly or he calls to say goodnight. He performs like a dependable, caring partner. But his dialogue seems mechanical and impersonal, and his tone is lukewarm and reserved. When he hangs up you ask yourself, *"What the heck are we doing?"*

- You feel uncertain when he leaves your house. You're not sure when you'll hear from him again. He leaves you hanging— even though you've been dating him for a while.

He leaves you feeling emotionally void ...

- Your relationship feels like a "push and pull" game. One day he really likes you, and the next day he disappears or shuts down. His behavior creates an addictive relationship. You feel he cares about you, so you keep trying to figure him out. When he withdraws from you, you suffer from his rejection and you instinctively seek his approval and validation.

- His compliments don't feel authentic; you find yourself "fishing" for his praise and validation. You seem to always hug and kiss him first.

- He leaves you sexually frustrated. His foreplay is perfunctory, minimal or non-existent. He doesn't take time to pleasure you during sex. He doesn't cuddle, touch or hold you after sex. You feel unfulfilled, lonely or sad after you sleep with him. He may even creep out and go home after sleeping with you.

- He says he wants to get married, but there is no sign of a ring, no mention of a date and years are going by. Some EUM's will cough up an engagement ring, but put off the wedding date indefinitely—that's because he never intends to marry you.

He withdraws but keeps you dangling ...

- He doesn't call when he is supposed to; he disappears and then resurfaces with little or no explanation.

- He lives out-of-town and he texts you flirty and sexual messages. He may call you and have long conversations, but he never mentions coming to see you. He says he is coming to see you—but nothing ever materializes.

- His pursuit subsides; you seem to initiate the dates. He pulls back or he disappears; you text or call him to restore the relationship. His behavior leaves you confused and it makes you want him even more.

- He doesn't answer your calls and he fails to return your calls/texts/emails/Facebook posts/tweets—or he calls you several days later when it is convenient for him.

- He no longer asks you out, but he calls or texts you on his way home from work, after happy hour or late at night. Your relationship has turned into a "booty call."

- Finally—he is married, he has a girlfriend or he is in a long-distance relationship with someone else. He is a momma's boy or he's a woman hater ... don't be a ninny—run, Shoe Sista, run!

Pay attention to your gut about how a man makes you feel. If a man continually makes your heart ache and your stomach wrench—or you are constantly confused about how he feels about you, and you're are uncertain about your future with him—chances are you are with an emotionally unavailable man.

My Rejected, Frustrated Girlfriend Within stepped between her dead-pan boyfriend and his TV, and announced, I want a divorce! He chugs his beer, belches and remarks, *Oh, yeah, sure, doll. Can it wait till half-time?*

Booze Tank

An addict doesn't control his addiction,
the addiction controls the addict.

I enjoy a glass wine—but Dr. Dirtbag gave a gin martini new meaning.

Dr. Dirtbag and I were both high energy, class "A" personalities who enjoyed cooking, dining and socializing. I guess that's why I ignored his drinking problem in the beginning—cocktails were a part of our lifestyle.

For me a glass of wine was a way to relax and have fun with my friends. For Dr. Dirtbag it was a 24/7/365 way of life. He drank when he got home from work. He drank beer while mowing the lawn, working on a house project or puttering in the garage. He drank double-time when he played golf with his buddies. *Come to think of it*—the only time he didn't drink was when he was sleeping or he had a scalpel in his hand.

Traveling was the perfect excuse for Dr. Dirtbag to start partying early. He would have a noonday margarita while waiting to board a plane in the airport, a couple of beers while in flight, happy hour martinis in our hotel lobby and then a bottle or two of wine while having dinner at a nice restaurant. By night's end he was soused. The next day he would say, *"Let's go shopping"* and we would catch a cab to a trendy retail district. I thought our mission was to find me some really cute shoes, a bauble or two, a smart outfit and some souvenir thingamajigs. But instead, Dr. Dirtbag wanted to duck

He called cocktails and appetizers "grazing."

into every restaurant in our path to sit at the bar and order drinks and appetizers. He called it "grazing."

Grazing would start at lunchtime. Dr. Dirtbag and I would walk up and down the streets lined with boutiques and restaurants. He would follow me into a couple of stores, lagging several yards behind me with his wallet, allowing me to fondle and lust over the merchandise. After I made a purchase or two, he would exclaim, "I'm hungry. Let's get something to eat"—signifying that *grazing* had commenced.

In the beginning grazing was fun. We made out-of-town friends in the local bistros. We dined on yummy appetizers—and we got a happy buzz before sundown. In reality "shopping" was his excuse to "graze": a ploy to start drinking early and drink long. By the end of the day I was ready for a pitcher of ice tea, two Excedrin and a serious nap.

It was on our trip to Pittsburgh that I realized the extent of Dr. Dirtbag's drinking. We arrived at the airport at 7 a.m. for an early flight. We went to an eatery to get breakfast prior to boarding our plane. I drank coffee and ate a sausage, egg and biscuit. He skipped breakfast and downed two beers on an empty stomach. He drank two vodka cranberries during our flight. We checked into our hotel mid-afternoon and he immediately wanted to go grazing. We walked to a nearby retail area, patronized three different restaurants, had multiple drinks and a couple of light-fare appetizers. The more Dr. Dirtbag drank the more disconnected, sullen and belligerent he became. By the end of the weekend I saw him for who he was—a stumbling lambasting lush.

Dishonorable Mention

An alcoholic will spend hours outside alone doing yard work or working in the garage to conceal their drinking.

Donnie was a charming gentlemanly tuxedo at the beginning of a party. After a couple of drinks he was a glassy-eyed, flushed-face drunk. His wife was fed up with obnoxious drinking behavior, chauffeuring him home from most parties because he was too intoxicated to drive. She threatened to divorce him if he didn't stop drinking. He promised to stop drinking—and then she caught him drinking vodka from a sports bottle while working in the garage.

Cooking on the holidays was an excuse for Bradley to start drinking before noon, said Amy. He ruined our holidays with his obnoxious, bumbling behavior. He got drunk and he torched his rack of ribs on July 4th and on Memorial Day. He charred the ham for Thanksgiving and he incinerated the Christmas turkey. By the time the holiday dinner was served Bradley was a stewed, incoherent sot.

Candace couldn't get her husband to eat when he's drinking. Candice said, "Alcohol killed his appetite. Food ruined his buzz. We would sit down to a nice meal; he would pick at his food, say he wasn't hungry and then he would mix himself another drink. He would put his untouched dinner in the refrigerator, claiming he would eat it for lunch tomorrow. The next day he ate the meat off his plate and threw the rest of the food in the disposal"

Dana's handsome, wealthy guy friend Aaron always reeked of strong mouthwash. One evening, because Aaron was wearing a cast for a broken arm, Dana drove them in his car to an art show. At the event they both had drinks. After the show Dana

was driving them home when Aaron reached into his car door side pocket and he pulled out a mini bottle of mouthwash. "Here, take a swig," he told Dana, handing her the mouthwash bottle. "I've been doing this for a long time." That's when she realized he was a professional drinker.

Normally Robert drank bourbon, but he switched to vodka because it was colorless, almost odorless. He bought eight-packs of small airplane bottles of vodka because they were easy to hide, sneak a quick drink and dispose of. His wife Jillian found several of the empty miniature vodka bottles in the outdoors trash bin. He told her the pool guy must have put them there.

Red Flags:

Warning signs of a drinking problem: They get juiced regularly at happy hour. They become inebriated while doing chores or yard work. They had rather drink than eat. They constantly drink alone. They lie and hide how much they drink. They're moody, irritable, withdrawn, and will even shake when they try to stop drinking. They get a DUI and they continue to drive while intoxicated.

My Lindsey Lohan Girlfriend Within is hobbling around the house wearing her arrest ankle bracelet. She can't remember where she hid her vodka bottle. *Her inner girlfriend slurs, Well, I dunno ... last time I saw it—hiccup!—it was in the toilet tank.*

Epilogue:
Don't Be One Either

"If only there were a magical mirror in which we could see ourselves as others see us."

—Nancy Nichols

Change begins with the willingness to accept the idea that: I may be the one who is wrong.

It has taken me a lifetime to identify and correct, and hopefully minimize, my behaviors which contributed to the demise of my relationships. I am the first to admit women are often flawed with our naïve, deceptive and self-serving behaviors. We attract, date and fall in love with the wrong man. We reject or run off a good man. We many times, I am ashamed to say, use men for our own personal gain. Where women are duped and injured by men who are abusers, cheaters and romance-artists—men are snookered by women who are cheaters, batterers, clingers and gold-diggers.

In my book *God, Please Fix Me!* I explore the dysfunctional issues which cause our relationship difficulties. I discuss emotional filters. Dr. Phil says, "Some filters may be *Faulty filters warp* healthy and constructive, while others *our reality.* may be distorted and destructive." Our emotional filters are at the core of our relationship decisions. It's why we choose to be with some people—and not others. If we view our world through fear, anxiety, anger, greed, resentment, sadness, hatred, jealousy and envy, our unhealthy filters distort our perception of a potential mate. We will push away a quality man—and instead—we bond to a man whose dysfunctional behavior supports and agrees with our own defective mindset. We gravitate toward a man who will accept and love us in spite of our unstable personality.

My phobia in life was that I believed I couldn't take care of myself. I was afraid of being alone and lonely. This flawed belief perpetuated my innermost need in life—security. It is why I married and divorced three times—I married for the wrong reason to the wrong men. The first time I naively married a high school boyfriend to escape my unhappy home life. We were both emotionally retarded. I shrugged off our marriage and a year later we divorced. Ten years later, still searching for emotional and financial safety, I recklessly married a pathological liar. Ten years later I divorced him. Then I married a tight-lipped Zombie. Unable to bear his cauldron of rejecting silence, I divorced him a decade later. I blamed all three of my husbands for my unhappy marriages. But in all fairness, their hurtful behavior was immensely apparent during their courtships—and I choose to marry them.

After my last divorce, I spent years in self-discovery and personal healing. I identified my critical, judgmental, negative mindset—and I corrected it. My soul-searching spawned my self-actualization. I learned self-acceptance and self-love, and an acceptance and appreciation for others. I discovered my inner potential and my independence. All of which inspired my writing "Secrets of the Ultimate Husband Hunter," a book of positive thought, self-esteem building and take-charge actions. Nevertheless—I still longed for the love, companionship and support of a man.

Loneliness and neediness is a mighty magnet for attracting trouble—that's when I met and foolishly fell in love with the man-from-hell. From the get-go Dr. Dirtbag sensed my core relationship need—everything he said and did spelled—S-E-C-U-R-I-T-Y! He boasted of wealth, position and privileges. He showered me with clothing, jewelry and gifts. He told me, "I'll take care of you forever." I evaluated Dr. Dirtbag through my security-driven filtering system—and I closed my eyes to the obvious fact that he was an arrogant, deceitful, pernicious douchebag—and I blamed him for the failure of our relationship.

Pain-bodies keep us tied to a harmful relationship.

Another emotional flaw which contributes to our relationship demise is what Eckard Tolle calls the "pain-body." Tolle says that almost everyone has within them an accumulation of old emotional pain that is "revived continuously" and becomes "part of our sense of self." Our pain body causes us to seek the emotional pain from our past, for that pain is familiar and oddly comfortable. We may feel a "magnetic pull" to someone who we sense will give us "more of the same pain," states Tolle, "That pain is sometimes misinterpreted as falling in love." Sometimes, when similar pain-bodies collide, men and women believe they have met their soul-mate.

The more hurtful our past experiences, the more intense our present-day emotional pain. The more intense our present-day emotional pain, the more severe is our pain-body. Women (and men) with heavy pain-bodies will accept insufferable abusive treatment from their partners.

It is our responsibility to heal our pain-body which causes us to sub-consciously bond to partners who will overlook and mirror our dysfunctional, destructive emotional issues.

Self-serving agendas induce our bad behavior.

Everyone has a relationship agenda. Like faulty filters, an agenda may be healthy and constructive, while other agendas may be self-serving and destructive. If we are close-minded and opinionated, emotionally stunted, or self-important and self-seeking, we will blame our partner when our relationship is problematic, or it fails.

Wendy used her good looks and alluring wily ways to get men to spend money on her and support her lifestyle. The problem was: men who are attracted to "arm candy" are often narcissistic, controlling, and often abusive. Needa was co-dependent and desperately looking for love. She gravitated to men who manipulated, controlled and abused her. Margaret married for stability; her husband, 20 years her senior, was her father figure. When they dated he was aloof and uncommunicative. Six months after they were married her brain-dead hubby disappeared into his emotionally-unavailable cave. Allie hungered for the love she never received from her father. She slept with a lot of men and she had affairs with married men trying to fill the hole in her soul. Her unstable, steamy relationships repeatedly ended in a fiery crash. Judith, a psychologist, dated her male clients. Her male clients became her live-in lovers and she began to mistreat them. When they stood up to her abuse, she blamed them for their relationship problems, she kicked them out of her house, and she told everyone they were impossible to live with. Lisa's problem was *never* that men did NOT ask her out; her problem was when a desirable man pursued her, she drank too much and she slept with them on the first or second date. Afterwards she was sick-at-heart for screwing up her chances, *yet again*, with a really great guy. She dealt with her heartbreak by lying to herself and to her girlfriends, claiming, "I don't have time for a man. I need to focus on my career." Patty, normally an attractive, intelligent, engaging woman, ran men off with her babble-mouth inebriated behavior. She found fault with them to deal with their rejection: "He's emotionally unavailable, he's a selfish jerk, he's a player, he can't get an erection, he's untrustworthy, on and on, etc. Vanna married a close-mouthed Zombie. Her ex-husband said, "I could never say or do anything right around Vanna. I learned to keep my mouth shut and I threw myself into my work and hobbies." Vanna divorced him, blaming his inability to communicate. Brook, a spoiled rich suburbanite, cheated on her husband with a man twenty years her junior—*because she could.* Her attorney husband hired a private investigator and divorced her, winning custody of their two children and child support.

Take Responsibility

We are each accountable for our own life. We are accountable for our harmful, destructive behaviors which erode our relationships. We are accountable for our faulty filters and emotional issues which bond us to emotionally unavailable, unstable and abusive partners. We are responsible for seeking out partners who will overlook our excessive drinking and harmful addictions. We are responsible for our naïve, fearful, co-dependent mindsets which cause us to attract, fall in love with, commit to and marry men who have proven they are untrustworthy. We are responsible for our self-centered agendas which land us with men who are jealous and controlling. We are responsible for our close-minded, hyper-critical, negative attitudes which run good men off.

> *Accepting your role in your problems, acknowledging that you are accountable means that you get it ... that you understand that the solutions lie within you, said Dr. Phil. While everyone else is still out there blaming those who aren't responsible for the results in their life, you can be as on target as a laser-guided missile, and therefore, work only on those things that will truly change your life.*

If you persistently experience dating disappointments, relationship failures, and *heaven forbid*, multiple divorces—you may want to examine your "faulty filters." If you blame the men in your life for your unhappiness and conflict—*as I once did*—it would behoove you to examine your negative attitudes, control issues and self-serving agendas which sabotage your relationships. If you are repeatedly drawn to men who mistreat you, or you are immersed in a relationship with an abusive man, it is imperative that you identify your "pain body" which tolerates maltreatment from a man—*or anyone.*

The designer questions are:

- Are you sick and tired of relationship conflict and failure?
- Do you *truly*, and I mean *earnestly* and *sincerely*, seek rapport, mutuality and stability within your relationships?
- Are you willing to dig deep into your emotional issues?

- Are you able to put aside your expectations and preconceived opinions of who is at fault with the men you date, within your relationships or marriage, and even in your friendships?

If you answered a rousing "yes" to all four questions, it's time to put on your big-girl jeans and red high heels and go to work on YOUR emotional issues and negative attitudes.

Step 1: You must acknowledge your impaired mindset which perpetuates your bad choices in men.

Step 2: You must admit to your self-absorbed, self-protecting agendas which evoke discord and contribute to the downfall of your relationships.

Step 3: You must work the *rest of your life* to change the negative thought patterns and harmful behavior which have caused you a lifetime of strife, misgivings, despair and heartbreak.

Otherwise, Shoe Sistas, enjoy dragging your luggage around.

My Carrie Bradshaw Girlfriend Within goes to Bloomingdale's to look for a new Dior suitcase LARGE enough to carry her emotional baggage.

Never date a dead animal, and for pity's gosh sakes—don't be one either!

Resources

The following books opened my eyes to the manipulative, under-handed, controlling behavior of abusive men. I give intellectual credit to these two books for contributing to my personal journey and inspiring my book *Never Date a Date Animal*.

- *Why Does He Do That? Inside the Minds of Angry and Controlling Men*, by Lundy Bancroft, Lundy (Berkley Books, 2003) www.lundybancroft.com.

This excellent book describes the nine types of abusers and how to deal with them. Bancroft explains the early warning signs of abusive relationships; the myths about abusers (such as: alcohol consumption causes abuse); the covert and manipulative tactics of an abuser; the traumatic effects of living with an abuser; counseling with an abusive personality, his ability to con the therapist and what you can and cannot fix; the abuser's "endgame," and how to safely leave an abusive relationship.

- *The Verbally Abusive Relationship: How to Recognize It and How to Respond*, by Patricia Evans, (Adams Media; 2010, 1996, 1992) www.verbalabuse.com.

This book gives terrific insight into the dynamics of an abusive relationship. Evans explores overt and covert abuse and introduces the fifteen categories of verbal abuse, such as: Withholding, Blocking and Diverting, Countering, Discounting, Verbal Abuse Disguised as Jokes, Accusing and Blaming, Judging and Criticizing, Trivializing, Undermining, Name Calling, Forgetting, Ordering, Abusive Anger, & Crazy-Making. She describes the thoughts and feelings of abused women, validating that their partner's covert abuse is not "all in your head." Evans provides effective responses to verbal abuse; the guidelines for protecting children from verbal abuse, and recovery and healing.

Source Notes

Chapter 4: It's Not My Fault—*Or Is It?*

"Women usually experience an attentive and affectionate person ... his approach to her is conciliatory." Patricia Evans, *The Verbally Abusive Relationship*, (Adams Media; 3 edition, 2010), p. 209.

Chapter 5: The Controlling, Abusive Personality

"Signs of an Abusive Personality" and "Signs of an Abusive Relationship," referenced, paraphrased and/or adapted in part from Patricia Evans, *The Verbally Abusive Relationship*, (Adams Media; 3 edition, 2010), Lundy Bancroft, *Why Does He Do That?* (Berkley Books, 2003), WomanSavers. com, Relationship.LifeTips.com, HelpGuide.com, Lindsey Ann Burke Memorial Fund, "Project for Victims of Family Violence" Fayetteville, AZ, and Domestic Violence Resource Center of South County.

"Abusive men are never abusive in the beginning if they were ..." Stephany Alexander, *"Top 10 Signs of an Abusive Man,"* www.womansavers.com (2012).

"Abuse is used for one purpose ... maintain total control over you." "Domestic Violence and Abuse," Melinda Smith, M.A. and Jeanne Segal, Ph.D., "Domestic Violence and Abuse," www.helpguide.org (2012).

Chapter 6: No! Oh, Hell No! Verbal Abuse

Referenced, paraphrased and/or adapted in part from Patricia Evans, *The Verbally Abusive Relationship*, (Adams Media; 3 edition, 2010), Lundy Bancroft, *Why Does He Do That?* (Berkley Books, 2003), WomanSavers. com, Relationship.LifeTips.com, HelpGuide.com, Lindsey Ann Burke Memorial Fund, "Project for Victims of Family Violence" Fayetteville, AZ, and Domestic Violence Resource Center of South County.

"Control and dominance seem to give the abuser a sense of power, security, and identity as a male." Lundy Bancroft, *Why Does He Do That?* (Berkley Books, 2003), p. 42.

"Just because you're not battered and bruised does not mean you're not being abused." Melinda Smith, M.A. and Jeanne Segal, Ph.D., "Domestic Violence and Abuse," www.helpguide.org (2012).

If the partner is told with gradually increasing frequency that she is illogical ... This conditioning is like brainwashing." Patricia Evans, *The Verbally Abusive Relationship*, (Adams Media; 3 edition, 2010), p. 113.

"This means there may not be anyone who has seen what has happened to you." Rape and Abuse Crisis Center of Fargo-Moorhead, www.raccfm. com (2012).

Chapter 7: Psychological Warfare

Referenced, paraphrased and/or adapted in part from Patricia Evans, *The Verbally Abusive Relationship*, (Adams Media; 3 edition, 2010), Lundy Bancroft, *Why Does He Do That?* (Berkley Books, 2003), WomanSavers. com, Relationship.LifeTips.com, HelpGuide.com, Lindsey Ann Burke Memorial Fund, "Project for Victims of Family Violence" Fayetteville, AZ, and Domestic Violence Resource Center of South County.

"Disparaging comments disguised as jokes often refer ... to her competency." Patricia Evans, *The Verbally Abusive Relationship*, (Adams Media; 3 edition, 2010), p. 93.

"What else is she to conclude ... so she pours herself into figuring out what happened." Lundy Bancroft, *Why Does He Do That?* (Berkley Books, 2003), p.110.

"The gaslighting abuser attempts to make the victim doubt her own perceptions ..." Susan Meindl, MA, psychologist, "Emotional Abuse - Are You Being "Too Sensitive"? Probably Not," Article Source: http:// EzineArticles.com/?expert=Susan_Meindl (May 2009).

"Most 'you' statements are judgmental, critical and abusive." Patricia Evans, *The Verbally Abusive Relationship*, (Adams Media; 3 edition, 2010), p. 97.

"Forgetting involves both denial ... what occurred didn't occur is abusive." Patricia Evans, *The Verbally Abusive Relationship*, (Adams Media; 3 edition, 2010), p. 102.

"Ordering denies the equality and autonomy of the partner ..." Patricia Evans, *The Verbally Abusive Relationship*, (Adams Media; 3 edition, 2010), p. 103.

"If your partner is abusive, it is not your fault ..." Rape and Abuse Crisis Center of Fargo-Moorhead, www.raccfm.com (2012).

"This is one of the reasons that verbal abuse increases over time ..." Patricia Evans, *The Verbally Abusive Relationship*, (Adams Media; 3 edition, 2010), p. 107.

Chapter 8: Don't You Dare Hit Me!

"People whose partners abuse them physically and sexually are at a higher risk of being seriously injured or killed." Melinda Smith, M.A. and Jeanne Segal, Ph.D., "Domestic Violence and Abuse," www.helpguide.org, (2012).

Chapter 9: Cycle of Abuse

"During every stage in the cycle, the abuser is fully in control of themselves ..." Domestic Violence Services, "About Domestic Violence," www.domesticviolenceservices.com (2012).

"cycle of violence can help the victim recognize they are not to blame ..." Domestic Violence Services, "About Domestic Violence," www.domesticviolenceservices.com (2012).

"Six distinct stages make up the cycle of violence ..." Domestic Violence Services, "About Domestic Violence," www.domesticviolenceservices.com (2012).

"Life with an abuser can be a dizzying wave of exciting good times ..." Lundy Bancroft, *Why Does He Do That?* (Berkley Books, 2003), p. 147.

"The goal of covert abuse is to manipulate ... the other is defending and explaining." Patricia Evans, *The Verbal Abuse Site*, www.verbalabuse.com (2012).

Chapter 10: Antisocial Personality Disorder

"3 million to 12 million sociopaths in the United States," Donna Andersen, "Beware the sociopath, No heart, no conscience, no remorse," www.lovefraud.com (2012).

"One of the most effective skills psychopaths ..." Dr. Robert Hare and Dr. Paul Babiak, *Snakes in Suits* (HarperBusiness; Reprint edition, May 2007), p. 48.

"Sociopaths live on the edge and verbal outbursts and punishing behavior ... without guilt, remorse or shame." Paraphrased from "Profile of the Sociopath," R. Preston McAfee, http://www.mcafee.cc/Bin/sb.html (2012).

"Some sociopaths use their professional role as a mask to hide their real personalities." Dr. Martha Stout, *The Sociopath Next Door*, (Three Rivers Press, 2006)

"If they happen to be intelligent, "well-bred," and physically attractive psychopaths ..." Dr. Robert Hare and Dr. Paul Babiak, *Snakes in Suits* (HarperBusiness; Reprint edition, May 2007), p. 72.

"Life is reduced to a contest ... used as shields or ejected." Dr. Martha Stout, *The Sociopath Next Door*, (Three Rivers Press, 2006), p. 46.

"four important messages ..." Dr. Robert Hare and Dr. Paul Babiak, *Snakes in Suits* (HarperBusiness; Reprint edition, May 2007), p. 74.

"That is why psychopaths often feel like soul-mates in a relationship ..." Dr. Robert Hare and Dr. Paul Babiak, *Snakes in Suits* (HarperBusiness; Reprint edition, May 2007), p. 74.

"Psychopaths [sociopaths] play on the fact that most of us are trusting and forgiving people." Michael Seto, Ph.D. Psychologist, Director of Forensic Rehabilitation Research at Royal Ottawa Health Care Group, "Profile of the Sociopath," www.mcafee.cc/Bin/sb.html (2012).

"the borderline personality frequently has a distorted ... but feel unable to change it." Mayo Clinic, "Borderline personality disorder," www.mayoclinic.com (2011).

"borderline personality disorder treatment may include ... can live happy, peaceful lives." Mayo Clinic, "Borderline personality disorder," www.mayoclinic.com (2011).

Chapter 11: Bonding with the Enemy

"The longer you have been living ... known as traumatic bonding." Lundy Bancroft, *Why Does He Do That?* (Berkley Books, 2003), p. 134.

"The three phases involved in the cycle of violence ... strengthens her emotional attachment." Domestic Violence Services, "About Domestic Violence," www.domesticviolenceservices.com (2012).

"By recognizing abuse for what it is ... natural state of personal power." Patricia Evans, *The Verbally Abusive Relationship*, (Adams Media; 3 edition, 2010), p. 6.

Chapter 12: Dead Animal in Therapy

"Signs of a ASPD 'first become evident ... the disorder is almost certainly permanent." Michael Seto, Ph.D. Psychologist, Director of Forensic Rehabilitation Research at Royal Ottawa Health Care Group, "Profile of the Sociopath," http://www.mcafee.cc/Bin/sb.html (2012).

"To a psychopath ... therapist is convinced of his or her 'rehabilitation." Michael Seto, Ph.D. Psychologist, Director of Forensic Rehabilitation Research at Royal Ottawa Health Care Group, "Profile of the Sociopath," http://www.mcafee.cc/Bin/sb.html (2012).

"The antisocial personality disorder is notoriously difficult to treat ... denial, distortion and deception." Mayo Clinic, "Antisocial personality disorder," www.mayoclinic.com (2012).

"Couples counseling can be a big setback for the abused woman ... she has to defend herself." Lundy Bancroft, *Why Does He Do That?* (Berkley Books, 2003), pp. 352, 353, 355.

Chapter 13: Alcohol, Drugs and a Dirtbag

"Addiction does not cause partner abuse ... " Lundy Bancroft, *Why Does He Do That?* (Berkley Books, 2003), p. 191.

"Alcohol does not change a person's fundamental value system ... unleash his innate and pent-up anger." Lundy Bancroft, *Why Does He Do That?* (Berkley Books, 2003) pp. 201, 203.

"Even when men who batter ... during substance abuse recovery." Lundy Bancroft, *Why Does He Do That?* (Berkley Books, 2003), p. 203

"Medication or therapy may temporarily lessen ... need close, long-term care and follow-up." Mayo Clinic, Mayo Clinic, "Antisocial personality disorder," www.mayoclinic.com (2011).

"No medication yet discovered ... quit the medication in a few months." Lundy Bancroft, *Why Does He Do That?* (Berkley Books, 2003), p. 40.

Chapter 14: His End Game

"He knows he used to be able to control you ... " Lundy Bancroft, *Why Does He Do That?* (Berkley Books, 2003), p. 215.

"Every year, 1 in 3 women who is a victim ... killed by an intimate partner than men." Safe Horizon, "Domestic Violence: Statistics & Facts," www.safehorizon.org. (2012).

"Because he is sicker than you are smart ... Once you know this the battle is over." Sandra L. Brown, M.A., The Institute for Relationship Harm Reduction, saferelationshipsmagazine.com.

Chapter 15: Cyber Playground

"1 in 5 singles are currently in a committed relationship ..." Current Online Dating and Dating Services Facts & Statistics, DatingSitesReviews.com (2010).

Chapter 17: Married Men Hunting

"30% of the men using an online dating service are married." MSNBC survey, source: www.onlinedatingsafetytips.com (2011).

Chapter 20: Protect Yourself

"Forty percent of all Facebook profiles are fake ..." "Five Hidden Dangers of Facebook," CBS News, www.cbsnews.com (May 11, 2010).

Chapter 21: Soul-mate? Think Again!

"I cannot exist without you ... as though I were dissolving ..." John Keats, "Letter to Fanny Brawne" (October, 13 1819).

Chapter 24: Jack-Ass Busted on Facebook

"I guess I just lost my husband ... So what? I'm still a rock star!" "So What," Pink recording artist, written by Pink, Max Martin and Shellback (2008).

Chapter 31: Jealousy the Monster

"What the ego calls love is possessiveness ..." Eckhart Tolle, *A New Earth*, (Penguin; Reprint edition, January 2008), p. 137.

Chapter 32: The Water Torturer

"He assaults his victim without even raising his voice ... blame herself for his hurtful behavior." Lundy Bancroft, *Why Does He Do That?* (Berkley Books, 2003), pp. 83, 84.

"The central attitudes driving the Water Torturer are: You are crazy ... I know exactly how to get under your skin." Lundy Bancroft, *Why Does He Do That?* (Berkley Books, 2003), p. 85.

"If you are involved with a Water Torturer ..." Lundy Bancroft, *Why Does He Do That?* (Berkley Books, 2003), p.85.

Chapter 34: Liar, Liar, Pants on Fire!

"Once you've realized he has lied, you can then question the validity ..." Patricia Evans, *Verbal Abuse Survivors Speak Out* (Adams Media, 2003), p. 74.

Epilogue: Don't Be One Either

"Some filters may be healthy and constructive ... " Phillip C. McGraw, Ph.D., *Life Strategies*, (Hyperion, August 2001) p. 155.

"Pain bodies," Eckhart Tolle, *A New Earth*, (Penguin; Reprint edition, January 2008), pp. 140, 178, 179

"Accepting your role in your problems ..." Phillip C. McGraw, Ph.D., *Life Strategies*, (Hyperion, August 2001) p. 59.

Due to the dynamics of the Internet, any web addresses or links in this book may have changed since publication and may no longer be valid.

About the Author

Nancy Nichols is an author, self-esteem leader and national motivational speaker. Her life's quest has been to understand the attitudes and behavior which create relationship harmony, business success and personal happiness. It was Nancy's lifetime of relationship failures and heartbreak which illuminated her insight into women's low self-esteem issues and inspired her writing career. As a women's advocate she imparts self-actualization and relationship understanding; her profound message empowers women with logical reasoning, intuitive decision-making and the power of positive thought. Her *God, Please Fix Me! Trilogy* concludes her 10-year writing journey. Her book trilogy includes: *Secrets of the Ultimate Husband Hunter, Never Date a Dead Animal* and *God, Please Fix Me!*

To book Nancy Nichols for a seminar or group presentation, contact: info@godpleasefix.com.

Also by Nancy Nichols

A Trilogy of Personal Healing for Women

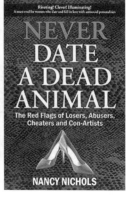

ISBN: 978-0-9795791-0-3   ISBN: 978-0-9795791-1-0   ISBN: 978-0-9795791-2-7

Trade Paperback, 5.5 x 8.5; Also Available in eBooks

Published by Epiphany Imprint; Email info@epiphanyimprint.com

Available everywhere books and eBooks are sold.

Available at www.godpleasefixme.com